THE JAPANESE SUPREME COURT: CONSTITUTIONAL POLICIES

THE JAPANESE SUPREME COURT:
CONSTITUTIONAL POLICIES

By
Hiroshi Itoh
State University of New York
at Plattsburgh

Markus Wiener Publishing, Inc.
New York

This book was published with help of the Japan Foundation.

© Copyright 1989 by Hiroshi Itoh
All rights reserved. No part may be reproduced in any form without prior permission from the copyright holder. For information write to: Markus Wiener Publishing, Inc.
225 Lafayette Street
New York, NY 10012

Library of Congress Cataloging-in-Publication Data
Itoh, Hiroshi.
    The Japanese Supreme Court.

    Includes bibliographical references.
    1. Japan. Saikō Saibansho—History. 2. Courts of last resort—Japan—History. 3. Judicial process--Japan—History. I. Title.
LAW   347.52'035'09   89-24844
ISBN 0-910129-81-9   345.2073509

Printed in the United States of America

To My Parents

Table of Contents

Introduction   1

Chapter One. The Judicial System in Japan   9
    1. The Courts, Judges, and Laws under the Meiji Constitution   9
    2. The Making of the Supreme Court   12
    3. Recruitment of Judges   19
    4. Avenues and Bases of Constitutional Trials   30

Chapter Two. Judicial Conversion: The Judicial Mind Probed   43
    1. Conceptualistic Jurisprudence and the Free Law Movement   44
    2. Neo-conceptualism and Marxism   49
    3. Behavioralist Perspectives on Judicial Conversion   54

Chapter Three. The Process of Judicial Decision Making   73
    1. Judicial Input   73
    2. Judicial Output   93
    3. Effects of Judicial Decisions   106

Chapter Four. How the Supreme Court Decided the Popolo Players Case   117
    1. Academic Freedom and University Autonomy in Japan   118

2. The Popolo Players Incident and the Lower Courts — 123
3. The Supreme Court Remands the Case — 133
4. The Popolo Players Decision and *Stare Decisis* — 141
5. Academic Freedom of Students in Changing Social Environments — 147

Chapter Five. The Self-Restrained Supreme Court — 159
1. Judicial Restraint vis-a-vis the Diet and the Cabinet — 162
2. Judicial Restraint vis-a-vis the Administrative Agencies — 175
3. Judicial Restraint vis-a-vis Local Governments — 182
4. Three Types of Judicial Activism — 186
5. The Activist Supreme Court vis-a-vis the Administrative Agencies — 197
6. Antecedents of Judicial Restraint — 204

Chapter Six. The Conservative Supreme Court — 221
1. Judicial Attitudes: Liberalism and Conservatism — 222
2. Conservative Judicial Antecedents — 232

Chapter Seven. Judicial Administration — 249
1. Administrative Functions of the Supreme Court — 249
2. Judicial Decision Making and Activist Judges — 256
3. Judicial Administration in Turmoil — 261
4. The Supreme Court and Lower Courts Compared — 269
5. Concluding Remarks — 276

Contents

Appendix 283
The Constitution of Japan 283

Abbreviations and Legends 297

Selected Bibliography 303

Index 309

Preface

The Supreme Court of Japan is in its fifth decade. The newly-created highest tribunal has enjoyed an elevated position coequal to the Diet and the Cabinet. With its increased power and prestige, the Court has attracted much attention from among various court observers, including political scientists, as a major political institution. Yet, when compared with the other two branches of the national government, the Supreme Court has been the least analyzed.

The Court was extremely active in turning out many new constitutional decisions during its first three decades. Many of its interpretations of the 1947 Constitution have become important judicial precedents for the political system of Japan. A steady flow of literature has started to emerge on the functions and roles of the Court. After the mid-1970s, however, the Court, and especially its full-member grand bench, gradually but noticeably stopped rendering constitutional decisions. At the same time, intensive and incessant scrutiny by court observers seemed to wane, and be replaced by a somewhat subdued attention to occasional constitutional decision-making activities by the Court. The present work focuses primarily on the Supreme Court at the peak of such activity during its first thirty-some years. It analyzes the structure and process of judicial decision making as well as the major typologies of constitutional policies made during the most active period of the Court to date.

I am grateful for information and research materials to many people in both Japan and the United States. On the Japanese side I would like to express special appreciation to the Supreme Court library in Tokyo, and particularly to Mr. Kazuo Tomura and to public law scholars including Professors Hideo

Wada, Takeo Hayakawa, Naoki Kobayashi, and Nobuyoshi Ashibe. I am also most appreciative to many former Supreme Court justices and *chosakan* like Judge Itsuo Sonobe for the interviews they granted to me. On the American side, warm thanks are due Professors John M. Maki, Dan F. Henderson, Lawrence W. Beer, and David J. Danelski for their valuable advice and suggestions.

I would also like to convey sincere gratitude to the Japan Foundation for its generous research and publication assistance.

Finally, I am greatly indebted to my wife, Nobu, for her painstaking research assistance and for typing the entire manuscript.

June 1989
Plattsburgh, New York

Introduction

Japan is one of a small number of democracies in the family of more than 160 nations. With just over forty years of history behind it, the Japanese Constitution of 1947 has already become one of the older constitutions in the world. The preamble of the Constitution purports to achieve peaceful international cooperation, national security, justice, and liberty. These constitutional ideals and aspirations have made the Constitution the supreme, basic, and organic law of the land. As one of the three major branches of national government, the Supreme Court has been deeply involved in constitutional politics.

The present work addresses itself to the question of how the Supreme Court decides constitutional disputes in Japan. It attempts to describe, for most typical situations, the structure and process of constitutional decision making by the Court and to explain some causal relationships among basic variables and parameters of constitutional litigation. It is an endeavor to prove the performance of the Court by paying special attention to analytical frameworks, especially a systems model.

The Supreme Court was established in 1947 under the Constitution written largely by the American occupation government. Its immediate predecessor was the Great Court of Cassation which had been created before the 1889 Meiji constitution. The latter's judicial power was primarily confined to the adjudication of private disputes, and did not cover constitutional litigation in which a court might have been able to examine public acts and actions and decide upon their constitutionality. The courts were a part of the executive branch. The power to decide the constitutionality of government actions was conferred on the perfunctory privy council, not on the Great Court of Cassation. In the absence of judicial review under the Meiji constitution, it required the making of a new constitution and a complete restructuring of the Japanese judicial system to graft the American common law tradition of judicial review and judicial supremacy upon the civil law tradition of prewar Japan. As a result of a full-scale constitutional reform, effected by the American occupation government, the Supreme Court has become the court of last resort and the repository of judicial administration. In that capacity, the Court has come to play a vital role in molding many important and basic national policies.

The French philosopher Montesquieu, in *The Spirit of the Laws* (1748), sought a device to promote political liberty by taking the monarch's law-making power and vesting it in a legislature. The Americans later advanced Montesquieu's two-division of legislature and executive to a three-division, by elevating the judiciary to an equal level. The power of judicial review, which remains an implied power in the American constitution, has been made an explicit power under the 1947 Japanese Constitution.

The Japanese Constitution with its preamble and 103 articles serves as the highest law of the land. Situated at the apex of the legal hierarchy, it acts as a yardstick for determining the legality of legislative laws and administrative ordinances. Here, the courts are assigned the task of reviewing and nullifying those public acts and actions that violate the highest law of the land. Since 1947 the Court has reviewed the constitutionality of the Criminal Code and administrative laws in a large number of cases, followed by the Criminal Procedural Code and various labor laws. In contrast, the Civil Code and the Commercial Code have seldom been involved in a constitutional litigation. In general, the Supreme Court has made constitutional decisions in the public law realm much more often than the private law realm.

While constitutional litigation is probably the single most important new function assigned to the judiciary by the 1947 Constitution, no single procedural code governs adjudication of constitutional disputes. Consequently, a number of basic questions have been raised ever since the early postwar days concerning the nature, function, and procedure of constitutional trials. Instead of having any single statute legislated covering constitutional litigation, the Supreme Court has relied upon the civil, criminal, and administrative procedural codes; adopted, on an incremental basis, practices and case laws of the United States Supreme Court; and has also made its own rules and regulations to carry out the newly assigned task of judicial review. The institutional framework of constitutional litigation in Japan has been firmly established, and is now less subject to borrowing from the United States or Europe.

The process of judicial decision making has been perceived differently by various judges and court observers. A judge might ask the question, "How do I decide a case?" while a court observer might ask, "How does a judge decide a case?" Different questions have been matched by just as many different answers. In the light of the developmental nature of judicial decision-making analysis, this book attempts to analyze constitutional litigation of the Supreme Court from various perspectives. A historical approach would focus on a transition from the Great Court of Cassation to the present Supreme Court and contrast similarities and differences between the two. An institutional approach would examine the structure, functions, and powers of the Supreme Court in the context of the entire judicial system. A legal approach would probe legal procedures and practices of constitutional and other forms of litigation, and examine rules and regulations governing legal professionals and court operations.

Chapter One will start with the examination of institutional developments of Japanese courts and judicial roles. Such an inquiry will help clarify the nature of the judicial system and provide a setting for an analysis of the changing research frontiers of judicial behavior in Chapter Two. The 1947 Constitution expanded greatly the function of the Supreme Court by giving it the authority to determine the legality of judicial review exercised by the lower courts and to oversee the uniformity of judicial interpretations at all levels. Here the Court is caught in a dilemma: the function of the Supreme Court as the court of last resort dictates, on the one hand, that the Court makes itself available for review of as many lower court decisions as possible, and, on the other hand, that lower courts' adjudication of legal disputes be given finality as much as possible, thereby allowing relatively small numbers of appeals to reach the Supreme Court. Judicial roles and judicial environments have also gone through a great transformation, as was manifested with the inquisitorial system under the Meiji constitution and the accusatorial system under the present Constitution. A classical controversy over judicial roles as either law-discoverer or law-maker also points to the different roles a judge has been expected to play under a new legal system.

The single most overriding feature of judicial decision-making analysis is that the Japanese legal and judicial systems as well as the methodology of judicial decision-making analysis, all originated in the West. First, the French court system was introduced, and its impact was clearly manifested by the naming of the highest court of Japan in 1875 after the *Cour de Cassation* in France. Then, the German influence grew with the adoption of the Meiji constitution in 1889, which was patterned after a Prussian-German constitution. It permeated the entire judicial system under the Court Organization Code for half a century until 1945. German civil law practices still manifest themselves prominently in Japan. Finally, the American common law is the most recent foreign influence on the Japanese legal and judicial systems. The American notion of judicial review and the rule of law are firmly incorporated in the constitutional politics of post-1945 Japan.

Chapter Two will undertake a historical review of scholarly attempts to examine the nature, function, and scope of judicial decision making in Japan. Since the question of how the Supreme Court decides constitutional cases involves human behavior, or, more precisely, judicial behavior, it will probe the judicial mind and judicial value judgment as an important medium of converting judicial input into output. After comparing and contrasting neoconceptualism and behavioralism, this work basically subscribes to the behavioral school of judicial decision-making analysis. It analyzes judicial value judgments or ideology, and also written judicial reasonings as a means to rationalize a judicial decision.

Introduction

Ever since the end of World War I, Japanese scholars have energetically been engaged in the task of studying a wide range of Western legal science ranging from Marxism to neo-Hegelianism, neo-Kantianism, Kelsenianism, phenomenology, pragmatism, and neo-scholasticism. However, only a few of them were to stay on Japanese soil, and fewer still were integrated into the study of the judicial process. First, neo-conceptualistic jurisprudence was used to focus on the analysis of judicial precedents; second, Marxism attempted to find, through court decisions, judicial ideologies in Japanese capitalistic society; and third, behavioralistic perspectives were adopted from the United States and were characterized by their pragmatic approach. These three philosophies have been intertwined in the minds of many Japanese legal scholars.

Chapter Three examines constitutional litigation of the Supreme Court as a system with structure and functions. Demands and support of litigants are major components of the input structure. Input process consists of an initiation of litigation, an accommodation of legal conflicts, and links the input structure to the conversion. A litigant seeks judicial protection of his legal interests. Through appeal briefs and/or oral hearings, his attorney presents his legal demands with supporting materials such as witness' testimonies, judicial precedents, and scholars' opinions. A judge defines and responds to a litigant's demands, and converts input into output. Issues raised in the input are questions of fact, law, and such extraneous factors as the competence of attorneys, which are a function of the different types of litigants. Any combination of these will stimulate different responses from a judge. Judges are the most important judicial decision makers, but prosecutors, attorneys, lower court judges and, above all, *chosakan*, the Japanese counterpart of a United States Supreme Court law clerk, may also act as important co-decision makers or influencers of the judicial process.

The output process consists of persuasion and decision making, and links conversion to the output structure, which is made up of decisions and norms. The output process is a culmination of persuasions among judicial actors deciding issues and writing opinions. It is highly integrated in the mind of a judge who interacts with his co-decision makers and other persons of a court in a face-to-face small group relationship. An output is an authoritative decision made to resolve conflicting legal interests of the parties in the case.

Finally the implementation and reconsideration of judicial decisions are the main elements of the feedback process. With the implementation of the Supreme Court decision, the wheel of justice will have completed its turn. But a decision, when fed back into a much wider political system, may generate a new case which might cause the Supreme Court to reconsider its previous policy. Negative or positive reactions from lower courts also become an important input for the Supreme Court. The Supreme Court decision constitutes the highest level of judicial order, and at the same time, provides a basis for *stare decisis* in deciding similar cases in the future.

An analytical framework has been missing in much of the existing literature on judicial behavior in Japan. Legal scholars have long confined their focus on judicial interpretation of law to its revelation in written court opinions. Seldom have they extended their research to cover the structure and process of judicial decision making. An uneven scholarly preoccupation with the normative aspects of the judicial process, coupled with a strict confidentiality among judges guarding their work, has been responsible for the dearth of empirical data and a conceptual framework of judicial decision-making analysis. This is painfully illustrated in the analysis of a major Supreme Court decision on academic freedom and university autonomy in Chapter Four.

Of several behavioral approaches, the political approach fails to differentiate judicial process from legislative or executive process, because it focuses on the decision-making process of those policy makers who are expected to behave by the drive for power, prestige, and personal interests. The Weberian bureaucratic approach is also inadequate in providing a comprehensive framework of creative policy making by the Supreme Court. It is still suitable for the simple rule application of the lower courts, or activities that take place outside the judicial system, like support and feedback.

Central to the systems approach is the concept of judicial value judgment. A judge perceives and responds to an issue through his values and beliefs. The manner by which judicial values or attitudes are acquired and the way in which they are expressed differ from one judge to another. But while an issue fluctuates widely from case to case, judicial values, internal to judges, are assumed to be relatively stable and consistent. On the assumption of consistency and rationality of judicial value judgment or attitude, one of the major objectives of a judicial voting analysis is to probe judicial values (intervening variable) by first determining the issue of a case (independent variable) as revealed in a judicial opinion, and then by examining the judicial vote (dependent variable).

In this context, the working principle of *stare decisis* tends to contribute to the stability and predictability of judicial decision making at different levels. Chapter Five, which focuses on the self-restraint of the Supreme Court, examines the entire Court, which often feels itself bound by its own prior decisions.

The relationship between parliamentary sovereignty and the rule of law is one in which the sovereign of parliament does not always favor the supremacy of law while the latter necessitates the former. Here lies the difficulty of reconciling the rule of law with parliamentary sovereignty. The prewar court was designed to enforce parliamentary supremacy and the rule by law whereas the postwar Supreme Court is intended to realize judicial supremacy and the rule of law. Since the Supreme Court delineates the power and function of each branch of government through constitutional litigations, Chapter Five will examine the conflict and harmony between the Supreme Court and political branches of government in terms of judicial activism and judicial self-restraint.

Chapter Six probes judges of some subgroup (usually with similar judicial attitudes) who often feel bound by prior decisions of an earlier subgroup of similar-minded judges and also an individual judge, who, in the majority of cases, is consistent with himself and has a strong tendency to follow his own voting pattern.

Many constitutional scholars in Japan advocate a more active use of judicial review by the Supreme Court. These progressive scholars construe the rule of law to embrace not only procedural regularity by an independent judiciary and judicial reviews of legislative and executive actions, but also certain substantive rights. For them, the rule of law is understood to signify not only the diffusion of the governing power but also individual dignity and fundamental human rights. For them, the government may not interfere with the citizen except in accordance with fair and general rules previously in force. The Japanese public often passes its judgment on the performance of the Supreme Court on the basis of the Court's decisions involving civil rights and civil liberties. Chapter Six will examine the Supreme Court's performance in discharging its task as a guardian of civil rights and liberties in terms of judicial liberalism and conservatism.

No discussion of the Supreme Court in Japan is complete without relating judicial administration to judicial decision making. The Supreme Court functions not only as the court of last resort but also as the highest administrative decision-making body for the entire court system. The minister of justice used to control all administrative matters such as the appointment and promotion of judges and the allocation of budgets for all the courts. As a part of strengthening judicial independence, the Constitution has transferred to the Supreme Court jurisdiction over all administrative matters, including the new tasks of supervising the Supreme Court's general secretariat and the Judicial Research and Training Institute (JRTI). Indeed, the intensity of concentration of judicial administration in the hands of the Supreme Court is unmatched anywhere in the world. The Court has invited, from time to time, criticism for its alleged undue administrative guidance over lower courts and JRTI. Against this background, Chapter Seven will test a widely held view that the Supreme Court is more conservative and inclined toward self-restraint than the lower courts and that the direction of influence flows only from the top down.

CHAPTER 1

The Judicial System in Japan

1. The Courts, Judges, and Laws Under the Meiji Constitution

One can trace the antecedents of the present court system to the Tokugawa period (1615–1867). A dominant feature of the Tokugawa judicial system was the prevalence of conciliation in lieu of a formal trial. Judicial officers first attempted a private settlement having the same force as a formal binding judgment. Conciliation in a civil suit was induced with penal threats of imprisonment against unwilling litigants, and only after a conciliation attempt had failed, would there be a formal trial. Thus the Tokugawa policy to encourage conciliation long stood in the way of a rapid development of the modern judicial system. Officials of the conference chamber in Edo (Tokyo), who were members of the three commissions (*sanbugyo*), served as quasi-judges, performing judicial functions along with administrative tasks.[1] Two of the four finance commissioners (*kujikata*) and other administrative officials who were versed in legal case and trial practice concurrently presided over hearings as examiners, and settled disputes.

The conference chamber was renamed a court (*saibansho*) after 1868, but its administrative and judicial functions remained indistinguishable. There was no centralized or independent court. The prefectural governors also acted as judges along with quasi-judicial officials.

The modern Japanese legal system began with the adoption of the European legal codes and judicial systems. The desire to eliminate the unequal treaties with Western powers was an immediate cause of legal modernization. The extraterritoriality clause, which conceded trial jurisdiction over a foreign resident who committed a crime in Japan to foreign consuls, was a special source of humiliation for the Japanese who, in turn, put pressure on the Japanese government to establish a modern judicial system as a prerequisite to the removal of the unequal treaties. Pressured by this urgent task, the government started with the relatively easy task of translating and adopting Western legal codes and copying Western court structures. The more difficult task of training legal professionals, especially lawyers, was largely neglected.

The French court system was the first introduced. Its impact was clearly manifested by the naming of the highest court of Japan in 1875 after the *Cour de Cassation* in France. In 1875 a three-tiered court system made up of prefectural or local courts, high courts, and the Great Court of Cassation was established. *Chian-saibansho* (Justice of Peace), *shishin-saibansho* (the Court of First Instances), and *koso-saibansho* (the Court of Appeals), all established in 1881, were literal translations of *Justice de paix, tribunal de premiere instance* and *tribunal d'appel*, respectively. Also, *koso-saibansho* (the Court of Appeals) was renamed *kosoin* in 1886 when the French counterpart was changed to *Cour d'appel*. In 1882 the Judicial Duties Rules were enacted to resolve judicial disputes between the ministry of justice and the prefectural governments, and to administer justice more uniformly throughout the country. The prefectural or local courts functioned as the court of fact-finding and were concerned primarily with ascertaining and finalizing factual questions of a case, while the Great Court of Cassation served as the court of last resort and was devoted to reviewing legal questions raised in appeals. The first phase of legal modernization was devoted to the adoption of Western legal codes through domestic legislation, with the main interests of Japanese scholars centering on the comparative study of those codes.[2] The Napoleonic legal codes were copied as they were considered to be the most systematic and advanced form in the world. The whole legal system was soon predominantly occupied with the legislation of laws, some of which were adopted almost verbatim from the French.

The Meiji government promised in an imperial proclamation in 1881 to open the Diet in ten years, and immediately set out to draft a constitution. About 1881, however, the interest in the French legal system waned and was replaced by enthusiasm for the German system. Attributing the rapidly growing national power of Germany to her monarchical constitutionalism, the Japanese government decided to exchange the optimistic liberalism of the early Meiji years for a more absolutist and conservative government, and to pattern the Japanese constitution after the German model. Underlying this shift was the new feeling that the German legal codes were more suitable for a new and powerful modern nation.

The abortive attempt in 1890 to legislate a civil code epitomizes this shift. A draft civil code was patterned after the French model. Yet it became subject to attack from so many legal practitioners, scholars, and politicians that it was tabled for eight years. A committee was formed to draft a new civil code. The final draft, which became effective in 1898 after heated debates in both Houses of the Imperial Diet, clearly reveals the victory of the German *Pandekten* model over the French system.

Despite some lingering influence of the French model in the criminal law, the controversy over the civil code precipitated a wholesale trend toward the German legal system in all Japanese legal codes, including the Court Organization Code and the Code of Civil Procedure. The decision to adopt a German-style constitution determined the framework of the court system and its functions. Following the German system, regular courts were divided into civil and criminal sections. The Meiji constitution of 1889, which was patterned after the Prussian-German constitution, followed the civilian law principle that separated law into public and private spheres and established two separate court structures: the judicial courts, headed by the Great Court of Cassation, to adjudicate private law disputes, and the administrative court, which was designed for public law litigation. The Court Martial (boards) and the Patent Bureau were also created as special courts separate from the judicial courts established by Article 60 of the Meiji constitution. The German influence permeated the entire judicial system under the Court Organization Code. German civil law practices still manifest themselves in Japan. A heavy reliance on statutory laws in judicial decision making, and a lower court practice of publishing only one opinion of the court without disclosing the vote of each judge are prime examples. The Supreme Court also seems to follow the German practice of deciding a case as a whole instead of each issue within a case separately.

Although there was some influence of British law on Japanese law, the possible adoption of Anglo-American case law was dismissed as being too complicated and time-consuming to meet the urgent task of revising the unequal treaties with the West. If English law had been practiced in this period, it would not have been case law but legal principles extracted from case law, and would not have differed much from codified law. "Although it would be most natural to assume that judges and lawyers who were trained in the English law might have influenced Japanese law in some cases, it is hard to ascertain such influence."[3]

The German-influenced judiciary shaped the machinery of administering justice over half a century until the collapse of Meiji constitutionalism in 1945. Subsequent judicial reforms were effected under the strong supervision of the American occupation authorities as part of the constitutional overhaul.

2. The Making of the Supreme Court

In the Potsdam Declaration of July 1945, the United States, Great Britain, and the Soviet Union demanded that the Japanese government remove all obstacles to the revival and strengthening of democracy among the Japanese people and establish "freedom of speech, of religion, and of thought, as well as respect for the fundamental human rights." On August 29, 1945, upon Japan's surrender, the U.S. President Harry S Truman advanced the Potsdam policy by stating in Section III of the Initial Post-Surrender Policy for Japan that ". . . those [*i.e.*, laws] which conflict with the objectives and policies outlined in this document shall be replaced, suspended or amended as required; and agencies charged specifically with their enforcement shall be abolished or appropriately modified."[4] Subsequently, on October 11, 1945, General Douglas MacArthur ordered the Japanese government to enact a liberal constitution as an essential part of the overall democratization of Japan. Yet, as it turned out, a constitutional reform was undertaken in a narrow and evasive manner by the Japanese government headed by Prime Minister Kijyuro Shidehara, who wanted to preserve the Meiji constitution wherever possible. Shidehara was also reluctant to initiate any constitutional changes in the absence of a popular mandate by the general election slated for April 1946. The confusion created by the purges of high-ranking Japanese government officials in December 1945 also slowed down the constitutional reform work. However, no sooner had the first draft of the constitution been submitted by the committee appointed by the Shidehara Cabinet than MacArthur called it so unprogressive as to require the direct intervention of the General Headquarters, the Supreme Commander for the Allied Powers (GHQ,SCAP) in preparing a new constitutional draft. Thus, contrary to his initial decision that democratization should not be imposed on the Japanese and that the Japanese government should not be pressured into any predetermined constitution, MacArthur, after February 1946, adopted a "direct and rapid" American approach to bring about a new constitution in Japan.

Next, we shall review the process through which the Supreme Court and lower courts were established.[5]

As part of the overall constitutional reform, the privy council, the Cabinet, and the ministry of justice all set out in October 1945 to reorganize the judiciary and revise the Court Organization Code. They were all guided by the Potsdam Declaration calling for democratization of the judiciary. The task force of the privy council was headed by Fumimaro Konoe and Soichi Sasaki, the latter of whom had advanced the concept of a constitutional court under which judicial review could be sought by the government, the Imperial Diet, and the highest judicial and administrative courts, as well as by the litigants themselves. The Shidehara Cabinet created the Constitutional Issues Investigatory Committee chaired by State Minister Jyoji Matsumoto. This committee proposed, among other changes, the abolition of the administrative court and the transfer of administrative cases to the judicial courts. The Judicial Reform Deliberation Council established by the justice ministry also studied possible reforms of criminal proceedings, including the prosecution, trial, and human rights of the accused. The council disclosed the following reform proposals: the public prosecutor's office should be separated from the courts; the administrative court should be abolished and its jurisdiction transferred to the judicial courts; the Great Court of Cassation should be granted the power of judicial review; the President of the Great Court of Cassation should henceforth be called Chief Justice; and the administrative work of the Great Court of Cassation should be removed from the jurisdiction of the justice ministry.

At the urging of GHQ,SCAP, the Japanese government published on March 6, 1946, a summary draft of the revised constitution and on April 17 its full text. According to the March 6 summary draft, the judges of the highest court would be appointed by the Cabinet, reviewed by the people, and be retired at the age of seventy. Furthermore, the Court would be empowered to make its own rules and regulations, and all special courts which existed under the Meiji constitution would be abolished. The April 17 draft left the compulsory retirement age to legislation rather than fixing it at age seventy. The summary draft, with the privy council's changes attached, was submitted to the 19th Special Session (1946) of the House of Representatives where an amendment was passed that the Chief Justice, as designated by the Cabinet, be appointed by the Emperor, in order to place the Chief Justice on the same level as the Prime Minister.

In June 1946 the minister of justice established the Provisional Judiciary Reform Council to prepare judicial reform plans. The seventeen-member provisional council (one vice justice minister, and representatives from each bureau of the ministry of justice, courts, prosecutors' office, bar associations, and the administrative court, all located in Tokyo) came up with the following proposals: the new highest court should be called either the Great Court of Cassation or the Supreme Court; such a court should have either nine or sixteen justices; justices should retire at the age of seventy five; *chosakan* should be assigned to justices; and the courts should be separated from the prosecutor's office. Finally, some councillors favored the retention of the justice ministry while others favored its abolition. The minister of justice then established the Judicial and Legal System Deliberation Council to finalize these proposals, but this council was also made part of the Provisional Legal System Investigation Council established by Prime Minister Shigeru Yoshida in July 1946 to revise major legal codes under the new Constitution. Both councils came to work closely with each other.

The Judicial and Legal System Deliberation Council revised its proposal seven times until the final draft was formally adopted by the Provisional Legal System Investigation Council's plenary meeting on October 23, 1946. According to the final draft, the highest court would be called the Supreme Court and there would be one Chief Justice and fourteen associate justices. A total of fifteen justices would correspond to the number of the state ministers, and constitute the maximum number for the Supreme Court to function effectively as a collective decision-making body. At least ten justices would be appointed from among legal practitioners or law professors, each of whom should have at least twenty years of experience, or its equivalent. Compulsory retirement age would be seventy-five years for the Chief Justice and seventy years for associate justices. The status of the Chief Justice would be the same as that of the Prime Minister, while the associate justices would enjoy the same status as state ministers. The judicial function of the Court would be to determine any alleged unconstitutionality of laws and ordinances as well as to ensure uniformity of legal interpretation and application. The jurisdiction of the Court would extend to review various kinds of appeals from a lower court, contending alleged unconstitutionality. The Supreme Court would function either as one grand bench with the full membership, or as three five-judge petty benches. The quorum would be nine for the grand bench, and three for a petty bench. A petty bench would first handle all appeals, and would not need to refer a case to the grand bench when all members present decided a case by unanimous vote. Only the grand bench, however, would be empowered to change existing judicial precedents or render law and ordinances unconstitutional. Each justice on the grand bench would express his decision. Thirty-five *chosakan* would be assigned to assist the justices.

The ministry of justice drafted a new Court Code based on this final draft and submitted it to the GHQ,SCAP for approval. Brigadier General Courtney Whitney, Chief of Government Section, reviewed it and strongly advised the adoption of the following points: 1) Five justices were to be recruited from non-legal professionals no younger than forty years old and possessed of sound judgment and legal capability. Also, an advisory committee should be established to assist the Cabinet in the selection of justices. Finally, all justices including the Chief Justice should retire at the age of seventy. 2) In the light of the relatively small number of Supreme Court justices compared with the justices of the Great Court of Cassation, the lower courts should be given the power of judicial review and an appeal from a summary court should be limited to a high court. 3) The structure and procedures on judicial process in the grand and petty benches should be decided by the Supreme Court itself, and each justice should be allowed to write his own opinions. With these GHQ changes incorporated, the draft Court Code passed the privy council and the 92nd ordinary session of the Diet in October 1946. The new Constitution and the Court Code were put into effect and the Supreme Court was formally established on May 3, 1947. Established by legislation were high courts, district courts, family courts, and summary courts. The administrative court was abolished, and any extraordinary tribunals were prohibited.

American influence on the new court system is very clear. The provision of Article 81 of the Constitution, which confers the power of judicial review upon the courts, has been viewed as a codification of *Marbury v. Madison* (1 *Cranch* 137: 1803). The provision of Article 98, Paragraph 1 is believed to have been derived from the judicial supremacy clause of the U.S. constitution (Article 3, Section 1). The introduction of the American federal judicial system and its decision-making practices was so extensive as to raise the question of how much the Meiji judiciary, rooted for half a century in the German model, lost its character and practice in the overhaul carried out under the American influence. The Supreme Court addressed itself to this issue when it dismissed an appeal in *Okimoto v. Japan* (1948).[6] In this case the appellant challenged the constitutionality of the provision of Article 1 of the Court Enforcement Ordinance, which required that pending appeals which had been filed with the Great Court of Cassation prior to the end of World War II be transferred to the Tokyo high court. In the opinion of the Court:[7]

> The Great Court of Cassation was organized and empowered under the authority of the Meiji constitution and the Court Organization Code whereas the Supreme Court was instituted by the Constitution of Japan and the Court Code. To the extent that the former was the highest level of court equipped with judicial power like the latter is, there may be some similarities, but there are major differences in terms of the structure, nature, authority, and functions of the two courts. Thus, the latter is neither the same entity as, nor a successor to the former.

Concerning the nature of judicial review, the Supreme Court passed the judgment that the provision of Article 81 of the Constitution did not confer upon a court established under the 1947 Constitution the power to review the conformity to the Meiji constitution of a law which had been enacted and operative under the Meiji constitution.[8] At the same time, the Court ruled that Article 98 of the Constitution established a standard with which to determine the constitutionality and validity of the laws enacted before the effective date of the 1947 Constitution and that the Food Control Code which had been enacted before the Constitution, for instance, continued to be effective even after the Constitution came into force.[9] Thus judicial review is conducted only in relation to the 1947 Constitution, even though it extends to public acts and actions effected prior to the new Constitution. This judicial interpretation of the nature of judicial review is designed to maintain a balance between the stability and continuity of legal order from the Meiji constitution, on the one hand, and the rule of law under the new Constitution, on the other. Judicial reorganization as part of the 1947 constitutional reform was rather extensive. The new court hierarchy is headed by the Supreme Court, while all special courts including the administrative court have been abolished. Except for the Supreme Court and the summary courts, all other courts are staffed by career judges and assistant judges. Judicial independence is greatly strengthened in relation to the political branches of government. Judicial review was spelled out for the first time in the Constitution itself. All in all, the role of judge-made law is increased as a result of the introduction of American common law practice to the civil law tradition of Japan.

The judicial role in Japan has gone through a great deal of change too. Prewar Japan adopted the inquisitorial type of judicial decision making from Europe. Under it a judge was empowered to investigate facts of a case and appoint experts of his own for fact-finding and direct evidence-gathering, without being bound by the assertion and offerings of either party to a case. The judicial proceedings in criminal cases concentrated on interrogation of the accused and questioning of witnesses. Furthermore, a prewar judge was fully informed of all that had transpired at the pretrial stage. Postwar Japan shifted to the Anglo-American adversary procedure under which a judge supposedly acts as a neutral referee or arbitrator between contending parties. Although he can still take a decisive part in the trial, such as through the arrangement of the evidence, a "judge-arbitrator" who makes a go of what parties may have to offer, faces just as stiff an uphill fight as a "judge-official" who enters a trial with strong preconceptions about the "gestalt"[10] of his case, if he wants to arrive at the best possible result.

Thus, the American common law system is the most recent foreign influence on the Japanese legal and judicial systems. The American notion of judicial review and the rule of law are now firmly incorporated in the constitutional politics of post-1945 Japan. At the same time, German conceptualistic jurisprudence retains its interest among Japanese scholars interested in judicial process analysis, studying it alongside American legal realism and behavioralism.

We now turn to the recruitment process of Supreme Court justices and lower court judges.

3. Recruitment of Judges

Regarding the question of how the initial fifteen members of the Supreme Court were appointed, the 1947 Constitution stipulates that the Emperor shall appoint a Chief Justice of the Supreme Court as designated by the Cabinet (Article 6, Paragraph 2) and that associate justices shall be appointed by the Cabinet (Article 79). The Court Code, enacted to implement the constitutional provisions on the courts, elaborates in Article 41 the qualifications of the Supreme Court justices as follows:[11]

> The Supreme Court justices shall be appointed from among persons, not less than forty years of age, who possess broad vision and extensive knowledge of law. At least ten of them should have held either one or both of the positions mentioned in Items (1) and (2) below for not less than ten years, or one or more of the positions in the following items for the total period of twenty years or more: Items (1) high court presidents, (2) judges, (3) summary court judges, (4) prosecutors, (5) private attorneys, and (6) university professors of legal science. . . . If positions such as assistant judge, *chosakan*, court secretary, Judicial Research and Training Institute instructor, or vice-minister, secretary, or educational official of the justice ministry have also been held by persons who have held the positions in Items (1) and (2) above for at least five years, or by persons who have held, for not less than ten years, one or more of the positions in Items (3) to (6) above, such positions shall be deemed to be equivalent to those mentioned in Items (3) to (6) above.

Pursuant to the provisions above, Prime Minister Shigeru Yoshida, with the advice of Justice Minister Tokutaro Kimura, issued Cabinet Ordinance No. 14 of April 16, 1947, creating the Advisory Committee for the Nomination of Supreme Court Justices. The following were selected to serve on the committee: the Chief Justice of the Great Court of Cassation, one lower court judge, the Chief Justice of the administrative court, the vice-minister of the justice ministry, the speakers of both Houses, the chief of the first department of the Imperial Academy, the president of Tokyo Imperial University, and the chairmen of the three major bar associations. The committee set out immediately to nominate thirty candidates, including three candidates for the chief justiceship, and reported their nominations to the Cabinet. From the list of candidates thus recommended, the Cabinet selected one Chief Justice and fourteen associate justices and was ready to have them formally appointed on May 3, 1947.

However, the proposed appointments were unexpectedly delayed by General MacArthur who instructed Prime Minister Yoshida to postpone the appointments until the first elections for the Diet had been held under the new Constitution. One, for the House of Councillors, was slated for April 20, and another, for the House of Representatives, for April 25, 1947. MacArthur might have echoed a strong feeling among many Japanese that the new Supreme Court justices should be appointed by a new Cabinet which would be selected by both Houses after the first election, rather than by the transitional caretaker Cabinet operating under the old constitution. Yoshida was expected to be reelected and appoint the Supreme Court justices from among the candidates recommended by the advisory committee during the previous term of his Cabinet. However, the unexpected victory of Tetsu Katayama of the Socialist Party over Shigeru Yoshida (the Liberal Party) in the general election had a great impact on the subsequent selection of the justices.

Immediately after the elections, the new Prime Minister Katayama told the public of the significance of appointing Supreme Court justices who would reflect a new constitutional spirit, and appointed Yoshio Suzuki as the new minister of justice, who would be given overall supervisory power over the selection process. Suzuki decided to rely on a similar type of advisory body which had existed under the Yoshida Cabinet in order to avoid any appearance of singlehanded appointment by the Cabinet. Convinced that the new Supreme Court should be built on a broad consensus of both legal professionals and the public, he convened a meeting of all legal professionals to select the members of the advisory body. He also added the chairmen of both Houses, and other men of knowledge and experience to its membership. Finally, in the light of the old animosity between the Great Court of Cassation and the minister of justice who used to appoint all judges, including the justices of the Great Court of Cassation, he made it explicit that the selection was the collective action of the Katayama Cabinet, and he was merely assisting the Prime Minister and other Cabinet members in his capacity as a state minister without portfolio. In order to stress this point he personally drafted many proposals for the selection of candidates and had the personnel bureau of the Prime Minister's Office rather than the ministry of justice handle all the work of judicial selection.

Between June 5 and June 17, 1947, a large number of people presented various suggestions and petitions concerning the composition and the function of the Advisory Committee. On June 17 the Cabinet promulgated the Advisory Committee Regulations for the Appointment of Supreme Court Justices (Cabinet Ordinance No. 83) which provided that: (1) the committee would have sixteen members with the speaker of the House of Representatives serving as the committee chairman; the committee would include the speaker of the House of Councillors, four judges, one prosecutor, the Chief Justice of the administrative court, one assessor, four practicing attorneys, three law professors, and one person of knowledge and experience to be appointed by the Prime Minister; (2) each committee member would submit in writing to the committee a list of fifteen to thirty candidates; (3) the committee would choose thirty candidates from the list thus submitted and report their selections to the Cabinet; and (4) that any candidate should report his unwillingness to serve to the committee within one week of the first recommendation. This last provision was inserted in the light of the large number of people who had declined recommendations by the Yoshida Cabinet.

An election for the advisory committee was held by mail between July 10 and 18, 1947, in an atmosphere that was tense and competitive, so much so that the election among the judges resulted in a Great Court of Cassation justice suing a district court judge for an alleged smear campaign. Finally, a double-ballot election returned the following delegates to the advisory committee. Representing the judges were Tamotsu Shima, (former justice of the Great Court of Cassation), Katsumi Tarumi (president of the Sendai High Court), Hachiro Fujita (president of the Osaka Court of Appeals), and Saburo Iwamatsu (president of the Fukuoka High Court). One thousand one hundred and thirteen votes were cast altogether with 7 invalid votes and 38 abstentions. Minoru Miyagi (former justice of the Great Court of Cassation) was a runner-up.

Representing the prosecutors was Attorney General Morita Fukui. There were 633 votes cast, of which 111 were cast by prosecutors of the former Administrative Court, with 6 invalid votes and 11 abstentions. The runner-up was Yoshihiro Kishimoto, chief prosecutor of the Sapporo High Prosecutors' Office.

Elected from among the lawyers were Naoyoshi Tsukasaki, chairman of the Tokyo Bar Association, Yoshio Konishi, chairman of the Osaka Bar Association, Ichiro Hasegawa, chairman of the First Tokyo Bar Association, and Kunisuke Nagano, member of the Tokyo Bar Association. Tsuyoshi Mano, chairman of the Second Tokyo Bar Association, was the runner-up. A total of 4,590 votes was cast, with 16 invalid votes and 1,702 abstentions.

The Cabinet appointed Sakae Wagatsuma, chairman of the faculty of law at Tokyo University, Koshin Takigawa, chairman of the faculty of law at Kyoto University, Rikisaburo Imamura, president of Senshu University, and Koichi Shimada, president of Waseda University, to represent law professors and "the men of knowledge and experience" in the advisory committee. Under the chairmanship of Komakichi Matsuoka, speaker of the House of Representatives, the committee held its first meeting where the names of eighty candidates were submitted for consideration of a Supreme Court justiceship. Justice Minister Suzuki seemed to have initially hoped that the committee would refrain from recommending its members for the post, but later dropped such an idea when he saw the names of the committee members who were just as well qualified for justiceships as those recommended. Indeed, several committee members were eventually appointed to the Supreme Court. On July 22, at its second meeting, as many as 139 additional names were submitted including those of Kotaro Tanaka, Tadaichiro Tanimura, and Shunzo Kobayashi. The committee finally managed to reduce the list to thirty candidates and submit their names to the Cabinet.

Prime Minister Kayatama and other Cabinet members showed a keen interest in the selection process. Heated discussions ensued at several Cabinet meetings reviewing the background, personality, and expertise of each of the thirty nominees. A few names were mentioned as possible candidates for the Chief Justiceship, and eventually Tadahiko Mibuchi was unanimously chosen for the post. The selection of Seiichi Shimoyama, former Chief Justice of the Great Court of Cassation, was apparently motivated by the government's desire that his nomination might add to the prestige of the new Court. On August 4, 1947, exactly three months after the creation of the Supreme Court, a Chief Justice and fourteen associate justices were finally sworn in.

Chief Justice Mibuchi was appointed at the recommendation of the advisory body who believed that the strong-willed Mibuchi would not become a yes-man to the occupation authorities, and would help enhance judicial independence. Subsequently, GHQ,SCAP and the Japanese government apparently felt that an advisory body might stand in the way of the discretionary power of the Cabinet to appoint justices. They quickly abolished it on the grounds that the constitutional provision which gave the executive branch the power to appoint Supreme Court justices might be violated by the use of the advisory committee.[12] A bill to revive the advisory committee was submitted to the Diet in 1947, but was tabled indefinitely.

Thus, except for the initial fifteen justices placed on the Court by the Socialist Cabinet, all the justices who succeeded them were appointed by Prime Ministers of the ruling Liberal Democratic Party (LDP) or its predecessors. Although the process of nominating and appointing justices after 1947 remains unclear, it appears that a Prime Minister and a handful of advisors, including an incumbent Chief Justice of the Court, are directly responsible for the selection of final candidates.

An analysis of the fifteen justices appointed by the Katayama Socialist Cabinet in 1947 reveals the following major occupational backgrounds: six career judges (Inoue, Iwamatsu, Shima, Fujita, Shimoyama, Mibuchi), five private attorneys (Shono, Tsukasaki, Hasegawa, Mano, Kotani), one prosecutor (Y. Saito), one law professor (M. Kawamura), one judicial administrator (Sawada), and one diplomat (Kuriyama). Some observers classify Mibuchi, Sawada, and Shimoyama along with Kawamura and Kuriyama, both of whom are classified as "intellectuals," and see the 1947 Supreme Court membership as consisting of five practicing attorneys, five judicial officials (*i.e.*, four career judges and one prosecutor), and five intellectuals.

Analyzing prior occupations of justices appointed after 1947 by the LDP and other conservative parties, these court observers deplore the fact that the equal ratio of 5:5:5 among these three groups has been abandoned at the expense of nonlegal intellectuals who have broad vision and political ideals, and that career judges and prosecutors have come to outnumber other groups. In response, former Justice Minister Suzuki recalls in his memoirs that each candidate's qualifications were the single most important factor for selection, and that if such equal ratios among practicing attorneys, judicial officials, and intellectuals, had existed, it must have been a mere coincidence.

Be that as it may, the equal ratio among these groups came to be seen almost as a vested right of each group. Whenever a vacancy arose, the group which had lost the position acted as if it were entitled to have one of its men fill the vacancy. For instance, the Eisaku Sato government decided to appoint Tsuda, former vice-justice minister, to succeed retiring Chief Justice Kazuto Ishida. However, Ishida and a new Chief Justice Tomokazu Murakami reportedly pushed for the appointment of Judge Yutaka Yoshida on the grounds that with the retirement of Ishida and the promotion of Murakami to the Chief Justiceship, the second petty bench would be left with only ex-lawyers and prosecutors and that the vacancy should be filled by a career judge. This argument prevailed and Yoshida, after serving only three months as President of Osaka High Court, was appointed a Supreme Court justice.

By the end of 1980 the LDP's ten Prime Ministers, starting with Prime Minister Yoshida, appointed a total of sixty-three justices to the Court. The major occupational backgrounds of these justices are listed as follows: twenty-four career judges, twenty practicing attorneys, seven prosecutors, seven law professors, three judicial administrators and two diplomats. Furthermore, at the time of this review in 1980, the Court consisted of six career judges, four private attorneys, two professors, two prosecutors, and one diplomat. Compared with the Socialist Court of 1947, the categories of prosecutors and professors each gained one additional position, and the categories of attorneys and judicial administrators each lost one. This meant a ratio of 8:4:3 among the judicial officials (*i.e.*, career judges and prosecutors), private attorneys, and the intellectuals.

A further analysis of the backgrounds of the seventy-eight justices appointed between 1947 and 1980 produces the following patterns of judicial recruitments. First, a total of thirty justices included career judges of the following lower courts: nine presidents and two judges of the Tokyo high court, eight presidents of the Osaka high court, two presidents of the Nagoya high court, one president of the Fukuoka high court, one director of the Tokyo district court, one Chief Justice and four associate justices of the former Great Court of Cassation, and two presidents of former courts of appeals. Second, a total of twenty-six practicing attorneys appointed to the Court included sixteen attorneys who had served as either president or vice-president of the following bar associations: five from the Tokyo Bar Association, three from the First Tokyo Bar Association, two from the Second Tokyo Bar Association, two from the Japan Federation of Bar Associations, two from the Osaka Bar Association, and one each from the Nagoya Bar Association and the Kobe Bar Association. Third, a total of eight prosecutors appointed to the Supreme Court included the following: one from the Supreme Prosecutors' Office, three from the Osaka High Prosecutors' Office, one each from the Nagoya and Tokyo High Prosecutors' Offices, and two prosecutors from the former Great Court of Cassation. Fourth, six law professors of Tokyo Imperial University, one law professor from Kyoto Imperial University and one from Kyushu Imperial University have been recruited to the Supreme Court so far. Fifth, three judicial administrators appointed to the Supreme Court had served in the former administrative court, in the legislative bureaus of the two Houses, or the Cabinet. Sixth, three former ambassadors (to the United States, the Netherlands, and French Indochina) have been appointed to the bench.

Thus, presidents of the Tokyo and Osaka high courts, presidents of the Tokyo and Osaka bar associations, Tokyo Imperial University law professors, Osaka high prosecutors and heads of legislative bureaus of the Diet or the Cabinet seem to have a very high chance of becoming Supreme Court justices. Indeed, a promotion to the position of secretary general of the Supreme Court, then a chief judgeship of a high court, especially in Tokyo, Osaka, and Nagoya, seems almost to assure an appointment to a Supreme Court justiceship and has come to be regarded in judicial circles as being "the elite" road to success.

In tune with the principle of recalling public officials, the popular review of Supreme Court justices has been institutionalized (Article 79, Paragraph 2 of the Constitution). A newly appointed justice is reviewed by the voting public in the first general election for the House of Representatives following his initial appointment, and is subsequently reviewed in a similar manner every ten years thereafter. He is subject to dismissal by a majority of voters, provided the total votes cast are no less than one percent of all registered voters. The Supreme Court, referring to the popular review system, was of the opinion in *Sasaki v. Yamashita, Chairman of the Popular Review Control Commission for the Supreme Court Justices*, (1950)[13] that the voting public does not directly select justices but can remove justices who are appointed by the Cabinet.

In the first popular review in which about 74 percent of the eligible voters participated, the justices reviewed received, on the average, a non-confidence vote of less than five percent. Chief Justice Mibuchi received the highest percentage (5.5 percent) of non-confidence votes while Justice Sawada got the lowest (4.0 percent). In the second review of 1952 the votes of non-confidence climbed a little bit, averaging around eight to nine percent. No record was made available to the voters about the judicial behavior of the justices at the first review: the electorate probably trusted the Cabinet's appointment of these justices. By the second review, however, the Court had handed down many decisions that drew some public criticism, which was reflected in an increased number of non-confidence votes.

Takezo Shimoda's 15.2 percent of non-confidence votes was the highest any individual justice has ever received. Of ten justices reviewed in 1976, Dando received the highest non-confidence vote (13.2 percent) while Motobayashi received the lowest (11.2 percent). The June 25, 1980, popular review of four justices produced the highest average rate (14.4 percent) of disapproval so far. But no justice has ever been recalled as a result of popular reviews conducted between 1949 and 1987. In reality, popular review of the Supreme Court justices has not affected the LDP-influenced judicial selection in the slightest degree.

Next, legal education, training, and judicial appointment of lower court judges will be briefly described. Legal education in Japan has always started at the university level. The faculties of law at major universities offer the law courses necessary to prepare for the national bar examination. Virtually all justices who have ever served on the highest bench graduated from the schools of law at major universities, specializing in German or French law, while judges of the postwar generation have focused on Anglo-American common law. Post-university legal training is given at JRTI to those who pass the bar examination. If one passes the bar examination before university graduation and starts two years of training immediately afterward, one can be a judge at the age of twenty-three. However, the bar examination is so hard that most university graduates must spend five to seven years after graduation studying to pass it. JRTI admits fewer than 500 people each year. Only 465, or less than 1.6 percent of 29,088 applicants, for instance, passed the bar examination in 1975. The average age of first-year students attending the institute is approximately twenty-eight.

Trainees must choose one of three legal careers, *i.e.*, judge, prosecutor, or private practice, during their two years of training at the institute. Upon graduation legal apprentices can apply for a position of judge or prosecutor or can be admitted to the bar to practice. Aspirants to be judges are often separated from those trainees who opt for prosecutorial positions or private practice. They receive intensive training, the rationale being that the judges are a special breed of government servant and require a high caliber of legal professionalism and a special sense of dedication to justice and the public interest. Top students at the institute are often persuaded to become judges rather than pursue other legal careers. A judge-aspirant becomes a freshman judge, on the average, at the age of thirty, which is still younger than either a new prosecutor or lawyer.

A new judge is normally appointed for ten years to the post of assistant judge, and sits on the left side of the presiding judge on a three-judge bench. Since 1972 a newly appointed assistant judge receives job training at the Tokyo district court, and also studies at JRTI for four months. Under the supervision of a presiding judge, he participates in collegiate decision making and assists in analyzing legal issues, the facts of a case, sentencing, and opinion writing. Also, since 1974 an assistant judge of less than five years of service has been assigned to a single bench in order to learn how to read trial records, sort out disputed points, deliberate, and draft a court opinion. However, he does not participate in decision making. In both instances the objectives of the job training have been to learn how to speedily handle cases and to acquire the techniques of writing court opinions that would withstand review by a higher court.

At the end of ten years, or approximately at age forty, the assistant judge is up for reappointment and promotion to full judge, and sits on the right side of the presiding judge or sits alone in a one-man court. In the early postwar years the number of litigations grew tremendously and there was an acute shortage of judges. The government encouraged prosecutors and lawyers to become judges. Some did, but after the mid-1950s only a few lawyers made such a switch. Only four lawyers responded in 1961 when the Supreme Court requested various bar associations to urge their members with the minimum of ten years of legal experience to become judges.[14] Even fewer public prosecutors have switched to judges. The reason for such a low rate of career change from lawyers and prosecutors to judges, seems to be not so much the low salaries of judges as their heavy work load. Judges' salaries have been fixed higher than those of prosecutors, but because of the relatively small number of judges and the large number of litigations, their work load is the heaviest of the three legal professions and has been more than the salary can compensate for.

Consequently, the limited number of newly available recruits affected the judicial assignment to lower courts. An assistant judge after the initial five years is expected to work as a full judge, five years later is made a full judge. Then he may be appointed as an acting high court judge to sit on the left side of a presiding judge; after another five years he may be promoted to the position of a regular high court judge.[15] When the first twenty years of service have passed, the seniority system is replaced by a merit system under which younger able judges pass over some older judges. Subject to reappointments at ten-year intervals, a judge becomes a lifelong career judge serving various district courts and high courts of both remote rural places and urban metropolitan areas. He may also serve in administrative posts throughout the country. The compulsory retirement age is seventy for the Supreme Court justices and summary court judges, and sixty-five for career judges of both the high courts and district courts.

4. Avenues and Bases of Constitutional Trials

One Supreme Court, fifteen high courts, 292 district courts, 388 family courts, and 575 summary courts comprise the Japanese court system. Fifteen Supreme Court justices, 278 high court judges, 805 judges and 399 assistant judges of the district courts, 193 judges and 148 assistant judges of the family courts, and 767 summary court judges fill the benches of the Japanese courts.[16] Two thousand six hundred and five judges serve the nation's population of over 121 million. All cases are channelled through either a civil or criminal court structure. Constitutional and administrative cases are disposed of in either a civil or criminal proceeding.

A criminal case deals with an offense against the state in a proceeding to which the state becomes a party, such as a theft which is criminally prosecuted by the state. The functions of the prosecutor are to conduct criminal investigations, initiate public prosecutions, and supervise the execution of judicial decisions. The system of the prosecutor's office is hierarchically structured. There are four levels, with each office located at the level of a corresponding court: the supreme prosecutor's office is parallel with the Supreme Court, the high prosecutor's office is parallel with the high court, the district prosecutor's office is parallel with the district court, and the ward prosecutor's office is parallel with the summary court. The supreme prosecutor's office is headed by the attorney general *(kenji socho)* and below him by the solicitor general *(kenji jicho)*. A prosecutor at each level is assigned functions related to the level of his court. The public prosecutor submits his charge in the form of an affidavit of evidence, supported by sworn statements, and conducts a preliminary examination. A prosecutor lacks the inquisitorial power of the grand jury and cannot compel attendance or testimony.

A civil case deals with an offense against a private person at the suit of the injured person; a trespasser, for instance, is sued by those whose rights he has violated. But note that while a refusal to pay tax is an offense against the state and is dealt with at the suit of the state, it is handled as a civil case just as is a refusal to repay money lent to a private person. Likewise, an action by the state for damages is civil, although the "person" injured is the state.

The three-tiered court system adopted under the Meiji constitution has been preserved in the form of trial *de novo* used in criminal procedure; the function of the first two levels of courts is primarily to find facts, while that of a third level of court is mostly to review questions of law. Continuous trial as practiced in civil procedure is one variation of the same idea.

For the purpose of criminal trials, the courts are divided into three levels: 1) the district court, the summary court and the family court, 2) the high court, and 3) the Supreme Court. For the purpose of civil cases, the courts are divided into four levels: 1) the summary court, 2) the district court and the family court, 3) the high court, and 4) the Supreme Court. Summary courts, which used to be called local courts, constitute the lowest echelon of courts, and their number has increased to twice that of the former local courts. Each summary court has three judges, distinct from career judges. They are similar to the justices of peace or judges of small claims courts in the United States. Jurisdictions of lower courts over both civil and criminal matters are as follows: the summary court handles claims of less than 300,000 yen; crimes such as gambling, theft, or attempted theft (against which a penalty of a fine or less is optional); embezzlement; and transactions involving stolen goods. A single judge always sits on the bench at a summary court level. Decisions rendered by a summary court can be appealed to no higher than a high court.

The family court conducts an adjustment *(shimpan)* or conciliation *(chotei)* in family matters, and a protective adjustment *(kajishimpan)* of juvenile delinquents. An adjustment is conducted by a court-designated officer in the presence of, or on the advice of, a counsellor with whom the family court can dispense. A domestic conciliation *(kajichotei)* is conducted by a commission composed of a domestic conciliation officer and conciliation committee members, also with whom the family court can dispense. Neither a conciliation nor an adjustment is required to follow litigious procedures such as an open trial and a confrontation of witnesses. The family court can also act as a first instance trial court on matters related to an adjustment or conciliation of family matters, and a protective measure of juvenile smoking, drinking, or other delinquencies. As a rule, only one judge sits at a family court. If otherwise stipulated by law, three judges act *en banc*.

A district court becomes a first instance court on a claim of not less than 300,000 yen or one based on an administrative suit excluding the crime of domestic disturbance. It is ordinarily presided over by one judge. However, a three-judge panel can take up these cases at its own discretion and is needed to conduct a trial involving capital punishment or imprisonment of an indefinite, or no less than one-year term.

Judges render three types of decisions at a district court level and up. *Hanketsu* is a court decision rendered after an oral hearing. *Kettei* is a court decision without an oral hearing, and is used in cases in which objection is made either to the way a judge conducts a trial or the qualification of a judge to hear a case. *Meirei* is a ruling of a judge (often a presiding judge) or judges regarding a courtroom procedure such as the time limit for oral argument or permission to excuse the defendant from a courtroom. Whereas a *koso* appeal challenges a decision of a first instance court on questions of fact-finding, a *jokoku* appeal is confined to the question of legal interpretation and application made by a second instance court. Whereas a *koso* appeal is made against a *hanketsu* form of decision, a *kokoku* appeal is made against *kettei* or *meirei* form.

A high court accepts a *koso* appeal challenging fact-findings contained in the *hanketsu* decision of a district court, a family court, or a summary court on criminal matters. It also accepts a *kokoku* appeal and reviews *kettei* or *meirei* of a district court, a family court, or a summary court on criminal matters. Finally, it accepts a *jokoku* appeal made against *hanketsu* of a district court or *kettei* of a summary court on non-criminal matters. In each of the above three instances, the high court conducts a trial as a three-judge panel. Otherwise it conducts a trial as a first instance court in a case involving a crime of national disturbance with five judges *en banc*. There are few restrictions on the right to review in appellate courts in Japan. *Jokoku* appeal on civil matters is open to any kind of summary case, as long as a contention is based on the breach of law or ordinance.[17]

There is no practice of gatekeeping which enables the Supreme Court to screen and reject appeals on purely procedural grounds at its own discretion. Even a frivolous appeal automatically placed on the Court's docket receives a pro forma review before being dismissed.[18] Five different avenues are open to seek a review by the Supreme Court as the court of last resort. Routes that may be taken in civil cases include: 1) *jokoku* appeal against a high court which adjudicated special administrative cases; 2) *jokoku* appeal against a high court which has decided on an appeal coming from a district court in an ordinary administrative case involving a claim of more than 300,000 yen; 3) special *jokoku* appeal against a high court which decided on an appeal coming from a summary court through a district court in a case involving a claim of less than 300,000 yen; 4) special *kokoku* appeal against a high court which ruled on an appeal lodged against a district court; and finally 5) jumping appeal directly to the Supreme Court against a district court which acted as a first instance court. A jumping appeal can be made even by a party to a case, challenging a first instance court decision despite its contract with the other party to forsake his right to *koso* appeal.

There are also five different avenues for an appeal to the Supreme Court in criminal cases: 1) *jokoku* appeal against a high court decision; 2) special *kokoku* appeal against a high court, a district court, a family court, or a summary court or judges thereof on the ground of an alleged violation of the Constitution or a judicial precedent; 3) a jumping *jokoku* appeal by either a prosecutor or defendant challenging a decision of a first instance court, which holds that a law, order, regulation, or official act violates the Constitution or that ordinances or regulations of a local government violate law; this can also be lodged by the prosecutor who challenges the judgment upholding the constitutionality or lawfulness of an ordinance or regulation passed by a local government as in the *Sunagawa* case (1959);[19] 4) a transfer from a high court on a *hanketsu* decision; and 5) quasi-*jokoku* against a Supreme Court justice(s) who dismiss(es) a petition seeking disqualification of a judge, and against a disposition by a prosecutor and judicial officer regarding a defendant's right to legal counsel or lawful search and seizure.

The Great Court of Cassation (five civil divisions and four criminal divisions with each division having five judges) handled all *jokoku* appeals in both criminal and civil matters. Despite the fact that the 1947 Constitution greatly enlarged the functions of the Supreme Court compared with the Great Court of Cassation, the number of justices was reduced from forty-five to fifteen. In less than five years after its inception the Supreme Court accumulated more than 7,000 cases pending in its docket. Alarmed by the delay of trial and the familiar public outcry of "justice delayed is justice denied," the Japan Bar Association and the Court itself made various reform plans. The Japan Bar Association proposed that: 1) the number of the Supreme Court justices be doubled to thirty; 2) the Court be composed of a grand bench (one Chief Justice and eight associate justices, all appointed by the Cabinet) and several petty benches with each petty bench having one grand bench justice and no fewer than two justices; and 3) only the grand bench be empowered to decide constitutional issues while petty benches be confined to the function of reviewing judicial precedents.

In May 1956 the non-partisan Council on the Legal System proposed that: 1) grand bench justices and a presiding justice from each of the six petty benches be appointed by the Cabinet; 2) grand bench justices be nominated by a selection committee composed of judges, prosecutors, private attorneys, and intellectuals appointed by the Cabinet, and be popularly reviewed at regular intervals thereafter; and 3) thirty judges be appointed to six petty benches.

Whereas the Japan Bar Association sought to alleviate the Court's overload by increasing the number of judges while decreasing the jurisdiction of the petty benches, the Supreme Court attempted to solve the same problems by proposing that 1) the Supreme Court have only one bench with either nine or eleven justices; 2) the jurisdiction of the Supreme Court be expanded to encompass not only the questions of unconstitutionality and inconsistency with judicial precedent, but also the interpretation and application of socially important laws and ordinances; and 3) an additional court be established to dispose of *jokoku* appeals involving alleged violations of laws and ordinances of ordinary importance. The proposal of the council on the legal system was introduced by the justice ministry to the twenty-eighth session of the Diet in December 1957, but was never legislated. As the total of pending cases decreased from the peak of 7,000 to 2,000, all reform plans died and to date no action has been taken.[20]

Emergency control measures were enacted at the same time in both criminal and civil areas to mitigate the impact of a flood of appeals to the Supreme Court. The Civil Procedure Emergency Control Code *(minji okyu sochiho)* conferred upon the high courts jurisdiction over appeals from summary courts. Likewise, the Criminal Procedure Emergency Control Code *(keiji okyu sochiho)* prohibited those appeals to the Supreme Court that would challenge only a fact-finding or the propriety of penalties imposed by a trial court. With these measures designed to ease its increased workload, the Supreme Court has come to perform two main functions. The first is to review, as the court of last appeal, the constitutionality of a law, order, regulation or official act; and, second, to supervise the uniformity of judicial interpretation and application of law.

In civil cases, the rapidly increasing number of appeals excessively overloaded the Supreme Court and it became necessary to remove an alleged violation of a law or regulation as a proper ground for appeal available to the Court. In December 1949, the Commission to Investigate the Legal System advised the justice minister to revise the grounds for *jokoku* appeals to the Supreme Court. It proposed to give the Court mandatory jurisdiction over cases involving constitutional questions or an incompatibility of a lower court decision with Supreme Court precedents, and a discretionary power to review those cases which the Court holds to involve an important interpretation of a law or ordinance. The commission also advised establishment of a special court to dispose of cases involving a violation of statutory law. Although the idea of a special court met opposition from GHQ,SCAP, other recommendations of the commission were adopted as a temporary measure effective for two years beginning June 1, 1950. After extending the measure for another two years in 1952, the commission, in its subcommittee on civil litigation, made an interim report in January 1954 advising a further restriction of *jokoku* appeals by: 1) expanding the summary court's jurisdiction to cover civil matters involving claims up to 100,000 yen (the amount was raised to 300,000 yen in 1970), 2) by conferring the finality of judgment on high court review of an appeal coming from a summary court in cases involving these issues, and 3) by restricting cases not involving a constitutional issue from *jokoku* appeal to the Supreme Court.

The present Code of Civil Procedure, which was passed at the nineteenth session of Diet in 1954, consequently allows a special *jokoku* appeal *(tokubetsu jokoku)* from a high court only if constitutional issues are involved. In the field of criminal cases, the Code of Criminal Procedure, which became effective on January 1, 1949, had the same effect of greatly reducing the number of *jokoku* appeals to the Supreme Court. Article 405 therein limits grounds for *jokoku* appeal to: 1) alleged violations of the Constitution or an error in the interpretation or application; 2) an alleged incompatibility of a lower court decision with Supreme Court decisions; and 3) a case which the Court deems to involve an important interpretation of law. An emergency *jokoku* appeal *(hijo jokoku)* can be lodged by the attorney general with the Supreme Court on the contention of a gross violation of laws and regulations. Further, in both civil and criminal cases, a reference to a specific constitutional provision is required in challenging the constitutionality of a lower court decision.[21]

The introduction of an American type of judicial review raised a host of questions concerning constitutional litigation in Japan. Such questions range from the standing to sue,[22] the ripeness of a case, and estoppel, to legislative facts and political questions. In the absence of any separate procedural code governing constitutional litigation, constitutional disputes must take the form of civil, criminal, or administrative cases. There are several requirements which the Supreme Court imposes on constitutional decision making. It seems that the following judicial restraint rules set forth by Justice Brandeis' concurring opinion in *Ashwander v. T.V.A.* (297 U.S. 288: 1936) have formed the *modus operandi* of the Japanese Supreme Court: 1) the Court will not pass upon the constitutionality in a friendly, non-adversarial proceeding; 2) the Court will not anticipate a question of constitutional law in advance of the necessity for deciding it; 3) the Court will not formulate a rule of law broader than the facts of the case require; 4) if possible, the Court will dispose of a case on non-constitutional grounds; 5) the Court will not pass upon the validity of a statute on complaint of one who fails to show injury to person or property; 6) the Court will not pass upon the constitutionality of a statute at the insistence of one who has accepted its benefits; and 7) whenever possible, statutes will be construed so as to avoid a constitutional issue.

In 1952 shortly after the end of the American occupation, Mosaburo Suzuki, secretary general of the Social Democratic Party, filed a suit directly to the Supreme Court on the original jurisdiction against the state, seeking a judicial judgment declaring the National Police Reserve unconstitutional in contravention of Article 9 of the Constitution. Declining to issue any advisory judgment in *Suzuki v. Japan* (1952), the Court ruled that the present judicial power is not capable of abstract pronouncements on constitutional issues. In the opinion of the Court, "If anyone could bring before the Court suits claiming unconstitutionality, the validity of laws, orders, and the like, would be frequently assailed and there would be a danger of the Court's assuming the appearance of an organ superior to all other powers in the land, thereby running counter to the basic principle of democratic government that the three powers are independent, equal, and immune from each other's interference."[23]

This decision was to eliminate from the Supreme Court any attribute of a "constitutional court," as was expounded by such scholars as Soichi Sasaki. According to him, while all and any courts are empowered to determine the constitutionality of a law as a premise for disposing of concrete and actual disputes, the Supreme Court can review the constitutionality of law even in an abstract manner. The dictum of the *Suzuki* case, which was unanimously reached, was followed in *Tomabechi v. Japan* (1953)[24] in which Dietman Tomabechi appealed to the Supreme Court to issue an advisory judgment making the House dissolution void. In dismissing his appeal, the Court ruled that an advisory judgment pronouncing such a dissolution null and void would not be in conformity with law in the absence of any concrete legal dispute between the two parties to the suit.

The Court also refuses to hear an appeal which becomes moot. For instance, a labor union applied to the government for a permit to hold a rally at the Imperial Palace plaza on the occasion of May Day in 1952. Because of the time it took the case to reach the Supreme Court for review, the date of the scheduled rally had passed. In *The General Council of Japanese Labor Unions v. Welfare Minister* (1953),[25] the Supreme Court dismissed the appeal and gave its opinion that since May 1, 1952, the date for which the appellant had applied for a permit to hold a rally, had passed while an appeal was pending, the appellant had lost a legal interest. These and other court decisions have become important procedural rules, which regulate not only access to a court, but also an outcome of the litigant's substantive rights and duties. Since judges are central to judicial decision making, we shall next probe the judicial mind to learn how judges have historically perceived the nature and functions of their work.

Footnotes to Chapter One

1. Dan F. Henderson, "Law and Political Modernization in Japan," in Robert E. Ward (ed.), *Political Development in Modern Japan*, Princeton, N.J.: Princeton University Press, 1968, p. 408.

2. Kenzo Takayanagi, "A century of innovation: The development of Japanese law, 1868–1961," in Arthur T. Von Mehren (ed.), *Law in Japan: The Legal Order in a Changing Society*, Cambridge, Mass.: Harvard University Press, 1963, p. 34.

3. Masami Ito, "Eikokuho" (English Law), in Masami Ito (ed.), *Gendaiho 14; Gaikokuho to Nihonho* (Modern Law 14; Foreign and Japanese Law), Tokyo: Iwanami Shoten, 1966, pp. 278–279.

4. U.S. Department of State, *Occupation of Japan: Policy and Program*, Washington D.C.: Government Printing Office, 1946, p. 55.

5. Yorihiro Naito, "Saikosai no soshiki kengen ga kimarumade" (The history of the organization and authority of the Supreme Court), in *Jurisuto* No. 385, 1967, pp. 84–87. Also, see Yorihiro Naito, "Shusengo no shihoseido kaikaku no keika" (The history of the postwar reform of the judicial system), in *Shihokenkyu Hokokusho* (The Report on Judicial Analysis), Vol. 8, No. 10, 1971, and Alfred C. Oppler, *Legal Reform in Occupied Japan: A Participant Looks Back*, Princeton, N.J.: Princeton University Press, 1976.

6. Sup. Ct., G.B.; July 19, 1948; 2 *Keishu* 922.

7. *Komatsu v. Japan* (Sup. Ct., G.B.; July 8, 1948; 2 *Keishu* 801) ruled that a case filed with and pending before the administrative court or the Great Court of Cassation at the time the Court Code went into effect be disposed of by the Tokyo high court.

8. *Okamura v. Meiji Mutual Life Insurance Co.*; Sup. Ct. G.B.; July 8, 1959; 13 *Minshu* 911.

9. *Yanagi v. Japan*; Sup. Ct., G.B.; February 1, 1950.

10. Otto Kirchheimer, *Political Justice: The Use of Legal Procedure for Political Ends*, Princeton, N.J.: Princeton University Press, 1961, p. 347.

11. Saikosaibansho Jimusokyoku, *Saibanshobinran* (The Court Handbook), May 1976, p. 1.

12. Hiroshi Sugawara, "Saikosai chokan no senko ni omou—Sankenbunritsu no kakuritsu o nozomu" (At the occasion of selecting a Chief Justice of the Supreme Court—Hope for an establishment of the separation of powers), in 11 *Jiyu to Seigi* 11, 1960, pp. 4–7. See also Kazuo Tanaka, "Saikosai chokan no sennin" (The selection of a Supreme Court Chief Justice), in *Toki no Horei* No. 367, 1960, p. 25.

13. Sup. Ct., G.B.; February 20, 1950; 6 *Minshu* 122.

14. Chuichi Suzuki, "Wagakuni shiho no genjyo to mondaiten: Hansei to kibo" (Present conditions and problems of our judiciary: Reflections and hopes), in *Jurisuto* No. 265, 1963, p. 10.

15. Takeo Hayakawa, "Age and judiciary in Japan," a paper presented at the 1974 Annual Meeting of International Political Science Association in Montreal, Canada, p. 5.

16. These figures are provided by the Supreme Court General Secretariat.

17. In *Morita v. Morisawa* (October 13, 1954; 8 *Minshu* 1846) the Supreme Court grand bench upheld the constitutionality of the following provisions: 1) Article 393 of the Civil Procedural Code which stipulates that a final judgment rendered by a high court as either a second or first instance may be *jokoku*-appealed to the Supreme Court, while final judgment, which a district court renders as a second instance, may be *jokoku*-appealed to a high court; where both litigants consent not to *koso*-appeal while leaving an avenue open for *jokoku*-appeal, a district court judgment may be *jokoku*-appealed without delay to the Supreme Court; a summary court judgment may similarly be appealed to a high court; 2) Article 16, Item 3, of the Court Code which stipulates in part that a high court shall process jurisdiction over a *jokoku*-appeal against a summary court judgment or a judgment which a district court renders as a second instance, excluding criminal matters.

18. *Shimura v. Japan* (Sup. Ct., G.B.; April 21, 1950; 4 *Keishu* 675) upheld the constitutionality of Article 387 of the old Criminal Procedural Code denying a right to *jokoku*-appeal which had been lost by the lapse of the deadline for such an appeal due to a fault of proxy. Similarly, *Yamada v. Japan* (Sup. Ct., G.B.; December 8, 1948; 2 *Keishu* 1711) dismissed the contention that the first instance court violated Article 38, Paragraph 3 of the Constitution in its fact-finding proceedings as insufficient grounds for jumping appeal, as stipulated in the Criminal Procedural Code.

19. Sup. Ct., G.B.; December 16, 1959; 13 *Keishu* 3225.

20. Saikosaibansho Jimusokyoku (ed.), *Saikosaibansho Kikokaikaku Mondai Kankei Shiryo* (Materials Related to the Issue of Structural Reforms of the Supreme Court), Vols. 1–6, 1957–1958.

21. *Masuda v. Japan;* Sup. Ct., G.B.; January 29, 1949; 3 *Keishu* 1135. See also *Matsui (Cousel) v. Japan;* Sup. Ct., G.B.; March 27, 1950; 4 *Keishu* 420.

22. See Yasuo Tokikuni, "Iken no soten o teiki suru tekikaku" (Qualifications to challenge constitutionality), in *Koho Kenkyu* No. 37, 1975, pp. 59–72. He finds five types of contentions challenging the constitutionality of public acts and actions. According to Tokikuni, a defense attorney for a criminally accused person raises some of the following five constitutional arguments in his brief for the Supreme Court review. The accused should not be held criminally liable for his action under prosecution because: 1) either his action is constitutionally protected or his victim committed an unconstitutional act; 2) the provision of a law that holds him criminally liable is inseparably tied to other provisions of the same law that is wholly or partly unconstitutional; 3) a law which provides for a license or permit is unconstitutional as a whole or in part by setting inadequate guidelines; 4) a law which fails to protect the constitutional rights of a given third party to a crime is unconstitutional when applied to the accused; or 5) a law is unclear and too broadly stated and is unconstitutional when applied to the accused, as it is to unspecified numbers of persons.

23. Sup. Ct., G.B.; October 8, 1952; 6 *Minshu* 783.

24. Sup. Ct., G.B.; April 15, 1953; 7 *Minshu* 305.

25. Sup. Ct., G.B.; December 23, 1953; 7 *Minshu* 1561.

Chapter 2
Judicial Conversion: The Judicial Mind Probed

This chapter starts by posing the question of how judges decide a constitutional case in Japan. Historical inquiries reveal a great deal of transformation parallel to similar developments in the West. They were characterized by a sharp contrast between conceptualistic jurisprudence, which minimized judicial rule making, and the free-law school, which contained the danger of unchecked judicial discretion. Postwar study was expanded to include the Marxist perspective of finding judicial ideologies in capitalist Japan. The main schools of contemporary studies are neoconceptualism and the American-influenced behavioralism.

Many Japanese judges are still influenced by neoconceptualism and tend to view legal judgments as something that derives from abstract rules and principles as they are applied to the concrete facts of a case. Justice Yusuke Saito seemed to reflect such a tendency when he stated in *Aomori Prefectural Assembly v. Yoneuchiyama* (1953)[1] that a trial is nothing more than a syllogism in which a conclusion is derived from an application of abstract rules of law as a major premise to a concrete set of facts as a minor premise. More recently Justice Ken'ichi Okuno revealed the same preoccupation as Saito with the niceties of logical reasoning and abstract legal construction.[2]

Reflecting the influence of judicial realism, Justice Tsuyoshi Mano, however, stressed the role of individual value judgments and extra-legal factors in judicial decision making. Critical of prevailing syllogistic judicial reasoning which tends to minimize the role of value judgment in the judicial process, Mano stressed that "a judge, in interpreting constitutional provisions, should make his decisions reflect a great deal of his own views on law, life, the world, and social philosophy."[3] Jiro Tanaka was more like Mano and exercised a wide latitude in fact-finding and legal interpretation in search of a reasonable solution satisfactory to both parties to a dispute. These two schools of thought disagree over the nature and function of fact-finding, legal interpretation, and the whole judicial process.

1. Conceptualistic Jurisprudence and the Free-Law Movement

With the completion of the judicial system and legal codification through legislation, Japanese judges and lawyers began to interpret statutory laws under the influence of French and German conceptualistic jurisprudence. According to this legal technique, the rule of law for every judicial decision must be derived from legislative provisions or what can be read into them, and the quest for the intention of the legislature is the sole function of judicial interpretation. "The nearer free government is approached, the more tightly should judges be held to the mechanical application of the law."[4] There was always only one correct meaning of a judicial concept and such an innate meaning could only be extracted by the time-honored method of deductive logic, especially syllogism. When the meaning of legal provisions was clear, the legislative intent would be made known to the judges through a literal interpretation of the words. Otherwise, judges would exercise what Ihering called "logical interpretation," that is, find the legislative will "in the spirit of law."[5]

They would also use analogy and contrast mechanically to deduce the will of the legislators from the law. A widely held view that the legislators had solved all conflicting interests in all contingencies, even where issues were not originally contemplated in the law, has led to the failure to give due consideration to conflicting legal interests and judicial fact finding in each dispute. The judicial process has predominantly been law-finding rather than law-making in that judges have felt themselves strongly bound by statutory laws.

Several legal and political factors contributed to the prevalence of conceptualistic jurisprudence after 1881 in Japan. First of all, during the turbulent years of the early Meiji era, conceptualism was conducive to the much-needed status quo and stability of Japanese society. Many Japanese scholars subscribed to the theories of Max Weber who postulated an underlying principle of predictability and calculability of capitalism in mid–nineteenth-century Germany. Second, the conceptualists' claim for a single correct interpretation of law gave the Meiji government a rationale to confer upon a court the appearance of prestige and authority while its denial of judicial creativeness enabled the government to keep judicial activities minimal and subordinate to the oligarchical leaders. Finally, believing in an innate meaning in every law, conceptualistic jurisprudence allegedly functioned as a pseudoscience capable of finding the truth. When conflicting interests were excluded from judicial consideration in favor of a total reliance on strict logic, especially syllogism, it was believed that legal science was capable of discovering *the* correct interpretation of the rule of law.

The stabilizing function attributed to the conceptualistic judicial analysis was soon found illusory. The rapid industrialization of Japan, emerging victorious out of the Sino-Japanese and Russo-Japanese Wars, rendered many codified laws, especially in the economic field, obsolete and incapable of meeting new social needs. Judicial creativeness became more and more apparent in narrowing the gap between rapid social changes and outdated legal norms, as revealed in some Great Court of Cassation cases during the first decade of the twentieth century. At issue in *Japan v. Fujimura* (1903),[6] for instance, was the question of whether electricity was a "possession" (shoyubutsu) as the term "possession" was used in the Criminal Code which penalized a theft of "possessions." By construing widely the term "possession" as to include the intangible, like electricity, the Court convicted the accused who had been indicted for stealing electricity. This legal construction of the Court was contrary to the prevailing interpretation which denoted a "possession" of only tangible things. In *Japan v. Shiraai* (1910),[7] however, the same Court acquitted a farmer who had been accused of consuming for his own use small amounts of tobacco leaves grown on his farm, though tobacco growers were required by law to sell all their tobacco produce to the government corporation. The Court's judgment that the legislators did not intend to punish such a petty crime was again contrary to the prevailing view of conceptualistic jurisprudence, which held a person guilty of an act of theft regardless of the amount involved. These decisions demonstrated that judicial decision making was a process in which judges, by identifying and resolving conflicting interests involved in a case, interpreted the legal code equitably rather than in strict compliance with logic and that by so doing judges were often creating legal norms. If conceptualistic jurisprudence disregarded the substantive aspects of conflict resolution and sought only formalistic, symmetrical perfection by logical deduction, the free-law school, which came as a reaction to the conceptualistic method, was in danger of going to the other extreme of allowing unwarranted discretion to the judge.

The free-law movements in France and Germany were introduced in Japan after World War I. Eiichi Makino subscribed to the free-law school and succeeded in challenging the then-prevalent conceptualistic analysis of judicial process. Convinced that many legal provisions were subject to more than one interpretation, Makino held it untenable to argue that deductive logical reasoning was capable of discovering the legislative will behind the law, and criticized judges, lawyers, and scholars for imputing to the legislator a will which the legislator never had. He then argued that judges should first identify conflicting interests raised in a case and then proceed to resolve them by taking into consideration extra-legal factors, social objectives, and the sense of equity that a given rule of law purported to serve.[8]

Even Chief Justices Kiichiro Hiranuma and Hideo Yokota of the Great Court of Cassation, addressing judicial conferences in 1922 and 1924 respectively, stressed the positive role which judges could play by freeing themselves from adherence to literal interpretations of law in favor of a more equitable resolution of conflicts. Yet, if the free-law approach succeeded in exposing the abuse of logic in the conceptualistic jurisprudence, it, too, led to the potential danger of judicial fascism in later years. The free-law theory, like conceptualistic jurisprudence, neglected to probe the judicial process of ascertaining factual relationships and instead rationalized, especially in criminal trials, subjective and arbitrary interpretations of equity, justice, and social policies under the guise of such broad legal terms as "public policy and good morals" *(kojyo ryozoku)*. Many cases involving the alleged violation of the Peace Preservation Code *(chian ijiho)* indicate the destruction of the very nature of the rule of law by the abuse of judicial discretion. The editorial note in the first issue of the *Study of Judicial Precedents (hanrei kenkyu)* published by Tokyo University in 1949 warned that the study of judicial precedents was more important than ever in order not to permit further abuse of judicial discretion in trials.

In the work of Izutaro Suehiro the prewar study of the judicial process attained its height of sophistication. Suehiro paid foremost attention to factual relations in a case, and also made explicit the inductive nature of judicial decision making. He postulated that fact-finding, the interpretation of legal provisions, and the will to derive a decision interact with each other simultaneously.[9] This view marked a significant departure from a traditional view of fact-finding, legal interpretation, and legal application, with each stage taking place in a separate but sequential manner. Emphasizing the uniqueness and particularity of facts involved in each case, he suggested that a study of judicial process should start with fact-finding and proceed to examine the adequacy of rules which a judge had chosen as controlling the concrete facts. However, it is unclear whether he made a distinction between a descriptive statement about empirical events which led to the conflict of interest in a case and an authoritative reconstruction of the past event by a judge.

On the one hand, Hiroshi Suekawa[10] and Takeyoshi Kawashima[11] have thought it sufficient to analyze those facts which a judge ascertains and includes in a written judgment in evaluating a judicial judgment, or a judicial use of precedents as a frame of reference in a later case. On the other hand, Koichi Bai[12] goes beyond a written judgment and compares his findings with those facts ascertained by a judge. Furthermore, Suehiro confined a source of a precedent contained in a written judgment only to those legal opinions which a judge expressed while addressing concrete facts. Thus it seems that he, like conceptualists before him, still thought it possible to distinguish between *ratio decidendi* and *obiter dicta* even though he was much more aware of the difficulty of making such a distinction.

In spite of the fact that judicial precedents were used by judges in later cases, judges and lawyers still refused to recognize judicial precedents as a source of law, and only a few scholars such as Jyoji Matsumoto conceded that customary law may grow out of the repeated use of the same court decisions.[13] Here again Izutaro Suehiro was the first to propose the judicial precedent as a source of law. According to him the legislature makes a framework of law, a court puts substance into it, and there is no practical difference between legislative and judge-made laws. In his view a study of judicial precedents should first find the concrete and specific facts of a case and then look, in a text of the whole judgment, for legal norms a judge creates to dispose of conflicting interests. Finally Suehiro pointed out the importance of studying the effect of judicial personality upon judicial decisions. Although he did not elaborate on this, his reference to the judicial personality was a great novelty in his day. Yet, conceptualistic jurisprudence continued to dominate the mainstream of judicial analysis. When Sakae Wagatsuma urged that scholars probe separately the "theoretical system of existing laws" (*i.e.*, the rule of law) and the "concrete evaluation of cases" (*i.e.*, factual relationships) in order to advance Suehiro's efforts, contemporary scholars, including Wagatsuma himself, compounded the two indistinguishably.

The absence of any noticeable advance throughout the days of the "dark valley of World War II" was partly due to conditions, under the militaristic authoritarian government, which were unfavorable to free academic pursuit, and also the rudimentary type of methodology used by Japanese researchers of the judicial process.

2. Neo-conceptualism and Marxism

Claiming to advance the pioneering efforts of Izutaro Suehiro, some legal scholars like Hiroshi Suekawa and Akira Takeda of Kyoto Imperial University and Nobuo Nishimura of Ritsumeikan University began after 1945 to present what might be called the neo-conceptualist view of judicial process in the *Journal of Civil and Commercial Laws (minshoho zasshi)*, an old, prestigious journal published in the *Kansai* area. These scholars explain judicial decision making as a process composed of three aspects: fact-finding, legal interpretation, and application of law to the ascertained facts. However, beyond this common premise, there are different views expressed within this group concerning the significance of each aspect.

For example, Hiroshi Suekawa, adhering to the traditional view that judicial reasoning relies on the deductive method, focuses his attention on the judicial interpretation of law and makes it his objective to evaluate each court decision according to "socially recognized" meanings, as revealed in court opinions. However, Masayasu Hasegawa construes the judicial process as essentially an inductive one and approaches judicial decision making from the standpoint of objectively ascertainable facts, instead of only the facts found by judges, and argues that the "ideology" of judges is the determining factor in fact finding, which, in turn, influences the judicial decision itself. Despite differences between Suekawa and Hasegawa, both men would agree that it is not so much the subjective and unpredictable type of judicial value judgment as it is objective and predictable legal norms that ultimately decide a case. Here judicial decision making is captured as a process which moves in the direction of fact-finding→rule of law→decision making, and the holding of a judicial decision can best be explained by judicial opinions that contain underlying legal norms as intermediaries between the facts in a case and the holding of a case. This group also treats judicial precedents as criteria with which to examine the normative question of how a particular case should be decided rather than the descriptive question of how a particular case is being decided. Some neo-conceptualists in the mid-1950s took up the no-war provision (Article 9) of the Constitution as interpreted by the government, and questioned whether the "arbitrary" and "inadequate" interpretation of the government should be regarded at all as one valid alternative interpretation of that provision. Yozo Watanabe points out that this line of questioning misses the point because it fails to distinguish between the multiplicity of legal interpretation and the correctness of such an interpretation.[14] Saburo Kurusu, a legal philosopher at Tokyo University, began to analyze the multiple nature of legal interpretations and the underlying value systems in a society.

Kaoru Yunoki, another proponent of neo-conceptualism, asserts that judicial opinion reveals just as much predictability as a holding in a case, because it contains a single *ratio decidendum*, a legal norm which may be applied to a similar case in the future. For him *ratio decidendi* are the only real sources of judicial decisions and precedents, although *obiter dicta* may have significant bearings upon judicial predictions since a judgment rendered in contradiction to apparent *obiter dicta* of a higher court may be overruled upon appeal.[15]

This position of Yunoki resembles very closely A.L. Goodhart's theory and the so-called classical theory of *ratio decidendi*. According to Goodhart, who strongly influenced Japanese scholars of Anglo-American law since World War I, the relation between the material facts in a case and a holding on these material facts forms, explicitly or implicitly, *ratio decidendi*, with the ratio consisting of that very reasoning which is necessary to explain the holding on the material facts, as found by a precedent judge. According to the classical theory the ratio is the principle formulated by a precedent judge as necessary for his decision. These two theories are based on the assumptions that there is normally one and only one *ratio decidendum* of a case which explains a holding on the material facts, and that such a ratio can be delimited from the examination of a particular case.

These assumptions, however, have been refuted by Julius Stone and others as being untenable. Stone argues that Goodhart committed a crucial error in failing to see several alternative *levels of statement* of each material fact of the precedent case, ranging from the "full unique concreteness of that actual case, through a series of widening generalizations."[16] Furthermore, even within a single case, choices available for a later court or observer can be enormously enlarged by the intrusion of judicial experience of life and judicially recognized social values or even socioeconomic pressures. Stone concludes that the question of what single principle a particular case establishes is "strictly nonsensical, that is, inherently incapable of being answered"[17] and that "both in logic and in law usually alternative *ratio* based on alternative characterizations" are also available for choice, though in the particular cases they are not chosen.

Yunoki and others in the neo-conceptualist group, instead of going in the direction suggested by Stone and trying to find such alternative *ratios*, have pursued, in a judicial opinion in a written judgment, a single *ratio decidendum* which is said to have led logically to a holding in a particular case. Underlying that is an assumption that psychological processes taking place within the judicial mind in deciding a case always correspond to whatever logical opinions the judge may construct in a written judgment of the case.

Marxist legal sociology has long competed with Western legal sociologists such as Eugen Ehrlich, Max Weber, and Roscoe Pound, and has attracted large numbers of Japanese legal scholars. Marxist historiography has also influenced legal history including the analysis of judicial process. Indeed, the

Marxist jurisprudence has influenced the analysis of judicial process in Japan almost as strongly as either the neo-conceptualistic or behavioralistic method.

During the occupation period when most scholars were preoccupied with interpretations of the new Constitution and laws or the quest for a "living law" in social norms, customs, and the *topoi* or seats of argument, commanding the consensus of the intellectuals, Marxists directed their attention toward the power structure of the Japanese ruling class under the occupation forces and presented their view that judicial norms are not necessarily reflective of "live laws" and that a "bourgeois state and its laws"[18] often destroy "people-oriented, progressive and even revolutionary" law. Caught between a rapidly growing domestic economy and a rather restrictive political atmosphere under the occupation, Marxists directed their attack on the American occupation force and the Japanese conservative ruling power.

To many Japanese Marxist-oriented scholars the occupational policies were self-contradictory as the American occupation government was assisting the democratic policy of abolishing absentee land ownership and the old family system while pursuing a reactionary policy in the fields of constitutional law and labor law. They have also devoted themselves to the critical examination of judicial value judgments, class-consciousness, and ideologies in capitalist trials.

In line with Marxist tradition, Masayasu Hasegawa puts judicial ideology at the center of judicial decision making and characterizes judicial ideology in a capitalist society as being fragmentary, arbitrary, and authoritarian. Some Marxists, however, have failed to distinguish between capitalism as an idea and capitalism as an actually existing system, and consequently have failed properly to analyze the legal structure and order of Japan. Yasuo Yamanaka, for example, claims to build his theory of Japanese law by first constructing a normative theory of law in conformity to a materialistic and idealistic doctrine of Marxism and then proceeding to make existing legal phenomena in Japan fit into his own model of the Japanese legal structure. This has invited criticism from such Marxists as Shun'ichi Suginohara who argued that inasmuch as legal norms are reflective of materialistic determinism, legal norms in the capitalistic society should be analyzed as they are revealed in concrete and unique facts in each case and not just in an abstract idea itself. Yamanaka's conceptualization of the capitalistic legal system in Japan has also been criticized by non-Marxists as too vague and oversimplified. Referring to judicial decision-making analysis, these critics also point out that by imposing their Marxian-imbued frame of reference upon the analysis of judicial behavior, Marxists are attributing to the judges those attitudes which the judge does not manifest.

There has been no unified theory among Japanese Marxists concerning the development of Japanese capitalism and the imperial system as well as the nature of the revolution to be carried out in Japan. According to a predominant and orthodox Marxist view of the *lecture (koza)* faction,[19] the Meiji Restoration was a bourgeois democratic revolution which brought Japan to the first stage of a capitalistic country, while in the prewar and early postwar periods Japanese capitalism was supported by its imperial system in which monopolistic capitalists and landlords, as a ruling class, exploited and oppressed Japanese workers and farmers. The *lecture* faction advocated a bourgeois democratic revolution to overthrow the ruling class and to prepare the way for a socialist revolution. Later, however, this faction began to regard American "imperialism" as a cause of Japanese capitalism and accordingly changed its immediate objective to national liberation.

The workers and farmers *(rono)* faction, however, assumed that Japan was already in the stage of socialist revolution and advocated more radical views of Marxist ideology. Some common features are discernible, however, between the two Marxist schools in their views on judicial thinking. Common among the Marxists is the characterization of Japanese judges into three categories: the first group exhibiting bureaucratic and artisan attributes; the second category devoted to individual human rights and constitutional democracy; and the third group of judges who "follow actively American imperialism and, as servants of Japanese monopolists, act in favor of anti-communism, anti-people, and anti-democracy."[20] This categorization of Japanese judges strongly reflects the old official position of the Japan Communist Party which claims that "the continuing process of revolution is in the democratic stage" and that "its main enemies are the American imperialists and the Japanese bureaucrats, landlords, and monopoly capitalists."[21] Many constitutional scholars have shared with Marxists their views on the ruling conservative government and its socioeconomic policies in Japan. They have also persistently criticized the Supreme Court decisions on civil liberties.

3. Behavioralist Perspectives on Judicial Conversion

The fact of a case is an authoritative supposition of empirical events in a particular case, while a law represents a normative supposition of human behavior which judges perceive and to which they respond. It is not always easy to distinguish between fact and law, and not a few cases have been decided in which a question of facts was transformed into the question of law, or vice versa. For instance, whether a particular bundle of printed sheets is a book or a magazine in the ordinary usage of language is a question of fact, but which of the two words as used in a statute applies to just that unit of printed material is a question of statutory construction. While neo-conceptualists dominated judicial process and analysis, a new breed of scholars began to reexamine many basic aspects of the structure and process of converting judicial input into judicial output. The behavioralistic perspective was first voiced in a journal called *Judicial Precedents on Civil Law (hanrei minjiho)* published by Tokyo Imperial University faculty members like Tatsukichi Minobe.

Heavily influenced by American realists like Benjamin Cardozo, Roscoe Pound, and Jerome Frank, Takeyoshi Kawashima saw a possibility of conceptualizing judicial decision making as a process composed of fact-finding→decision making→rationalization. Ichiro Kato, another proponent of behaviorism, explains judicial rationalization as follows:[22]

First, a formalistic rationalization, through theoretical construction, has the role of verifying the appropriateness (not the correctness) of the decision. It clarifies a connection with another system *(seido)* or a comparison with an analogous case which had been overlooked in the first decision-making process. Depending upon the situation, it is necessary to revise the first conclusion or, having abandoned the first conclusion, to seek another conclusion. Second, through theoretical construction it becomes clear where and how far the conclusion reached can be applied. For instance, even though one tries to broaden the scope of the application of a particular law, when after broadening, one cannot satisfactorily draw a limit to its application, one will abandon the enlarged scope of application since it is not advisable from the viewpoint of the administration of justice. Third, one increases the persuasive power of the conclusion through theoretical construction. The fact that the conclusion is reduced to a general rule or the fact that the conclusion is rationalized from general rules points out the fact that the conclusion is not an accidental and arbitrary decision. This gives a feeling of confidence concerning the appropriateness of the conclusion. It is not necessarily a simulation or a falsehood.

The behavioralists would stress the multiplicity of fact-ascertaining and legal interpretations as demonstrated by differences between judges of lower courts and higher courts, between majority and minority justices of the Supreme Court, or for that matter, between the opposing litigants in a case. And it is up to a given judge to decide which facts should be ascertained and which legal effects should be attached to such ascertained facts. Out of a fact in a case, which is a complex aggregate of an almost infinite and continuous chain of events, a judge selects and evaluates pertinent facts on the basis of his own discretion. In criminal cases the existence of alleged criminal acts is ascertained in strict compliance with rules of evidence, but the selection of facts is left entirely to a trial judge (Article 318 of the Criminal Procedural Code).

Individual differences in sentencing are striking in cases involving violations of the Public Office Election Code. A violation of the code (especially Article 252, Paragraph 3), if followed by conviction, would normally result in the suspension of the right to vote and/or the right to run for a public office. In 1954 the Aomori district court in Aomori prefecture was most lenient with only 11.5 percent of convicted persons having their voting right and the right to candidacy suspended while the Urawa district court in Saitama prefecture was the strictest with 76.8 percent of suspension. The Osaka district court was most lenient in granting the shortest suspension to 49.7 percent whereas district courts in Kobe, Fukushima, and Yamagata never granted the short period of suspension.[23]

The Supreme Court, as a rule, reviews only the question of law. In most instances, the justices make their own suppositions of empirical events on the basis of the facts of a case, as defined and constructed by lower court judges. A typical reference to facts of a case by the Supreme Court reads, "according to the factual relations, ascertained by the court below, . . ." Once in a great while the Court reviews whether or not lower court judges have made a gross error in their fact-finding through the lower court's proceedings or open hearings, even though it overturns only a few lower court decisions each year on the ground of error in fact-finding. Because of a contention challenging the constitutionality of a law, order, regulation, or official act is one of the few grounds available for an appeal to the Supreme Court, an appellant often attempts to construct his version of facts of a case in the manner most conducive to the presentation of a constitutional issue.

Take, for instance, *Tomabechi v. Japan* (1960),[24] the facts of which, as determined by the Supreme Court, were that then Prime Minister Shigeru Yoshida dissolved the House of Representatives on August 28, 1952, by means of an imperial rescript, and that Gizo Tomabechi of an opposition party sought a declaratory judgment invalidating the House dissolution. Tomabechi first contended in vain that the Constitution did not permit the dissolution in the way it was done because there were certain irregularities in the form of "advice and consent" to the Emperor. In the opinion of the Court, Tomabechi failed to show his personal injury due to such a dissolution. Only after this abortive attempt did he succeed in making a constitutional issue out of this incident by arguing that the dissolution deprived him of his status and salary as a House member. In *Fujii et al v. Japan* (1954)[25] appellants raised the issue of unconstitutionality of an action, but the Court turned them down without any reference to the issue.

A propensity for making a constitutional issue out of a given set of facts is differently perceived by different judges as in *Japan v. Hamazoe* (1956).[26] Also in spite of an apparently identical fact raised in two cases, the Court dealt with one case as raising only a statutory issue and in the other case as raising a constitutional issue. *Kaneshiro v. Japan* (1957),[27] dealing with the confiscation of property belonging to a third party to a crime, did not raise Article 31, but *Kunihiro v. Japan* (1962)[28] involving the same issue of confiscation did raise the Article 31 question. Similarly, in *Matsui v. Japan* (1953),[29] some judges raised the issue of alleged unconstitutionality but other judges did not refer to the same issue at all. Furthermore, some facts raise constitutional issues for some judges but only statutory ones for others. Chief Justice Kotaro Tanaka in *Sakata et al v. Japan* (1959)[30] saw no logical connection between the constitutionality of the United States armed forces stationed in Japan on the basis of the bilateral security agreement, on the one hand, and upholding the validity of a Special Criminal Code provision which convicted the accused, on the other hand, and applied only the Special Criminal Code to the present case. Different judges examined *Tamura v. Japan* (1957)[31] from different angles, and reached different constitutional judgments. Also, for some judges, the same facts presented in *Japan v. Komiya* (1948)[32] were related to Article 31 of the Constitution while for others they were related to Article 38 of the Constitution. Finally, in *Japan v. Nakamori* (1950)[33] some judges regarded the facts of the present case as being identical to that of the earlier case, while others perceived the facts of the present case and those of the earlier case to be so different that the constitutional decision in the earlier case could not and should not be applied to the present case.

It is generally recognized that the multiplicity of judicial interpretations primarily rests upon multiple value systems in a society, and that judges exercise their own value judgment to resolve conflicting interests. *Attorney General, Takamatsu High Prosecutors' Office v. Matsumoto* (1950)[34] involved an alleged violation by a company management of the right of workers to organize and bargain and act collectively (Article 28 of the Constitution). Since Article 11[35] of the Labor Union Code was apparently clear, the judicial decision making, given the facts found by lower courts, seemed to be limited to reviewing whether or not the action of the accused would fall within the proscription of Article 11 of the said law. Yet the Court was split over the interpretation of terms like "disadvantageous" treatment of workers. Acquitting the defendant, a company manager in a labor dispute, the majority of the Court construed the term "disadvantageous treatment" narrowly to penalize the company management only for a discharge or similar discriminatory treatments of workers set forth in the provision, and for any and all acts that might harm the workers' status, benefits, and rights.

The minority justices, however, interpreted the term broadly and stated that "discriminatory treatment" is only an example of an infringement upon the right to organize, and includes any acts of employers that are detrimental to whatever workers' rights and interests are protected by laws. Granted that Article 11 used the term "disadvantageous" *(furiekina)* rather than "discriminatory" *(sabetsuteki)*, the minority justices argued, limiting "discriminatory" to "tangible" acts would misinterpret the provision. Although the disagreement between the majority and minority justices was expressed ostensibly over legal interpretation, the real differences seemed to lie in the justices' attitudes toward labor-management relations, an attitude which was relatively consistent for each justice and which transcended variations in the facts of this case.

Approaching the question of legal interpretation from the standpoint of communication theory, Tadao Hozumi identifies two stages of judicial interpretation; the discovery of meanings and the assignment of meanings. It is generally recognized that there are three methods of legal discovery. One is to find the intent of the legal framers; the second is to find how words were used when the law was written; and the third is to find the meaning from current use. According to Hozumi, to discover meanings is to discover a socially accepted meaning of legal language and not *the* meaning innate to the language which the neo-conceptualistic scholars thought could be extracted by deductive methods.

Parties to a contract do not always contemplate all contingencies which may arise in the process of performing a contract. Should a dispute arise concerning the situation not anticipated by the contractual parties, a judge is called on to adjudicate the dispute in accordance with a rule of law, whether it be a statutory or case law. Where there is no applicable rule of law, a judge from time to time makes his own rule governing the disputed point, and then tries to justify his own rule making by saying that what he did was nothing but to discover an innate meaning in the contract.

For example, X sold Y a pregnant cow, and received a down payment with additional payments to be made after the cow had delivered a calf and produced more than a given amount of milk a day. Later Y refused to pay the remaining debt on the ground that the cow had failed to produce the amount of milk agreed on. In an ensuing suit the Great Court of Cassation in *Shinshi v. Okamura* (1929)[36] ruled against Y and gave the opinion that the contract should be construed that Y should milk a cow with a reasonable care and that if Y fails to produce the agreed upon amount of milk from a cow capable of doing so, due to his own negligence or malice, the contract inherently means that Y should make the rest of the payment.

The assigning of meanings is to switch from one meaning to another by taking advantage of the very nature of the meaning of meanings, which are both ambiguous and plural. A judge, whenever he attaches different meanings to different legal acts, is constantly evaluating what legal effect should be derived from given facts. If one legal effect thus derived does not seem to be acceptable to him, then it is abandoned in favor of a more acceptable one. If a judge wants to reach decision *Y*, for example, in accordance with a rule of law setting forth that if there exists fact *A*, a legal effect should be *Y*, he has to prove that fact *A'* which he found is the same as fact *A* which is prescribed in the rule of law. The desired legal effect *Y* can be attained either by changing ascertained fact A' into prescribed fact A, or by attaching to the rule of law such a meaning so that the legal effect Y can be applied to the fact A', or by doing both. He would repeat fact-finding and legal interpretation, on the one hand, and an evaluation of the propriety of a legal effect deriving from them, on the other, until he can reach a desired holding on the fact.

Even in cases where socially accepted meanings are easy to find, a judge will accept such a meaning only after he is convinced that the meaning he assigns can render the decision and a rationalization thereof acceptable to himself. Even where a socially acceptable meaning of a legal act is relatively clear, a judge sometimes assigns another meaning resulting in another legal consequence, when he feels that a socially acceptable meaning is not desirable from the standpoint of public policy. Here again the judicial act of assigning another meaning not based on the letter of a contract is rationalized on the ground that the meaning a judge gave was innate in the contract.

For example, Y bought a house and leased from X a lot on which Y's house stood. Their lease contained a provision that even during the effective period of the contract, Y must remove his house from the lot and vacate the premises within six months after notice from X. The Tokyo district court in *Reigenji Temple v. Sano* (1912)[37] ruled against X who was seeking Y's vacation, and the court expressed the opinion that a person will not be able to own a house at ease if he must remove his house from the leased lot and vacate the premises merely at the convenience of and a simple notice from a landowner. Then the court proceeded to attach the following meaning to the contract between X and Y: unless special circumstances exist, contractual parties normally would not make such a special arrangement. Y leased the lot from X who intended to buy and own a house on it; the contract Y made with X was quite customary, and contractual parties had no intention of being bound by the provision requiring a vacation of the premises within six months after notice. Therefore, the court concluded that such a provision was invalid.

As long as the judicial assigning of meanings to language

and other symbols of legal acts enables the judge to give one out of several alternative meanings to legal acts, a judge is engaged in policy making, although admittedly following existing authoritative legal principles by utilizing the authority of the principles accepted by the society in order to justify his desired conclusion in a case. In the context of changing power relationships among various forces in a society, then the assigning of meaning functions as an adaptive process by the court to maintain effective social control while the court, too, is adapting itself to the changing demands and expectations from the society.[38] Yet, the popular belief in only one innate meaning in a language and the pretense that the meaning selected is inherently included in the rule of law with the subsequent holding in a case being the only logical derivative of such an interpretation has tended to becloud the judicial maneuvering of assigning or discovering one meaning rather than another.

According to Takeyoshi Kawashima, the framework of legal interpretation is delineated by the balance of powers among the three branches of government and various political and economic forces within that framework, and an actual interpretation is determined by the interpreter's perception of and response to the institutional framework and socioeconomic forces in it.[39] Take, for instance, the governmental interpretation of the constitutional renunciation of war. Many constitutional scholars and lawyers long criticized as being unconstitutional the conservative governments' interpretation of Article 9 of the Constitution, which allowed the maintaining of Japanese forces for the purpose of "self-defense" and of United States bases in Japan. However the governmental interpretation has won a general acceptance from the public and also was referred to in the Supreme Court decision in *Japan v. Sakata et al* (1959)[40] involving the constitutionality of the United States military bases in Japan. By ruling the issue to be a non-justiciable political question, the Court, in effect, let the governmental interpretation of Article 9 prevail.

Other Japanese scholars who have been influenced by realists like Raymond Saleilles, Francois Geny, and Eugen Ehrlich would seek to balance competing interests in "the living law" or through "free scientific research." Julius Stone maintains that justice and social policy primarily determine the judicial interpretation of legal acts. Scholars have also considered various other facets of justice, ranging from psychological, procedural, or functional to metaphysical or moral aspects of justice.

Typical of a psychological approach is Edmond J. Cahn in *The Sense of Injustice: An Anthropocentric View of Law* (1949) and *The Moral Decision* (1956). Admitting that justice has been so beclouded by natural law writing that it brings to mind some ideal or static conditions, Cahn defines justice as the active process of remedying or preventing what would arouse the sense of injustice. Whereas Cahn observes that although the sense of justice speaks compellingly in particular cases, its disclosures have not been generalized. Arnold Brecht, in *Political Theory* (1959) attempts to construct the following five tentative universal postulates of justice:[41] 1) Justice demands an accordance with truth, objective or subjective. All relevant statements of facts must be objectively true, and a judging person must honestly think that the relevant statements are true. 2) Justice demands treatment as equal of what is equal under the accepted system. No arbitrary discrimination is allowed among equal cases. 3) Justice demands generality of the system of values, which is applied. No arbitrary selection of values is allowed in considering one case or another. 4) Justice demands no restriction of freedom beyond the requirements of the accepted system, thus, no arbitrary restriction of freedom. 5) Respect for the necessities of nature in the strict sense. No infliction of punishment is allowed against nonfulfillment of a law impossible to carry out.

Roscoe Pound's *Justice According to Law* (1951) and Hans Kelsen's *What is Justice* (1957) represent a procedural approach to justice in that both men are concerned with developing an apparatus that will serve as a fair means to the attainment of ends that procedural justice does not determine. This approach runs the risk of equating justice with efficiency or utility. While Pound conceives of justice to be an ideal relationship among men through conflict resolution by law functioning as social engineering, he takes a relativistic and particularistic view of ideal relations. Kelsen goes one step further and speaks only about what justice means to him. For Kelsen, justice is, *inter alia*, freedom, peace, democracy, and tolerance.

Finally, Eredell Jenkins, in "Justice as Ideal and Ideology"[42] presents a functional model of justice after defining justice as the order that man seeks to create through law. According to Jenkins, justice is an ideal in the sense that it pretends to be objectively grounded and universally relevant. The functions of law and the ends of justice are to realize: 1) the cultivation of human potentialities; 2) the inculcation and acceptance of responsibilities and authority; 3) the establishment and control of authority; and 4) assurance of continuity within society. The general and abstract ideal of justice, furthermore, must be supplemented by a specific and concrete ideology at a given time and place. Whichever approach and facet of justice a judge subscribes to will influence his value judgments and decision making.

While a judge arrives at an interpretation which not only will be compatible with his value orientation on the issue but which also will justify the holding, a judge is also bound by the Constitution and the law (Article 76, Paragraph 3 of the Constitution). In case of a clash between a judge's conscience and the rule of law, such a conflict will be resolved in favor of the latter. A judge whose conscience dictates him to oppose the institution of divorce or capital punishment, would still have to go against his conscience and grant divorce or to pronounce a death sentence, to abide by the legal order of his society. Thus, a judge will have to justify his decision within the framework of and with reference to the rule of law. Saburo Kurusu, subscribing to the Kelsenite jurisprudence, postulates that the rule of law establishes a "framework" for a correct and lawful interpretation of legal acts and that any judicial interpretation which exceeds such a framework should be construed to be incorrect and unlawful.

In a similar vein, Tadao Hozumi states that the possible alternative interpretations of legal acts are limited so that if a judge wants to assign meanings which will deviate too much from socially recognized meanings, then his interpretation will no longer be able effectively to rationalize his desired decision in a case. Shigeru Inoue, applying the "rule analysis" by H.L.A. Hart, attaches similar limitations to judicial interpretations. Comparing the judicial process to a chess game, Inoue argues that it is the judicial duty (or a "secondary rule," in Hart's words)[43] to apply as best he can the rule of law (or a "primary rule") which remains the same. A rule of law has a "core of settled meaning" as well as a gray area open to various interpretations, and it is the core of settled meaning from which the judge is not free to deviate inasmuch as it sets the standard of correct judgments. A gross deviation from the core of settled meaning would be seriously criticized and might even be overruled by a higher court upon appeal. For instance, if a judge sustains the government's confiscation of private lands with a grossly meager compensation, he will be held to have violated a constitutional requirement for "just compensation." Thus, while a judge reaches a decision by relying on his own evaluation, within reason and limits, of what is most appropriate to a society and legal stability, he must make a reference to rules of law.

Probably because of the strong influence of neo-conceptualistic jurisprudence, there are few Japanese academicians who explicitly subscribe to the "hunch" theory of judicial decision-making analysis. Ichiro Kato is probably one of a few who come very close to this position when he states that from purely formal logic it seems to be possible to draw any legal interpretation inasmuch as judges use their hunches first to decide the solution of conflicting interests and then try to justify their conclusions by the inductive process in a convincing and persuasive manner.[44] In some cases a judge first makes a decision intuitively or by hunches and then chooses merely among several alternatives one rule of law which resembles the instant case, and attempts to rationalize it by claiming that this was the rule of law which led to the decision. Most decisions are either derived through conforming to rules consciously taken as guiding standards of decision or, if reached by hunches, are justified by rules which a judge was "antecedently disposed to observe and whose relevance to the case in hand would generally be acknowledged."[45] Suppose that a judge does not have such a degree of value orientation as to overrule whatever decisions to which logical construction based on a given rule of law would lead. Then it is likely that the judge will reach a conclusion contrary to or, at least, irrespective of his own value orientation, as was probably the case immediately after the establishment of the new legal order in 1945.

In the early days of the new Constitution, much of the Supreme Court decision making was taken up by the task of giving authoritative interpretations to the Constitution and other legal policies. This was especially true in the public law realm where there had been no detectable policy making by the Great Court of Cassation under the Meiji constitution compared with private laws, particularly the Civil Code. Furthermore, a procedural technicality in a collegiate form of decision making can very well make a judge adopt a conclusion not necessarily reflecting his own value judgment. Thus, caution is needed in treating the contention that even where a conclusion seemed to be a logical consequence of following the rule of law, a judge adopted such a conclusion only after he had been convinced of its acceptability to his own value judgment.

Even in the judicial process of facts→conclusions→rationalization, the rule of law retains its control over judicial interpretation, with its efficacy dependent upon several factors. In the field of constitutional law where the judicial value judgment, or "ideology" is very broad, the framework of alternative interpretations is much wider than in less ideological and more technical statutory laws. The efficacy of the rule of law also depends upon the precision and specificity of the legislative law. The more general and broad a legislative rule is, the less restrictive the rule of law is to the judicial discretion. The very same concepts, like justice and public welfare, which permit multiple interpretations of legal acts, also function to limit alternative interpretations by setting a standard whereby a judge attempts to make and then rationalize whatever decisions he finds most acceptable. A judge is expected to consider the socioeconomic consequences of his decision, and here a cost and benefits calculation and a concern for public welfare could influence his value judgments. Likewise, broad concepts like public policy and good morals *(kojyo ryozoku)* and reasonable grounds *(seito na jiyu)*, which give a wide range of alternative interpretations, do not allow unreasonable and unwarranted alternative interpretations.

Given a framework for correct and lawful interpretations, several alternative interpretations are still available, inasmuch as the constitutional provision (Article 76, Paragraph 3) which binds a judge to the Constitution and the laws still guarantees him a free exercise of his conscience. In the words of the Supreme Court, a judge is thought to dispense justice, fulfilling the constitutional requirement of judicial conscience whenever he decides a case according to what he believes to be right within the limit set by existing laws and regulations, "without submitting himself to oppressions and temptations, and in conformity to good sense and ethics of his innermost thought."[46] Judicial conscience is a pair of spectacles which a judge wears in determining facts and the rule of law. Such spectacles have different decisional effects depending upon who wears what color. Some criminal trial judges in the wartime period were apparently convinced that their conscience dictated a faithful execution of governmental policies, right or wrong. Likewise, the subjective nature of judicial conscience was demonstrated by Chief Justice Kotaro Tanaka in *Suzuki et al v. Japan* (1959) or the *Matsukawa* case[47] when he commented that the majority opinion sounded as if it were logical and conscientious, because this line of argument would suggest that only those opinions that are acceptable to him are conscientious.

Because of a wide latitude of judicial conscience, virtually all appeals grounded in the alleged violation of judicial conscience requirement have been dismissed by the Supreme Court,[48] whether it be the conscience of Supreme Court Justices as in the *Lady Chatterley's Lover* case[49] or the conscience of lower courts as in *Nishikawa v. Japan* (1948).[50] In the latter case, the defendant argued in vain that Article 4 of the Poisonous Food and Drink Control Ordinance deprived a judge of the free exercise of his conscience by prohibiting him from sentencing less than what the provision stipulated even under the strong mitigating circumstances. Justice Noboru Inoue and Saburo Iwamatsu, in *Tanaka v. Japan* (1953),[51] involving a constitutional requirement of just compensation in a case of eminent domain, reasoned that since the objective of such a seizure was to transfer the farm land from the landowner to the tenants, it was not for public use and that the landowner should have been allowed to sell to the government at a competitive price. Justice Mano, also in dissenting, employed the fundamental human right argument and held that if the landowner was forced, as in this case, to sell his farm at a low price fixed by the government, then his fundamental right to own property would be violated. Thus, Inoue and Iwamatsu, on the one hand, and Mano, on the other, used different logical reasonings to reach the same decision. Given a framework for correct and lawful interpretations, several alternative interpretations are still available. In each of these cases, judicial value orientations are a major determining factor in choosing one out of several choices and a judge will link the fact ascertained to derivative conclusions until he reaches a logical reasoning that will maximize a rationalization of a preferred conclusion.

Karl Llewellyn discerns the "free law" or what he calls the "grand style" of judicial decision making and the "slot machine" or what he calls "formal style" decision-making situations. Likewise, Ichiro Kato classifies three thought patterns of the Japanese Supreme Court justices with free law and slot machine types at both ends and an in-between type. The centripetal tendencies between the neo-conceptualistic type and the behavioralistic type have been counterbalanced by the centrifugal forces between the two types of judicial decision making. In its present form, the neo-conceptualistic type should not be identified with the so-called mechanical or slot machine theory which postulates absolute legal norms, existing prior to and independent of judicial decision making, and which pays little, if any, attention to individual value judgments of the judge. Nor should the behavioralistic type be construed to exclude the rule of law from judicial behavior in favor of the free-law theory which postulates that the judge draws his conclusion exclusively from his own concepts and conscience influenced by his own backgrounds and by the socioeconomic considerations raised in a case.

Probably in their overeagerness to expose fallacies and myths of rigid conceptualistic jurisprudence in the past, some behavioralists tended to dramatize the intuitive decision-making model. The neo-conceptualists, in defense of their theory, stressed the importance of the rule of law to the point of almost equating it with the old natural law doctrine. In reality, the neo-conceptualist group does not exclude the personal value orientations of judges affecting the decisional process any more than the behavioralists deny legal norms which control and regulate the exercise of their value orientations. The difference between the two types of judicial process should be sought in the degree to which each group differs in taking cognizance of the rule of law and the judicial value orientations influencing the decision-making process.

At the same time, there still remain differences between the two schools of thought. Whereas neo-conceptualists argue that it is not so much judicial attitudes toward the rule of law as objectively definable rules of law that ultimately decide a case, behavioralists would counterargue that a judge's value system (or attitudinal variable) and his efforts to justify his decision in harmony with the rule of law, and not the rule of law itself, are the determining factors. Also, whereas the former perceives a written judicial opinion as the key in explaining causal relationships between facts and holdings in a case, the latter would regard such written judicial opinion as a reflection of judicial rationalization of his decision. On the one hand, the neo-conceptualist approach may have significant implications for a theory-building of judicial process, but it does not adequately explain reality. On the other hand, by scrutinizing neo-conceptualistic jurisprudence, still strong in Japan, behavioralist perspectives have given many judicial concepts new meanings and a new significance. They have also narrowed the gap between the reality and what they purport to describe regarding judicial decision making. They have failed, however, so far conclusively to demonstrate that judicial value judgment (or attitudinal variable) is the most important determinant of judicial decision making. Despite its limitations, the present work will basically subscribe to the behavioralist approach, and use it to analyze constitutional judicial decision making by the Court.

Footnotes to Chapter Two

1. Sup. Ct., G.B.; January 16, 1953; 7 *Minshu* 12.

2. *Hogaku Semina*, No. 261, December 1977, p. 57.

3. *Nishioka v. Japan;* Sup. Ct., G.B.; April 20, 1948; 3 *Keishu* 589.

4. Julius Stone, *Legal System and Lawyers' Reasoning*, Palo Alto, Cal.: Stanford University Press, 1964, p. 213.

5. *Ibid.*, p. 215.

6. Gr. Ct. Cass.; May 21, 1903; 9 *Keiroku* 874.

7. Gr. Ct. Cass.; October 11, 1910; 16 *Keiroku* 1620.

8. Eiichi Makino, *Horitsu niokeru Gutaiteki Datosei* (The Propriety of Law), Tokyo: Yuhikaku, 1948, pp. 1–104.

9. Izutaro Suehiro, *Hogaku Nyumon* (An Introduction to the Legal Study), Nihon Hyoron Shinsha, 1963, pp. 157–158.

10. Hiroshi Suekawa *et al.*, "Minji hanrei kenkyu no tenkai to genjyo" (The development and present status of the study of civil cases), in 34 *Horitsu Jiho* 1, 1962, p. 29.

11. Takeyoshi Kawashima, *Kagaku to shiteno Horitsugaku* (The Legal Study as Science), Tokyo: Kobundo, 1964, pp. 220–221.

12. Koichi Bai, "Kon'in yoyaku yuko hanketsu no saikento" (A reexamination of the decision upholding marriage engagement), in 31 *Horitsu Jiho* 3, 1959, pp. 56–61; No. 4, pp. 86–95; No. 10, pp. 95–101; No. 11, pp. 38–43.

13. Jyoji Matsumoto, *Hito, Hojin oyobi Mono* (Person, Corporation, and Property), Tokyo: Ganshodo, 1911, p. 17.

14. Yozo Watanabe (ed.), *Hoshakaigaku to Hokaishakugaku* (Legal Sociology and Legal Interpretation), Tokyo: Iwanami Shoten, 1962, p. 32, p. 94.

15. Kaoru Yunoki, "Hanrei kenkyu no mokuteki to hoho (mimpo)" [Objectives and methods of analyzing court decisions (civil law)], in *Hoshakaigaku Kenkyu* (The Study of Legal Sociology), No. 16, Tokyo: Yuhikaku, 1961, p. 13.

16. Julius Stone, *Op. Cit.*, p. 268.

17. Julius Stone, *Op. Cit.*, p. 269.

18. Shun'ichi Suginohara, "Ho towa nani ka: kihankoi to saibankoi" (What is law?: Behavioral norms and trials), in *Hoshakaigaku no Mondai* (Problems of Legal Sociology), 1950, p. 21, as quoted by Toshitaka Ushiomi in 15 *Gendaiho*, p. 91.

19. For historical descriptions of controversies between the two factions, see Hirotake Koyama, *Nihon Marukusu Shugi-shi* (A History of Marxism in Japan), Tokyo: Aoki Shoten, 1962, and Noboru Sato, *Nihon no Marukusu Shugi to Kokusai Kyosan Shugi Undo* (Japanese Marxism and the International Communist Movement), Tokyo: San'ichi Shobo, 1964.

20. Mitsuo Higashinaka, "Saibankan" (Judges), in Masayasu Hasegawa, Hiroshi Miyauchi, and Yozo Watanabe (eds.), *Nihon no Horitsuka* (Japanese Jurists), Tokyo: San'ichi Shobo, 1962, pp. 15–37, as cited in Naoki Kobayashi, *Nihonkoku Kempo no Mondai Jyokyo* (Problems of the Japanese Constitution), Tokyo: Iwanami Shoten, 1964, pp. 151–152.

21. George M. Beckmann, "Japanese adaptations of Marxism-Leninism," in *Asian Cultural Studies: Studies on Modernization of Japan by Western Scholars*, No. 3, Tokyo: International Christian University, October 1962, p. 111.

22. Ichiro Kato, "Hokaishakugaku niokeru ronri to riekikoryo" (Logic and balancing of interests in legal interpretations), as translated by Charles R. Stevens in *Law in Japan: An Annual* Vol. 2, 1968, pp. 102–103.

23. Hideo Saito, *Saibankanron* (On Judges), Tokyo: Ichiryusha, 1963, pp. 97–98.

24. Sup. Ct., G.B.; June 8, 1960; 14 *Minshu* 1206.

25. Sup. Ct., G.B.; November 10, 1954; 100 *Saibanshu Keiji* 307.

26. Sup. Ct., G.B.; January 25, 1956; 10 *Keishu* 105.

27. Sup. Ct., G.B.; November 27, 1957; 122 *Saibanshu Keiji* 409.

28. Sup. Ct., G.B.; November 28, 1962; 145 *Saibanshu Keiji* 207.

29. Sup. Ct., G.B.; June 10, 1953; 82 *Saibanshu Keiji* 489. See also *Japan v. Tanaka;* Sup. Ct., G.B.; February 15, 1950; 4 *Keishu* 167 and *Japan v. Shimazaki;* Sup. Ct., G.B.; October 25, 1950; 4 *Keishu* 2151. These cases raised constitutional issues for some justices but only statutory ones for other justices.

30. Sup. Ct., G.B.; December 16, 1959; 13 *Keishu* 3225.

31. Sup. Ct., G.B.; December 28, 1957; 122 *Saibanshu Keiji* 973.

32. Sup. Ct., G.B.; July 14, 1948; 2 *Keishu* 856.

33. Sup. Ct., G.B.; November 15, 1950; 35 *Saibanshu Keiji* 569.

34. Sup. Ct., G.B.; July 19, 1950; 4 *Keishu* 1402.

35. The provision of the Article reads, "An employer may not dismiss nor treat disadvantageously his workers on the grounds that they belong to, attempt to organize, or join a labor union or engage in justifiable union activities. He may not make it a condition of employment for his workers not to join a union or to withdraw from one."

36. Gr. Ct. Cass.: December 18, 1929; *Horitsu Shimbun* No. 3081, p. 10 as cited in Tadao Hozumi, "Horitsu koi no kaishaku no kozo to kino" (The structure and function of interpreting legal acts), in 78 *Hogaku Kyokai Zasshi* 1, 1961, pp. 31–33.

37. Gr. Ct. Cass.; July 3, 1912; *Horitsu Shimbun* No. 804, p. 24, as cited in Tadao Hozumi, *Ibid.,* pp. 35–36.

38. Tadao Hozumi, *Ibid.,* p. 30.

39. Takeyoshi Kawashima *et al.,* "Hokaishakugaku no 'kagakusei'" (The science of legal sociology), in 26 *Horitsu Jiho* 4, 1954, p. 57.

40. Sup. Ct., G.B.; December 16, 1959; 13 *Keishu* 3325.

41. Arnold Brecht, *Political Theory: The Foundations of Twentieth-Century Political Thought*, Princeton, N.J.: Princeton University Press, 1959, p. 396.

42. Eredell Jenkins, "Justice as ideal and ideology," in *Nomos* Vol. 6 (On Justices), 1963.

43. Herbert Lionel Adolphus Hart, *The Concept of Law*, Oxford, England: Clarendon Press, 1961, p. 140.

44. Ichiro Kato, *Op. Cit.*, p. 35.

45. H.L.A. Hart, *Op. Cit.*, pp. 136–137.

46. *Mutsuguruma v. Japan;* Sup. Ct., G.B.; November 17, 1948; 2 *Keishu* 1565, 1569.

47. *Suzuki et al. v. Japan;* Sup. Ct., G.B.; August 10, 1959; 13 *Keishu* 1419.

48. Shinobu Tabata (ed.), *Hanrei Kempogaku* (The Study of the Constitution through Judicial Precedents), Kyoto: Mineruba Shobo, 1958, p. 443. See also Hiroshi Masaki, "Jyokoku riyu toshite no saibankan no ryoshin ihan" (Grounds for *jokoku* appeal, asserting the violation of the judicial conscience), in 7 *Horitsu no Hiroba* 9, 1954, p. 32.

49. *Koyama et al v. Japan;* Sup. Ct., G.B.; March 13, 1957; 11 *Keishu* 997.

50. Sup. Ct., G.B.; December 15, 1948; 2 *Keishu* 1783, 1786.

51. Sup. Ct., G.B.; December 23, 1953; 7 *Minshu* 1523.

CHAPTER 3

The Process of Judicial Decision Making

Since all constitutional disputes are channelled through either a criminal or a civil procedure, it becomes necessary to examine the Supreme Court practice and case laws governing constitutional litigation. Here the institution of appeals to the Supreme Court constitutes input process. It is through appeals that issues of a case are converted into a judicial output. A comparison of decision-making methods and opinion writing between the Great Court of Cassation and the Supreme Court becomes relevant to our analysis.

While a Supreme Court decision becomes an order for a lower court to follow in a case, it often becomes the highest level of judicial norm for future cases, and lower court judges often feel compelled to follow Supreme Court precedents for fear of having their decisions overruled upon appeal. Furthermore the Supreme Court decisions and its opinions are subject to more than one interpretation and implementation, and it becomes necessary to examine legal effects of public policies rendered unconstitutional by the Supreme Court.

1. Judicial Input

A litigant asks a court to protect his legal interests. In so doing, he also supplies a judge with judicial precedents, legal theories, or various forms of evidence and witnesses in support of his legal interests. Facts and rules of law are objective components or issues of a case whereas types of litigants and competency of an attorney, *inter alia* are subjective extraneous components which stimulate different responses from a judge.

Within two weeks after a lower court mails its decision to the litigants, a dissatisfied party must express his intent to file an appeal to the Supreme Court. He must then submit an appeal brief to the lower court within fifty days after the court secretary and the presiding judge of the case acknowledges such an intent. The court conducts an examination to make sure that an appellant provides all the relevant provisions of legal codes and statutes being challenged and cites relevant precedents accurately. Then it forwards all materials to the Supreme Court for review.

The Supreme Court functions as the collective decision-making body of either a fifteen-member grand bench or three five-member petty benches. The Court goes into recess during a New Year's celebration, a summer vacation in August, and the week of Constitution Day, May 3. A new term starts in January and ends in December.

Concerning the division of labor among three petty benches, the Supreme Court judicial conference composed of all fifteen justices almost adopted in 1947 the practice of the Great Court of Cassation, whereby the first bench handles criminal cases, the second one civil cases, and the third one both constitutional and administrative cases. However, it was found that there were only three justices (Shima, Tsukasaki, and Y. Saito) who had any experience with criminal trials and that the Court had more criminal cases than civil cases to handle. So it was finally decided that each of the three benches would review all three types of appeals (civil, criminal, and administrative), and that a judge be assigned to a given petty bench by lot. The decision to assign all kinds of cases to each justice made many justices feel uneasy. Justice Matasuke Kawamura was a political scientist and a professor of constitutional law at Kyushu University at the time of his appointment to the bench. Lacking expertise in civil and criminal matters, he confided in Chief Justice Tadahiko Mibuchi about his inexperience, but the Chief Justice comforted him by saying that seasoned common sense was all that was needed.[1]

All the cases coming to the Supreme Court are first referred to a petty bench for judicial screening, except for those appeals which are required by law to be decided by the grand bench. Approximately 4,500 appeals come to the Supreme Court each year. Roughly 1,500 appeals forwarded to each petty bench are assigned equally among the five petty bench justices, excluding the Chief Justice who does not normally participate in petty bench deliberations. This would mean that a little over 100 civil and 200 criminal cases are assigned to each justice on a rotation basis. While no clear guidelines exist, difficult cases which may create new precedents or which involve constitutional or other important issues are distinguished from relatively easy and clearcut cases, which number over 90 percent of criminal and 50 to 60 percent of civil cases.[2]

Each justice assumes responsibility for his own cases and presides over a group discussion of his cases. With the assistance of a *chosakan*, he examines both the substance and the procedure of an appeal to determine whether or not it warrants the Court's review. He clarifies disputed points, prepares necessary materials, and drafts a proposed decision for a consideration of other justices at a group discussion. Thus, the role of a presiding judge clearly becomes one of great significance. The petty bench can dispose of detention, relief, bail, and suspension of compulsory execution. While discussions take place freely, confidentiality is required of all justices concerning what transpires at a group discussion. Indeed, Justice Shima later destroyed all his trial materials and his personal notes. Strict secrecy is observed during judicial group discussion, with no one else allowed in the conference chambers except for two groups: *chosakan* who may be called in to the grand and petty benches at the request of justices, and trainees of JRTI who, at the discretion of the justices, may be allowed in the chambers in order to observe deliberation processes.

In the case of the second petty bench, *chosakan* are called in in all cases, but in the first and third petty benches, they are called in only when needed. *Chosakan* can stay even while justices are deliberating a case. The petty benches convened their first meeting on October 1, 1947. The first petty bench meets on Mondays and Thursdays, the second petty bench on Mondays and Fridays, and the third petty bench on Tuesdays and Fridays. Judicial group discussion provides a forum for an exchange of opinions in which justices attempt to influence one another and settle their differences. Usually when a case is remanded to a petty bench with a grand bench's instructions on important issues, the petty bench proceeds to decide less important issues with the same presiding judge. Overall, cases have become more difficult and complex than before, and require detailed research. Justices usually read the transcript of the first and second instances' decisions, the appeal brief and rebuttals, and the research report prepared by their *chosakan*. They may also read various records and evidence if they determine it to be necessary. The work load has been so heavy, with each justice assigned as many as a dozen cases at a time, that most justices can spare little time for research on cases assigned to other judges, thereby increasing their dependence upon a presiding justice and *chosakan* for the formation of their opinions.

The legal culture of Japan has long encouraged informal, non-litigious types of conflict resolution among people. Thus, direct accommodation by negotiation takes place from time to time at the level of lower courts, but conciliation at the Supreme Court level is rare between private parties who are determined to fight to the end. Prosecutors may withdraw their appeals in criminal cases to the Supreme Court by failing to contest petitions by opposing counsels. Conciliation by the Court in civil cases has grown from a few to more than thirty cases per annum in recent years. The legal basis of conciliation is unclear, but justices rely on the provision of Article 130 of the Civil Procedural Code, which enables a presiding judge to handle a court mandate, and even commission another judge. An individual justice initiates conciliation and most of the actual conciliation process is done by a *chosakan*. Pretrial conferences are conducted to secure agreements and concessions on the question of facts that are not substantially in dispute, to narrow and simplify the disputed points, and dispense with unnecessary witnesses that may impede a shortened but fair and adequate trial. They are also designed to settle disputes with a minimum of trouble and court time, while both parties feel that they have had a fair hearing.

Conciliation is preferred when a judge tries to circumvent a judicial precedent which he feels should not bind the present dispute. Through the prestige and influence of his office a justice could conciliate an increased number of disputes to the satisfaction of both parties, but he would not normally encourage conciliation at this level lest he should deprive the Court of a chance to deliberate issues in a dispute and make a new precedent.

All appeals made to the Supreme Court are first reviewed by *chosakan*. Article 57 of the Court Code provides that a *chosakan* engage in the research necessary for justices to dispose of cases at their group discussions. Twenty-nine *chosakan*, including one chief *chosakan*, work for an average of five years for the Supreme Court, and are mostly recruited from among relatively young and able lower court judges. Unlike the justices who handle all kinds of cases, *chosakan* specialize in types of cases. Twelve *chosakan* take assignments in criminal cases, another twelve in civil cases, and the remaining four in administrative cases. The chief *chosakan* is not assigned to any type of case. In order to avoid a situation in which justices can pick and choose any *chosakan*, they, unlike their American law clerk counterparts, are not attached to any particular justice.[3]

In the criminal section, twelve *chosakan* are divided into three groups, with each group assigned to one of three petty benches. Judicial socialization is facilitated by the composition of each group in which a senior *chosakan* with over twenty years of experience as a trial judge assists a junior *chosakan* who may have about ten years of experience as a trial judge. They receive assignments from any of the five justices in the petty bench and stay with their petty bench for four months, rotating among all three in twelve months. Cases are assigned to each *chosakan* on a case by case basis. The *chosakan* in the civil section are divided into three groups and the remaining four *chosakan* form one group in the administrative section. They do not rotate in either the civil or administrative sections but each case gets assigned by rotation. In a criminal case proceedings of the first and second instance courts and appeal briefs need not be typed up. They are given to all five members of a petty bench, and a *chosakan* in charge of a given case.

A *chosakan's* work in the criminal section starts with careful readings of the briefs and proceedings of lower courts. He familiarizes himself with the facts of a case, past criminal records of the accused, and other circumstantial factors. If, for instance, an appellant contends that a judgment below has violated a statute or a judicial precedent, a *chosakan* goes back to the statute or the precedent to compare it with the present case, and then may point out any fine differences in factual relations in the two cases. In rare instances he may want to contact administrative agencies in order to know the administrative background of a law under dispute. Furthermore, he may consult with a *chosakan* who handled the precedent case.

Since 1954, *chosakan* have annually published for future reference a volume of their comments on the Supreme Court decisions they handled, which is also reprinted in the law journal *Horitsu Jiho*. As a rule, all *chosakan* hold a weekly study meeting where they exchange their opinions about each other's cases. If a *chosakan* feels that his court may be inclined to overturn the precedent, he cites all relevant cases, scholars' opinions, legislative backgrounds, and foreign case laws. If he feels, however, that an appellant lacks procedural grounds, he so reports by filling out a fixed form for dismissal. A *chosakan* submits his report not only to the presiding judge, but also to all four others one week before a scheduled group discussion. He advises his justice not to decide in his petty bench those cases which should be transferred to the grand bench.

In a civil case proceedings of all lower courts and appeal briefs are printed and distributed to all five justices and a *chosakan* in charge of a given case. After a *chosakan* submits his case report a date is fixed for a group discussion among the five justices. If a presiding justice feels that the case report is insufficient or that a group discussion raises further questions to be clarified, a *chosakan* continues his work.

Considering the fact that many *chosakan* are among the most able career judges of ten to twenty years of experience and expertise as trial judges, it is not difficult to assume that their case reports are more than mechanical, value-free research, and often reflect their own policy preferences. Also, considering the relatively advanced ages of most justices and their very heavy work load, many justices, especially those justices who have little prior judicial experience, are likely to rely heavily on *chosakan* for important input on their decision making. Former Justice Fujita once referred to such influence in creating the Supreme Court decisions which guide all lower courts in the country.[4]

The grand bench is a collegiate body composed of all fifteen justices. A quorum is nine, and unless a judge is excused on grounds of illness, official trip, expulsion, restraint, or challenge, he is required to participate in both grand and petty benches. A Chief Justice always serves as a presiding judge of the grand bench; in his absence his authority and duties are delegated to one of the associate justices according to an order established at a judicial conference. Since the petty bench exercises the judicial power delegated to it by the grand bench, the latter can order a referral of cases whenever it wishes. A petty bench usually decides by a simple majority vote whether or not to forward a case to the grand bench. Initially, the grand bench was called on to decide all issues, constitutional or otherwise, raised in a case, but now only relevant issues and not the whole case are forwarded to the grand bench.

As a rule a petty bench first examines the formal aspects of a case and then refers it to the grand bench whenever an appeal involves the following issues, as provided for in Article 10 of the Court Code: 1) When constitutionality is challenged either by an appellant or a petty bench itself, except regarding an issue which was already decided by the grand bench; 2) when an interpretation and/or application of law and regulation by a petty bench contradict those of the grand bench; 3) when the petty bench is equally divided; and 4) when a petty bench decides that an appeal raises legal issues that are so important as to have a great social impact.

The grand bench first met on November 21, 1947, and has scheduled itself to meet on Wednesdays ever since. There were initially some difficulties in creating common grounds for group discussions among the first fifteen justices due to their different backgrounds and experiences. Justice Saburo Iwamatsu critically recalls that some ex-lawyers and ex-scholars were not accustomed to listening to and accommodating opinions of other justices and kept insisting on their views to the end.[5] Discussions were unnecessarily prolonged, he continues, because many opinions were irrelevant to a solution of disputed points, and the debates were often carried out in the form of formal speeches rather than a free exchange of opinions, but it all gradually improved and became more orderly. Justice Daisuke Kawamura describes what transpired at those initial sessions of the Court:[6]

> Very rarely at the outset of group discussion was there consensus on a case. Disagreements arose very often and a compromise was worked out only after a considerable amount of deliberation. It is not difficult to imagine the development of heated discussion. But when the time was ripe to reach a decision, all the justices felt relieved and left no grudges.

Acknowledging the effect of judicial group discussion upon individual judicial behavior, Justices Iwamatsu and Shima in *Suzuki v. Ishigaki* (1956)[7] recall that they were defeated on the question of the constitutionality of conciliation in lieu of a judicial trial, and subsequently changed their opinion to conform to the majority.

Usually a presiding judge of a petty bench, which refers a case to the grand bench, continues in charge of the case in the grand bench by briefing his colleagues on disputed points in a case, and often drafts the opinion of the Court whenever he is in the majority. Justice Mano recalls his influence on other justices at the grand bench deliberation of *Japan v. Murakami* (1948),[8] a case involving manslaughter, as follows:

> There were occasions when my concurring opinions became the majority opinion of the Court. One such occasion was the reviewing of an appeal challenging the constitutionality of capital punishment in the Criminal Code. No justice on the grand bench held a provision in question unconstitutional and seemed to have agreed to the opinion drafted by the presiding justice. But I felt the draft to be too simplistic and insufficient. So I decided to write a concurring opinion of my own. Strangely enough, when I presented my opinion at a group discussion, one colleague after another changed his opinion and eventually all of them came to agree with my concurring opinion which eventually was adopted as the majority opinion of the Court without modification.

Justice Mano also recalls the stifling effect of the practice in which many justices heavily rely on the information provided by a presiding justice and simply follow the majority opinion with little or no discussion. Justice Jiro Tanaka wanted to have all his colleagues express their opinion in each case, but Chief Justice Kisaburo Yokota rejected this proposal for fear of slowing down the work. It seems that even now only about one third of the justices present at the grand bench deliberations express their opinions and engage in substantive discussion.

As far as the power of the Chief Justice is concerned, he has only one vote in a grand bench discussion and his role as the presiding judge in the grand bench does not seem to have any overt effect upon an outcome of a case. As a rule, unless his presence is required to meet a quorum, a Chief Justice does not participate in proceedings in his petty bench. Chief Justice Hattori was an exception to the rule. He took upon himself about one-half of the normal work load and participated in petty bench deliberations. When Saburo Ienaga[9] attributed certain court decisions to the personal influence of Chief Justice Kotaro Tanaka, Justice Noboru Inoue refuted such influence and described the role of a Chief Justice in judicial decision making as follows:[10]

> The judiciary has always been a place where a Chief Justice never exerts pressure on his associate justices, no pressure at all as far as judicial process is concerned. I think the public has misunderstood this. Those intellectuals who have been criticizing the *Lady Chatterley's Lover* decision as a religious trial influenced by Chief Justice Tanaka are wrong and naive. Each justice who participated in that case expressed what he believed to be a right opinion and the Chief Justice never exerted any pressure on him. Many justices have been on the bench longer than the Chief Justice and each of them claims to be an expert in his own field. Many critics ludicrously disregard this. It is true that an opinion of the Court which I presume was written by Chief Justice Tanaka smacked somewhat of religion but that was all.

This view of Justice Inoue has been widely shared. A Chief Justice in Japan does not seem to wield power influencing the Supreme Court decision making comparable to his counterpart in the United States Supreme Court.[11]

The Court very rarely holds an open hearing which enables the litigants to persuade justices directly. The majority of the cases that come before the Court are decided on the basis of examinations of the written records like proceedings of lower courts, appeal briefs, and the reports of the *chosakan*. In criminal cases, however, there are three types of situations in which the Court holds open hearings in accordance with either its own custom or statutory requirements. First, the Court holds an open hearing when the justices believe that a judgment below should be reversed. When informed of a hearing, an attorney of a litigant whose interests may be favorably affected by a Supreme Court review, tends to suspect that the judgment below may be reversed and gets busy in preparing for an open hearing. The Court invites the appellee to submit his response in writing. Second, the Supreme Court is likely to hold a hearing when reviewing capital punishment. It is not clear when and how this practice began, but Justice Mano made the following remarks concerning its origin in the Supreme Court:[12]

> With the *Mitaka* case [*Iida et al v. Japan* (1955)][13] as turning point, the grand bench began to hold it uncon-

stitutional for a second instance court to sustain without oral hearing the first instance court's conviction. I do not know if this change was due to the criticism I made a few months after the *Mitaka* trial but we can regard this as a by-product of the case. Thereafter, both the grand and petty benches began to hold oral arguments whenever they dealt with an appeal involving capital punishment.

Third, the Court tends to hold an open hearing when it reviews public security incidents as in the *Matsukawa* (1959) or *Sunagawa* (1959) cases. Whereas Article 408 of the Code of Criminal Procedure provides that when the court of last resort believes, on the basis of the appeal briefs or other documents, that the motion for appeal is not supported by reason, it may dismiss such an appeal by judgment without an oral argument. The Court apparently feels itself obliged to give a thorough review of such socially important issues as public security by holding open hearings. Furthermore, these cases often receive a great deal of publicity by mass media. If no hearing was held, the litigants might begin to speculate that the Court was going to dismiss an appeal on the grounds of Article 408 of the Criminal Procedural Code and such speculation might promptly spread to the public before a court announcement. The Court, therefore, may feel obliged to hold an oral argument partly to keep the mass media from guessing at the outcome of a trial.

An oral argument at open hearing is often characterized by an absence of lively questions and answers. Since the function of attorney is to advocate his client's legal interests before judges and to convince them that his client's interests deserve the protection of the legal system, poor oral presentation among Japanese attorneys tends to reduce this function.

A historical review of Japanese attorneys reveals a very slow development of their profession. During the Tokugawa era, legal experts in the suit inn *(kujiyado)* in Edo drafted legal documents, and served as negotiators and litigation guides for itinerant parties in civil suits only. It was not until 1882 that lawyers were provided for defendants in criminal actions. Even then it was not the custom for lawyers to appear before a court, nor to represent clients. The accused was detained sometimes for months without the right to counsel. In 1893 a new type of lawyer *(bengoshi)* appeared, but their roles remained very passive.[14] The prewar inquisitorial procedure gave judges an active role, and minimized the activities of the litigant and his lawyer before and during a trial. Both prosecutors and defense counsellors remained auxiliaries of the judge. Counsel was only able to develop gradually his pleadings and proofs along guidelines laid down by a judge who performed the function of clarifying substantive issues in a case. The prewar system, therefore, tended to encourage inertia, inactivity, and a casual attitude on the part of many lawyers. Some able lawyers took the initiative in collecting evidence without waiting for instructions from judges.

The Code of Civil Procedure, as revised in 1945, shifted the function of taking proof *sua sponte*, from a trial judge to litigants and their counsellors. However lawyers accustomed to the prewar trial practice often could not perform efficiently and competently their new trial function of examining and cross-examining witnesses. Koji Tanabe, former judge of the Mito district court in Ibaragi prefecture, describes Japanese lawyers during the early postwar days as follows:[15]

> Lacking experience, lawyers were clumsy amateurs in the examination of witnesses. Their questioning was inept and dragging. For a while after 1948, many lawyers simply read aloud "questions" in writing and asked a witness to answer yes or no. Asking gross leading questions was very common and cross-examination, though frequently used, was often repetitious of direct examinations or unduly argumentative. For many of them, cross-examination was a vehicle for arguing an error in testimony rather than testing a witness' credibility or eliciting additional testimony. Objections to improper or irrelevant questionings were rarely made, and also tended to lead witnesses in cross-examination. Elderly lawyers often felt personally insulted by an opponent's objection.

Several leading trial judges in Tokyo, commenting in the early 1960s, noted a steady improvement in lawyers' examination skills during the late 1950s. Even now evidence of ineffectual presentation by lawyers can be found in their briefs. Although Japanese lawyers, trained in the tradition of neo-conceptualist jurisprudence, were believed to be skilled in preparing briefs by marshalling various legal concepts and logic, failure of lawyers to present their cases effectively has been pointed out, often cynically, by justices who would state that a counsellor could have persuaded the Court in his favor had he brought out certain points of law or presented his arguments in a different manner.

A former Supreme Court *chosakan* also cites examples of inadequate briefs and an unskillful presentation of issues by some lawyers.[16] Some attorneys are hesitant to make the best use of a chance given at oral hearings to supplement and reinforce their briefs. They simply refer all their arguments to a written brief and would not add any new remarks. It is not difficult to imagine the poor reception these attorneys might receive from justices.

This is not to say, however, that all justices respond more favorably to a case presented by leading counsels. On the contrary, a judicial response in such a situation may be an unfavorable one. Sometimes an attorney may want to project the image of not outsmarting a judge or his opponent attorney, so as to elicit a judge's sympathy who may want to help an underdog and not ask very difficult questions. Furthermore, the judicial response is likely to be more intense when the stimulus or the argument *qua* issue has been reinforced by the advocacy of a recognized personality who is experienced in interacting with the justices. For this reason some retired Supreme Court justices go into practice at an appellate court level.

Judges respond differently to not only different types of attorneys but also different types of litigants. Certain judges are found to be disposed to react against the state as a function of a particular litigant in a civil rights and liberty case. Likewise, a judge who is found to be sympathetic with labor unions vis-a-vis management reacts in favor of a union not only because of the issue involved but also because of the labor union per se is involved. There also exists legal inequality between the parties regarding research, resources, and representation. Thus the status and competence of counsel to present the objective contents of a case are also perceived differently by different judges. At the same time, the balancing of pluralistic interests such as those between management and labor, the state and the individual, the executive and the judiciary, and the adversary relationship in each of these heterogeneous pairs is made fuzzy by the ambiguity of concepts like class and interest. Workers do not necessarily identify their own interests with those of the labor class as a whole, and the public and private interests are not always mutually exclusive. Such fuzziness complicates the personal attitudes of judges and the multiple judicial interpretations of legal acts.

Chosakan, prosecutors, private attorneys, and various types of litigants are all among the subjective kind of judicial input. More important are issues of a case, namely, facts and laws raised in a dispute. Included in this objective type of input are, among other things, judicial precedents, scholarly opinions, and legislative intent.

According to the prewar conceptualistic jurisprudence, a judicial precedent could not be used as a frame of reference in the adjudication of later cases. This rigid view began to loosen in the first decade of the present century. On the one hand, Cabinet Ordinance 103, Article 4 of 1875, continued to deny a source of law in judicial precedents and forbade a judge to follow judicial precedents in earlier cases. On the other hand, the same Cabinet Ordinance in Article 3 allowed a use of customs on civil matters in the absence of a codified law and a use of reason (jori) in the absence of appropriate customs. Furthermore, the justice ministry began in 1875 to compile and publish some Great Court of Cassation decisions. After 1921 the Great Court of Cassation began compiling its own decisions with the objective of establishing precedents for later cases. It summarized abstract principles in a form of the Court's holding and opinions, and attached a lower court's proceedings as facts ascertained, and appeal briefs to the Court. In *Shinhokan v. Vottokeismer* (1905)[17] the Court made ambivalent statements that although Article 57 of the Constitution prohibits the use of judicial precedents, judicial precedents are respected and relied on not because they apply precedents *qua* precedents but because they apply law. The Court eventually came to recognize a judicial norm extracted from judicial precedents and used it as a frame of reference in later cases.

The Court also began to employ scholars' case commentaries in its judicial opinions. Influenced by neo-conceptualistic jurisprudence, most scholars acted as if they would be able to find *the* correct meaning of the law just like judges. They would single out and treat only portions of the written opinion of the court as if they contained nothing but the *ratio decidendi* of a case. Thus they put themselves in the position of judicial decision makers and commented on court decisions against judgments which they constructed through their own spectacles of formal logic.

Practically all important judicial decisions have found either sympathetic or critical reception among the Japanese jurists. Judges are sensitive to legal scholars' opinions and cite them to justify and provide support for their decisions. Law journals are also important forums of professional opinions along with Western judicial decisions and legal theories. For example, admitting the difficulty of judging "what is scholarship and what is art" in observing various schools of art and new theories and trends in art and scholarship, Justice Katsumi Tarumi in the concurring opinion in the *Tokyo High Prosecutor v. Senda* (1963)[18] conceded the need to respect the common sense and good judgment of authoritative scholars and artists.

After 1945 courts began to cite even Western case laws, especially in the public law realm. For instance, Justice Sakuro Saito, in *Koshiyama v. Chairman, Tokyo Election Control Commission* (1964)[19] disagreed with the opinion of the Court which stated that in cases of extreme inequality of representation in election districts the question of malapportionment may be subject to judicial review. He used Justice Frankfurter's opinion in *Baker v. Carr* (369 US 186; 1962) to support his argument for a more restrained use of judicial power. It will also be recalled that in *Colegrove v. Green* (328 US 549; 1946) Frankfurter concluded that the question of legislative apportionment was not justiciable because the

Court was incapable of fashioning affirmative relief and that the U.S. constitution vested exclusive control of such matters in Congress. He dissented later in *Baker v. Carr* when the majority of the Court held the issue of legislative apportionment not to raise political questions.

Also, scholars' analyses of foreign case laws and legal doctrines have been cited by Japanese courts. Justices Hachiro Fujita and Toshio Irie in *Sakata et al v. Japan* (1959) state:[20]

> For many years there have been precedents for political questions in the countries of Europe and America: "acte de gouvernement" in France, "act of state" in Great Britain, or "political question" in the United States. In West Germany, "Regierungsakt" and "Hoheitsakt" have been approved in academic theory in relation to Article 19 of the Basic Law. In our own country, . . . this has also come to be recognized by many scholars of public law as included in the concept of state governance.

Likewise, Justice Katsumi Tarumi states in the same case:[21]

> In our country, although it may be difficult to define the concept of "state governance" or to list them exhaustively, there is the academic theory that there are some acts in both Diet and the Cabinet that should not be subjected to the right of constitutional review by the courts.

One can also discern reference to European court decisions in the judicial decision making by the Japanese Supreme Court. For instance, in *Kuwahara v. Governor, Hiroshima Prefecture* (1975),[22] the Supreme Court used as a basis of its reasoning the West German Federal Constitutional Court decision involving the freedom of occupation and trade (7 BVerfGE 377: June 11, 1958). Also, in *Kurokawa v. Chiba Prefecture Election Control Commission* (1976),[23] involving malapportionment in the House of Representatives, the Supreme Court appears to have considered scholars' arguments concerning the American practice of prospective effects of laws that are held unconstitutional,[24] and the German practice of judicial judgment either confirming or warning of unconstitutionality of laws and regulations.[25]

Judges have from time to time examined legislative intent of statutory laws under dispute. In using legislative intent in judicial decision making, a judge tries to ascertain, 1) reasons why a bill was brought forth and what the statute was aimed at accomplishing, 2) the consideration of the bill from the time it was introduced to the final enactment, and 3) history of the act since its enactment and how the government administered the law. The Supreme Court has made very little use of legislative intent as a frame of reference, and it has been somewhat arbitrary where it has relied on it. "Even in a case which seems to require proof, a judgment is reached by the use of formalistic logic or even a guess in ascertaining what amounts to be a legislative intent."[26]

Shimizu v. Japan (1955),[27] involving a violation of the Public Bathhouse Code, illustrates the Court's reference to a legislative intent in this fashion. In challenging the constitutionality of the provision in the said code (especially Article 2 as amended in 1950) and the Fukuoka prefectural ordinance enacted to implement this law, both of which stipulated that a governor could refuse to grant a license when he found a site for the construction of a new public bathhouse to be improperly located, the defendant contended in his brief filed for *jokoku* appeal to the Supreme Court that restricting the freedom of occupation in this instance would not promote public welfare.

The legislative history behind the present law reveals a great deal of interest group activity. The old Public Bathhouse Code did not have the provision, now found in Article 2,[28] which the public bathhouse operators wanted. When operators lobbied for an inclusion of the provision in the form of an ordinance or regulation, the bureau of legal opinions in the ministry of justice rejected the lobbyists and gave the opinion that an ordinance restricting bathhouse sites would not be warranted under the existing Public Bathhouse Code and might even violate the constitutional guarantee of the freedom of occupation. Then the lobbyists attempted to have the law revised in their favor, but the bureau was reluctant to have the

Cabinet submit the operators' proposal to Diet. Finally the bathhouse operators succeeded in persuading some Diet members to submit a bill authorizing a governor to refuse to grant a license on grounds of improper location. In explaining the proposed bill, their lobbyists gave the following reasons:[29]

> It is extremely important to have public bathhouse properly spaced so that they may provide as many people as possible with the service while giving public bathhouse operators an economically healthy basis which will, in turn, ensure the sanitary safety of the public bathhouses.

A comparison of this explanation with the opinion of the Supreme Court in the *Shimizu* case suggests that the Court did indeed accept this reasoning and used it almost verbatim as a legislative intent to rationalize its decision against the defendant who applied for a license to operate a new public bathhouse. Likewise, after having analyzed the legislative intent to eliminate the maldistribution of pharmacies and to prevent public health hazards caused by substandard drugs, the Court in *Sumiyoshi Co. v. Governor of Hiroshima Prefecture* (1975)[30] ruled the present restrictions on geographic locations of new pharmacies neither necessary nor reasonable and exceeding legislative discretion.

In *Hoashi v. Japan* (1958),[31] a case involving a passport denied by the minister of foreign affairs, however, many scholars have pointed out that the government made the following statement when it proposed the provision of Article 13, Paragraph 1, Item 5 in the Passport Code, and that the Court should have taken this statement into account as legislative background when it reviewed the action of the minister of foreign affairs in the principal case:[32]

> The minister of foreign affairs should be authorized to deny a passport to an applicant if he has sufficient reasons to believe that the applicant is likely to commit such criminal acts as "civil disorder as defined in the Criminal Code, troubles and disturbances in Japan's diplomacy, grave violations of the Foreign Exchange Control Code, the Drug Control Code, or the Weapons and Swords

Control Code." The minister should take into consideration the government's policies in reaching his decision.

The critics argued that the Court disregarded this legislative background in deciding the *Hoashi* case and gave little reason for upholding the minister's action when it simply stated that the provision in question was "in the interest of the public welfare and a reasonable restriction on the freedom of foreign travel." The Supreme Court practice of announcing its decisions and opinions makes it very difficult to identify the legislative intent which a judge constructed in reaching his decision unless the parties to litigation specifically referred to them in their briefs.

Finally various reactions to judicial decisions have come from both liberal and conservative groups and individuals, as often reported through mass media. A popular magazine, *the Comprehensive View* (zembo), termed the junior lawyers association (JLA) *(seihokyo)* a "communist-oriented organization." While another popular magazine, *the Economic Traffic (keizai orai)*, criticized the free jurist association *(jiyu hosodan)*, the national judicial association *(zenshiho)*, and JLA as being responsible for many lower court decisions in favor of labor unions or against public security. A more prestigious publication, *the Times of the Japan Federation of Employers Association (nikkeiren taimuzu)*, made similar remarks that the Japan Communist Party and the Federation of Japanese Democratic Youth had penetrated judicial circles. Furthermore, the LDP party congress was highly critical of the Supreme Court decision in *Hasegawa et al v. Japan* (1969),[33] better known as the *Tokyo Teachers Union* case and the Fukuoka district court decision in *Kaneko et al v. Japan* (1969),[34] or also known as the *Hakata Station Film* case, both of which had resulted in acquittals of the criminally accused labor union leaders and news cameramen. The party adopted in April 1969 a resolution to establish a special investigatory committee to probe the judicial process. It also urged the Cabinet to use more often not only judicial opinions as the basis for appointing and promoting judges but also the judge impeachment proceedings. In response, the secretary general of the Supreme Court warned against this sort of criticism as impairing judicial independence.

At the same time, popular criticism from the progressive quarters elicited a negative response from a Chief Justice of the Supreme Court in some instances. While the *Matsukawa* case was pending, several journalists wrote commentaries critical of a lower court's handling of the case.[35] Addressing a meeting of presidents and directors of the lower courts in May 1955, Chief Justice Kotaro Tanaka warned against what he called "the noise of the people,"[36] or public criticism of trials, and told judges not to pay any attention to it. It is doubtful whether public criticism of trials might provoke a judicial response in an actual decision-making process, but, in a wider context, judges are exposed to public sentiments and detect a prevailing opinion in the country. In recent years there is a growing feeling about environmental problems and a judge, deciding a claim of air pollution victims, probably cannot help but take into consideration what he considers to be the public sentiment on the issue. While there is no empirical research to date, some judges seem to consider impacts of their decision upon the society and the government. In the Osaka international airport noise pollution case,[37] the Supreme Court seemed to have calculated a gross sum of the government indemnity to affected residents if similar noise pollutions were to be litigated at many other airports throughout the country, in reaching a decision on how much the Court should award to each resident near the Osaka international airport. Although the psychological effect of public criticism on trial judges and Supreme Court justices is hard to ascertain, public criticism of trials is certainly a new phenomenon in postwar Japan.

All in all, interactions among the legislative, executive, and judicial branches often condition judicial decision making. Legislative codes become rules of law for judges to work with. Political branches can influence judicial administration. In criminal cases a law enforcement agency can set the judicial process in motion, and interactions between the executive and judicial branches continue at all levels, while in civil cases the government may appear as a direct party to a litigation involving commercial, labor, or utilities regulations. Even the general public, interest groups, and the mass media become relevant to constitutional litigation when they act in response to judicial decisions.

We have analyzed major variables of judicial input. They are representative and by no means exhaustive in real decision-making situations. Such an extraneous and even irrational variable like judicial temperament or mood in a morning of judicial hearing or group discussion may affect his final opinion on a case. Be that as it may, justices respond to both an objective type of input like issues of a case and a subjective type of input like types of litigants and attorneys all through their value judgments or ideologies. As analyzed in chapter two, judicial input is converted into judicial output primarily through a means of judicial attitudes toward major socioeconomic and political issues of a society.

Conversion is where a judge defines and responds to conflicting demands and support of opposing litigants, and makes an authoritative decision, affecting advantages and disadvantages of the parties involved. All this takes place through values and beliefs of a judge. Issues of a case then become an independent variable while judicial value judgments form the intervening attitudinal variable. We shall now turn to the process of judicial output.

2. Judicial Output

Group discussions and mutual persuasions are followed by decision making and opinion writing. On most occasions formal voting by either ballot or show of hands is not necessary nor practiced. Nodding or some form of implicit expression of decision is all it takes to reach a collective decision in both petty and grand benches. In the case of the grand bench a Chief Justice ranks the highest and each associate justice ranks according to his formal seniority. Seniority is determined by the date of appointment to the bench or, in the event two judges have the same appointment date, according to age. However, because a presiding judge changes from one case to another there is apparently no predetermined order to follow in expressing opinions or decision making at a petty bench group discussion. Neither does there seem to be any power advantage inherent in the discussion and voting sequence. This practice of the Japanese Supreme Court is in contrast with that of the United States Supreme Court where the Chief Justice states his opinion first, followed by the other justices in order of their seniority. Then the justices formally vote, also beginning with the Chief Justice and working down the seniority scale.

The Great Court of Cassation used a type of deliberation and voting patterned after the German method. Judicial voting proceeds, according to this method, from one disputed point to another, and each disputed point was usually arranged by the parties to a case in such a way as to contain one question of law or fact. The Court ordinarily followed the order arranged by a party in deciding each disputed point. When all the judges exhausted their opinions on each issue, they took a vote and differences were resolved by a majority vote. If they agreed on the disposition of an issue, however, they could omit voting and proceed to the next issue. A justice whose opinion was defeated in the voting had to conform to that of the majority of the Court and decide the next issue by accepting the premises favored by the majority. As the collegiate body of the Great Court of Cassation moved from one issue to another it eliminated minority opinions on each issue, so that when it finished its deliberations on all the points raised in a case, a decision was made on a final issue. Out of this came a single decision and a single opinion of the court for the case, with no dissenting opinions recorded. Under this method, therefore, there is no way of knowing the voting behavior of the justices nor is there a record of any dissenting opinion of the court.

Today the Court Code in Article 77, Paragraph 1 requires that the Supreme Court decide a case by a "majority opinion," unless otherwise stipulated in a Supreme Court regulation; Article 76 requires that each justice express his decision at a group discussion. Although a simple majority is generally sufficient to dispose of a case, both at petty and grand benches, the Supreme Court Business Disposition Rules (*ji-*

mushorikisoku), in Article 12 stipulates that whenever the grand bench holds any law, ordinance, regulation, or official act to be unconstitutional, at least eight justices must agree. But since the quorum of the grand bench is nine, a vote of five to four can render a law or ordinance unconstitutional. Typically, an opinion of the Court in a case which is decided by a divided opinion ends with a statement that the present judgment is made with the agreement of all the justices except for the dissenting opinions of Justices So-and-So.

So long as a case involves only one issue, a judicial decision on the particular issue will determine the outcome of the case as a whole. A decision made on the issue at the end of all the deliberations on such a case is expected to reflect a judicial attitude on the single issue in an unadulterated manner. For instance, if a decision is made on the issue of equality under law, the single issue involved in the case, judicial attitudes toward that particular issue will be the determinant.

However, where more than one issue is raised in a case, there has been a disagreement as to how the case should be decided. Justice Mano, favoring the method practiced by the United States Supreme Court, advocated making only one decision on the case as a whole. Since different judges employ different logical constructions and legal interpretations to arrive at different judgments, he argued, the spirit of a collegiate type of decision making will be reflected best by a decision made at the end of all deliberations to determine the judgment reached by a majority of the justices on the case as a whole, regardless of their different opinions on some issues in the case. Accordingly, he construed the provision of Article 11 of the Court Code which requires a written court judgment to state each justice's opinions to mean that a concurring opinion refers to an opinion of those justices who agree with the majority's judgment of the case but not with the majority's reasoning, in whole or in part, and that a dissenting opinion is an opinion of a justice who disagrees with both the holding and the reasoning of the majority.

According to some scholars, both constitutional and criminal cases should be decided by the votes on the conclusion whereas civil cases should be decided by the votes on each disputed point.[38] For example, a three-judge panel is divided three ways. Judge A holds the defendant committed no crime; Judge B feels that the defendant committed a crime but should be acquitted on the grounds of insanity; Judge C feels that the defendant's crime was an act of self defense. Thus, none of the three judges feels that the defendant should be convicted and go to jail if votes are taken on the conclusion of this case. But if votes are taken on the question of whether a crime was committed, Judge A would be outvoted by Judges B and C who believe that a crime was committed. Then the three judges would proceed to the next question of guilt or innocence. If there is no majority vote on either the insanity or self defense of the defendant, however, the accused may be convicted and sent to jail despite the fact that all three judges feel that he is not guilty.

It seems to be a settled practice of the Japanese Supreme Court to decide on each issue raised by the parties to a case, and not on the case as a whole. According to this method a separate decision made on each issue, when put together, will comprise the judgment of the Court on that case, provided each issue is independent of every other one. For example, in *Ueki v. Japan* (1956)[39] decisions were made on two issues at the grand bench of the Supreme Court. The first decision was made on the question of whether or not Article 45 of the Ordinance to Implement the Code to Regulate Weaponry and Explosives, under which a defendant was convicted, was made inoperative by a new law and fell into violation of Articles 31 and 98, Paragraph 1 of the Constitution. Justices Fujita, Iwamatsu, M. Kawamura, Kobayashi, Kotani, Kuriyama, Shima, and Tanimura held the provision of Article 45 to be inoperative and unconstitutional, while Justices Motomura, Y. Saito, and K. Tanaka upheld its constitutionality. The second decision was on the question of whether penalties for the crime of aiding the illegal departure of Koreans were abolished by the law enacted after the defendant had committed the alleged act. Justices Fujita, Kotani, Shima, and Tanimura held that the penalties should be regarded as having been abolished, and Justices Iwamatsu, M. Kawamura, Kobayashi, Kuriyama, Motomura, Y. Saito, and K.

Tanaka held it to be in conformity with the provisions of Articles 22 and 31 of the Constitution to apply the penalties prescribed to the principal case. Thus, four justices, *i.e.*, Iwamatsu, M. Kawamura, Kobayashi, and Kuriyama, decided for the defendant on the first issue but against him on the second one. The outcome of these two decisions was reflected in the judgment of the case in that the defendant prevailed on the first issue but was convicted on the basis of the second one. When two or more issues are independent of each other and a judgment on one issue does not affect a determination of another, a group of separate judgments rendered on the issues becomes the judgment of the case.

This judicial process, however, can be reconstructed by the method suggested by Justice Mano as well. Mano would explain that a judge has first reached his judgment on the case as a whole after having analyzed the entire set of facts and issues of the case. When called on to respond to each of the two issues brought out at the group discussion, he expressed his opinion on each point on the basis of his overall judgments on the case. Likewise, where a settlement of one issue becomes a premise for deciding a second issue in a case, many justices seem to follow the method used by the Great Court of Cassation under which a decision on a final issue will settle the case as a whole. Minority-opinion justices on the first issue will have to proceed to the second issue on the assumption that they agreed with the decision of the majority-opinion justices on the first issue. The attitudes of the minority justices toward a first issue or public policy will not be reflected in the second issue.

For instance, in a civil proceeding in which a plaintiff demands repayment in compliance with a contract, a respondent raises three arguments: 1) he made no such contract, 2) he has already paid his debt, and 3) a statute of limitation has nullified the contract. A three-judge panel proceeds deliberatively from issue to issue. Suppose Judge A disagrees with Judges B and C on the existence of such a contract. Judge A would accept the majority decision by his colleagues, who acknowledge such a contract, and proceed to the next issue. Suppose Judge B disagrees with Judges A and C on the evidence of repayment. Judge B would accept the majority decision of A and C, which holds that the debt has not been repaid, and proceed to the third issue. The three-man panel might compel the respondent to pay his debt if it decides by a majority vote that a statute of limitation had not nullified the contract, or it might invalidate the debt on the strength of the statute of limitation. However, if Justice Mano's method is to be followed, minority judges on each issue will continue to adhere to their own opinions independent of the majority opinion, and their final judgment on the case as a whole will be made differently from the majority judgment.

Takeuchi et al v. Japan (1955),[40] seeking a reversal of the Supreme Court judgment[41] which had convicted the defendants in the well-known *Mitaka* incident, reveals a significant ramification of the two different voting methods. All except Justice Mano dismissed the petition for reversal on the ground that the original judgment of the Court was not in error. There were two major issues to decide and the justices were sharply divided on both. The first issue arose over Article 127 of the Criminal Code.[42] The majority was of the opinion that Article 127 therein be construed to provide that Article 126, Paragraph 3 of the Criminal Code should be applied to the defendants' acts of destroying trains, electric cars or ships, which led to death, as stipulated in Article 125 therein. Justices Fujita, Kuriyama, Mano, Shima, and Tanimura dissented, arguing that Article 127 of the Criminal Code be construed to provide that when a person commits an offense stipulated in Article 125 he should be given the penalty of from three years to life imprisonment with hard labor provided by Article 125, Paragraphs 1 and 2 instead of the capital punishment in Article 126, Paragraph 3 which is given only to a premeditated homicide.

The second point of disagreement centered on the constitutionality for an appellate court to increase without oral hearing a sentence from life imprisonment rendered by a first instance court to capital punishment. The eleven justice majority upheld as being constitutional the increased penalty while four justices, Kobayashi, Kotani, Kuriyama, and Tanimura dissented. Against this background of the original judgment of

The Process of Judicial Decision Making

the Supreme Court, Mano argued that inasmuch as the original decision had been made by a one vote margin of eight to seven, it should be reconsidered with another open hearing. According to him, seven justices (presumably Fujita, Kuriyama, Mano, Shima, Tanimura, Kobayashi, and Kotani) thought the original judgment should be reversed. The eight other justices favored the dismissal of the appeal. In refuting Mano on this point, Iwamatsu argues that the original judgment of the Court dismissing the appeal was never made by such a narrow margin of eight to seven but by the unanimity of all the justices.

Likewise, *Suzuki v. Ishigaki* (1956),[43] involving a question of constitutionality of a conciliation conducted in lieu of judicial adjudication, illustrates the impact of the voting on each issue on individual judges. Justices Iwamatsu and Shima in the principal case were first of the opinion that such a conciliation, if made final and irrevocable, would not preclude a suit on the same claim later and would not violate the Constitution. However, upon rejection by the majority justices, the two men changed their opinion and conformed to the premise upheld by the majority that such a conciliation, once finalized, would have a legally binding force, and then joined the dissenting group who held the conciliation to be unconstitutional. Toward the end of their opinion, both justices commented that since their opinion was not shared with the majority, they had to reach the conclusion that such a conciliation in lieu of judicial trial would violate the provisions of Articles 32 and 82 of the Constitution guaranteeing an open trial administered by a judicial court.

Kazuo Tanaka points out an important implication of these two different methods in this case, as follows:[44]

> Had these two justices (*i.e.*, Justices Iwamatsu and Shima) followed the method advocated by Mano they would have joined the majority group in the case. As it was, they obviously changed their opinion and joined the dissenting group. Since this case was decided, by eight to seven, their joining the majority group would not have affected the outcome of the case except for changing the voting to ten to five. However, suppose that

one of the justices holding conciliation in lieu of judicial trial to be constitutional changed his opinion and joined the dissenting group, then the outcome of the judgment would have been decided depending upon which one of the two methods Iwamatsu and Shima might have followed.

The provision of Article 77[45] of the Court Code is designed for the situation in which there may be three or more separate opinions with no single opinion sufficient to command a majority of the court. But here again disagreements over the interpretation of this provision manifested themselves among several justices in *Sakagami v. Japan* (1953)[46] in which the defendant was criminally charged and convicted of violating a government ordinance ordering the suspension of the *Red Flag*, the Japan Communist Party's newspaper, and its successor. The fourteen-member grand bench was divided into three opinions concerning the effectiveness of the ordinance after the peace treaty had come into force. Six justices, Mano, Kotani, Shima, Fujita, Tanimura, and Irie were of the opinion that the defendant should be acquitted in accordance with Article 337 of the Code of Criminal Procedure which required acquittal in analogy to an abolition of a penalty. They held that the ordinance was unconstitutional and invalid when the occupation ended and the peace treaty went into effect. Four other justices, Inoue, Kuriyama, M. Kawamura, and Kobayashi, contended that the ordinance was not necessarily unconstitutional *en toto*, but that only those portions which punished a violation of the ordinance became unconstitutional and void after the peace treaty. Writing his concurring opinion, Justice Inoue stated, in part:[47]

> For the reason discussed above, we differ from Justice Mano and five others but we agree with them that it would be unconstitutional and impermissible after Japan's independence to punish the defendants in the present case by applying Ordinance 325. (Since six justices hold that the ordinance is completely abolished in its entirety, their decision will naturally encompass ours and these two opinions, put together, should be made the opinion of the Court.)

The remaining four justices, Tanaka, Shimoyama, Y. Saito, and Motomura, dissented by arguing that the ordinance was effective even after the peace treaty so long as it was applied to punish a crime committed prior to the effective date of the treaty, and that punishment provided by the ordinance should not be construed to have been abolished until and unless specifically so declared by the government. Y. Saito argued that the opinion of Mano's and Inoue's groups are not compatible and should be treated as separate minority opinions, and that in the absence of the majority opinion of the Court the appeal in the principal case should be dismissed by upholding the decision below.

Writing of judicial reasonings is the final stage of judicial decision making. A Chief Justice ordinarily assigns a justice who is charged with a particular case in a petty bench the task of drafting the opinion of the Supreme Court, provided the justice is in the majority group. If a justice in charge did not join the majority opinion, then another justice will be assigned the task from among the majority group. There does not seem to be any other working principle governing the assignment of writing opinions.

In many easy and clearcut cases justices may want to change a few places in a draft majority opinion prepared by a *chosakan*. After each justice initials the draft an official opinion is made, formally signed, and sealed by all the justices. However with difficult cases a copy of the draft is first circulated among the majority justices and then the minority group. Some may feel compelled to write, individually or jointly, a dissenting or concurring opinion. A copy of the modified majority opinion and all dissenting and/or concurring opinions, if any, are then distributed to each justice. At this point some justices may insist on changing the opinion while others may want to write a further opinion of their own, either for or against concurring or dissenting opinions. When each justice has read all the opinions of every other justice, he signs and affixes his seal to the final draft of the written judgment of the Court, including the majority opinion, the concurring opinions, and the dissenting opinions.

A justice who accepts the majority holding but who wishes

to supplement the majority reasoning writes a "supplementary opinion"; a justice who accepts the majority holding while rejecting the majority reasoning writes an "opinion." Both a "supplementary opinion" and an "opinion" fall under what the United States Supreme Court calls a concurring opinion, inasmuch as they accept the majority holding but disagree with the majority reasoning. Next, a judge who disagrees with a majority holding writes either a "minority opinion" or a "dissenting opinion."

According to former Supreme Court *chosakan* Giei Tabaru, the justices deliberate on all the legal constructions and their derivative conclusions prepared by a *chosakan* in charge of a given case, and then the majority usually selects and adopts one of these alternatives as its own holding and its underlying reasonings. If a judge disagrees with the selection made by the majority group, he writes a "minority opinion." A justice writes a "dissenting opinion" when he arrives at a holding opposed to the majority, with reasoning from his own sources, totally independent of the materials supplied by the *chosakan*. The difference between the minority and dissenting opinions, however, are minor and both fall under the category of dissenting opinions. In *Fujikawa v. Japan* (1955),[48] a case involving the violation of the Customs Code, six justices wrote one joint dissenting opinion. However, Justice Kobayashi, one of the six dissenters, wrote another opinion of his own, supplementing the joint dissenting opinion. He states, "I agree with the five other justices in that the crime committed in violation of the Customs Code should be dismissed, but since the reason for the dismissal, as expressed in the joint dissenting opinion is very simplistic, I would like to add my own opinions."

An analysis of the abridged Supreme Court reports reveals that a little over a quarter of constitutional cases were decided by divided opinions during the first decade of the Court. Studying a justice's ratio of concurring and dissenting opinions to his total participation in divided decisions, Takeyoshi Kawashima[49] found that there was a steadily increasing number of dissenting and concurring opinions voiced from 1947 through 1962, and that after the mid-1960s a tendency to write dissenting opinions decreased considerably. According to the same study, justices were inclined to dissent nearly twice as often as they concurred. In regard to the specialization of justices, Kawashima confirmed, both criminal and civil specialists were more prone to write concurring and dissenting opinions than their counterpart non-specialists in cases involving their specialty. Further, criminal specialists had a higher dissenting rate in criminal cases than civil cases, and civil specialists had a higher concurring rate in civil cases than criminal cases. Finally, it was found that criminal specialists were twice as likely to write their own opinions as civil specialists, especially in expressing concurring opinions.

The practice of writing concurring and dissenting opinions was introduced from the United States after World War II, since under the Meiji constitution the Great Court of Cassation followed the German practice of writing and publishing only the majority opinion. Some well-known opinions were attributed to Chief Justice Hideo Yokota (1862–1937)[50] of the Great Court of Cassation, on the basis of their style and wording, but, as a rule, it was impossible to associate judicial attitudes with judicial behavior. An underlying assumption of the old practice was that publishing any opinion other than the majority opinion would decrease a popular trust in legal stability and authority and would encourage more unnecessary litigation. The Meiji practice still persists in the provision of Article 75, Paragraph 2 of the Court Code which reads in part that, except as otherwise provided for in the law, strict secrecy shall be observed with respect to the proceeding of deliberation, the opinion of each judge, and the number of opinions.

The lower courts continue to publish only the majority opinion and do so anonymously. The rationales behind the Supreme Court practice of publishing both dissenting and concurring opinions are several. It is contended that concurring and dissenting opinions will further clarify legal issues and judicial policies in the case. Further, a dissenting opinion, once made known, might gain an increased acceptance in the society and perhaps become a majority opinion later. Also, it is hoped that publishing concurring and dissenting opinions would enable a voting public to know the views of individual justices at the time of popular review of Supreme Court justices.

It should be pointed out, however, that although Article 11 of the Court Code requires a written court judgment to state each justice's opinions, each judge is not required to write his own opinion. Except for a few majority opinions of which Justice Mano identified himself as a writer in 1948,[51] there is no way of knowing who drafts the majority opinion of the Court. The majority opinion is supposed to be the statement of rationales for the decision acceptable to each justice in the majority group. However, when the majority is large and diversified in its reasoning, an initial draft is so modified and adulterated by other members of the same group, the final draft of the Court and personal views of each justice tend to lack clarity and logical cohesion.

Exchanges of written opinions among some justices sometimes become amusing. Dissenting in *Oda v. Japan* (1952),[52] Justice Yusuke Saito complained about the clarity of the majority opinion, did not believe the majority to have agreed among themselves, and construed the majority to base its holding on the alleged unconstitutionality of the provision of Article 45 of the Weaponry and Powder Control Ordinance of 1911. Then Justices Kawamura and Irie wrote their joint concurring opinion on the ground that they joined the majority group, but not for the reason Saito had attributed to the majority.

When more than one justice concurs with or dissents from the majority, both abridged and unabridged Supreme Court reports simply state that the "following is the concurring or dissenting opinion of Justices A, B, and C." What is worse, the reports failed to cite the dissenting opinion of Naoyoshi Tsukazaki in *Asano v. Japan* (1952).[53] Thus, dissenting and concurring opinions when written jointly tend to suffer from the same problem of a lack of clarity and logical consistency as the majority opinion, thereby weakening the objectives of publishing various judicial opinions.

The Supreme Court decisions are announced in three different ways. In a small number of cases the Court hears an oral argument and renders its *hanketsu* judgment in an open court. Usually the Court announces its decision in the *hanketsu* form when it reverses a decision below. The Court reads its holding and reasons at open court and/or mails it to the litigants. If the Court does not hold oral hearings it need not specify the date of announcing its decision. In reversing a decision below, however, the date of announcement must be given to both parties to a case. A large majority of appeals made to the Supreme Court lack proper grounds and are dismissed in the form of *kettei*, which require neither open hearing nor open court announcement, in accordance with Article 381, Paragraph 1, Item 3 of the Code of Criminal Procedure. Only the first petty bench has traditionally announced its *kettei* judgment at open court. While *kettei* is rendered by a petty bench itself, *meirei* is issued by a justice(s) in his (their) individual capacity.

The Court need not give its opinion in dismissing a defense motion that a public prosecution is unconstitutional. The Court is also regarded to have upheld the constitutionality of a law or ordinance being challenged when it cites that law or ordinance in its opinion upholding the conviction.

The Supreme Court passes several judgments. It may uphold the decision below and dismiss an appeal, it may reverse the decision below and remand the case for further review in accordance with its own instruction, or it may reverse the decision below and pass its own judgment. In any case, Article 411 of the Criminal Procedural Code provides that the Supreme Court can reverse the judgment below on any of the following grounds: 1) there exists a material mistake of construction, in interpretation, or application of a law or ordinance; 2) the punishment has been imposed with gross injustice; 3) there is a gross error in the finding of facts that are material to the judgment; and 4) that there is a reason supporting the reopening of procedure. When the Supreme Court announces its decision, the wheel of justice completes a turn, different forms of judicial sentencing notwithstanding. As a rule, there will be no further recourse for appeal, although an appeal is occasionally attempted from a Supreme Court petty bench decision to its grand bench, invariably without success.

3. Effects of Judicial Decisions

The Supreme Court decision is the output of judicial decision making, and becomes a judicial order of the highest level, providing directions for other judicial actors in a principal case. The impact of judicial decision making is most significantly felt in the constitutional field where the basic framework of national polity is molded and remolded. The lower court is bound by the judgment of the Supreme Court. In a retrial of the *Sunagawa* case[54] the defense contended that the Supreme Court decision, which allegedly violated Article 9 of the Constitution, did not bind the lower court. However, the Tokyo district court,[55] dismissing the defense motion, ruled that Article 4 of the Court Code binds a lower court to abide by the instructions of the Supreme Court in deciding a case remanded by the latter, and that Article 66 of the Constitution, which sets up different levels of trials, does not allow a lower court to contradict such an instruction. There has not been any instance of non-compliance with the Supreme Court decision. Note that the courts have no independent enforcement machinery to compel compliance with their rulings, and coercion, when needed, must be supplied by the executive branch.

Judicial reasonings of the Supreme Court do not have the same effect. They are subject to different interpretations and implementations. In some cases alternative ratios are available for a later judge. Kawashima cites several cases[56] demonstrating that what was apparently considered as *ratio decidendi* were not used as a controlling factor in similar cases later, or that a judge may change ascertained facts in an immediate case to make them fit facts of a precedent case so that he can apply the holding in the precedent case to the immediate one. In so doing he may fail to account for social consequences of his decision. Or a judge might simply point out differences between a lower court decision under review and a precedent case which would overturn the lower court decision, if he does not want to use the precedent.

Koichi Bai discovered that an *obiter dictum* functioned as a precedent for later cases. According to Bai's study, a party to a matrimonial engagement sued the other party for damages and contended that the latter committed an unlawful act by dissolving the engagement.

On January 26, 1915, the Great Court of Cassation in *Yanaka v. Nozawa* (1915),[57] dismissed this claim for compensation and decided that a matrimonial engagement was a lawful and valid contract although a party to such a contract could not compel the other party to fulfill it and that the former, in good faith, could seek a compensation of damages, both tangible and intangible, if the latter refused to marry without good reason. After reexamining the facts ascertained by the Court and also the facts he himself gathered through readings of trial proceedings and interviews with villagers, Bai discovered that the Court was stating not *ratio decidendi* but an *obiter dictum* when it stated that a claim for damage in contract law would arise out of a non-performance of a matrimonial engagement inasmuch as the Court was called on to decide the claimant's contention that a claim for damage would arise out of the unlawful act of dissolving an engagement. Be that as it may, Bai concludes, later courts have come to use the *obiter dictum* in the 1915 Great Court of Cassation decision in granting a damage in contract law.

Similarly, Michitaka Kaino cites his own study of common rights *(iriaiken)* in which he finds a decision, in *Tonai Village v. Japan* (1915),[58] by the Great Court of Cassation which had denied common rights over state-owned land to have misconstrued a provision of a legal code which became a precedent in later cases. Finally, in *Ko Lin-mai v. Tokyo Immigration Control Chief Officer* (1957),[59] the Tokyo district court held that the justice minister had no absolute discretion in the matters of deportation and that the courts must determine the extent of his administrative discretion. However, the Tokyo high court[60] reversed this decision on the strength of grace, granting absolute discretion to administrative agencies. But, in *Liu Sun-chin v. Osaka Immigration Control Chief Officer*

(1957), the Osaka district court[61] denied the suspension of the deportation order by citing the Tokyo high court decision in the *Ko Lin-mai* case. Thereupon, the Osaka high court[62] reversed this decision on the similar grounds which the Tokyo district court had taken in the *Ko Lin-mai* case.

According to Kawashima, several different levels of abstraction should be extracted from each material fact of the precedent, and then the same process of abstracting should be made to generalize a ruling from a unique and concrete ruling in the precedent case. Next, a proposition should be constructed that given a set of abstracted legal facts, a given abstracted ruling will follow that is capable of accounting for the ruling on such material and relevant facts. Thus, a generalized judicial ruling on a generalized set of facts will constitute a frame of reference for later cases. Where this theoretical construction differs from logical constructions given by a judge, it provides a criterion with which to examine the adequacy of such a judicial reasoning.

Article 98 of the Constitution stipulates that "this Constitution shall be the supreme law of the nation and no law, ordinance, imperial rescript or other act of government, or part thereof, contrary to the provisions thereof, shall have legal force or validity." Likewise, no "law, order, regulation or official act" (Article 81 of the Constitution) contrary to the Constitution will be valid and have legal force.

Against the background of these constitutional provisions, *Nakamura v. Japan* (1962),[63] the first case to declare a public policy unconstitutional, raised an important question of the legal effect of an unconstitutional policy. Involved in this case was the provision of Article 118, Paragraph 1 of the Customs Code authorizing a customs official to confiscate a third party's property used in smuggling in contravention of the law. A host of questions were raised over the interpretation of the Supreme Court ruling in this case which held that such a confiscation, as was carried out in accordance with the law, would violate both the due process and property rights on the third party.

Shiro Kiyomiya[64] and many other constitutional scholars construed the Supreme Court in the *Nakamura* case to have rendered unconstitutional both the legal provision in question and the present act of confiscation. According to their void *ab initio* theory an unconstitutional law becomes null and void, not only with respect to the principal case but also all the past and future cases. The power of judicial review has the effect of abolishing such a law as if it never existed in order to discourage other people from bringing in similar suits designed to avoid the enforcement of such an unconstitutional law. An application of this view on the effect of an unconstitutional law on a criminal case, however, may interfere with the protection against double jeopardy.

Jiro Tanaka and Nobuyoshi Ashibe,[65] on their part, interpret the *Nakamura* decision to have invalidated, as in contravention of the due process clause of the Constitution, not so much the present confiscation under dispute as the provision of Article 118, Paragraph 1 of the Code. A statute which is declared unconstitutional is not necessarily rendered null and void, nor is it stricken from the book. It takes a legislative action to abolish the law, and until then, Tanaka and Ashibe continue, the legal provision, although no longer operative, remains in the book. If the statute in question is revised in such a way as to provide an innocent owner, a third party to a crime, with a guarantee of notice and hearing, then it may once again become operative and even be retroactively applicable to a crime.

Further, some people take a case by case approach whereby a statute declared unconstitutional is neither totally valid nor invalid: it may be operative under certain conditions and inoperative under some other circumstances. Still others argue that an unconstitutional statute may get some judicial recognition as one determining factor in a case. For example, an election result may be judged valid although the law authorizing or regulating such an election is unconstitutional as in *Kurokawa v. Chiba Prefecture Election Control Commission* (1976).[66] Likewise, in *Aoki v. Japan* (1967)[67] the Supreme Court grand bench dismissed an appeal on the grounds that while the court below violated Article 31 and Article 38, Paragraph 1 of the Constitution by using an unindicted criminal act in its sentencing, this unconstitutional judicial discretion did not significantly affect the overall judgment. Finally, concerning a question of whether a third party to a crime, whose property was confiscated, can initiate a new suit to recover his property on the grounds of a good faith and intent on his side, opinions are divided. Ashibe thinks affirmatively while J. Tanaka and Hirano hold otherwise.

The primary function of judicial policy making is conflict resolution of the contending litigants. In so doing a court also performs other functions like integration, goal attainment, and system maintenance, while generating support and legitimacy for the legal and political systems. Since a Supreme Court decision is bound to have its impact on the Japanese society, the Court is in a position to monitor impacts of its own decision, compliance or non-compliance, or changes in public support, and tries to minimize discontent or satisfy grievances that arise out of initial decisions. A new motion for a hearing to change announced decisions is rarely granted. A more common form of reconsideration by the Court is the same issue in a new case. Such reconsideration is likely to occur when the policy position of the administrative agency conflicts with that of the Supreme Court majority or when a minority of the Court becomes a majority. In any case, "without feedback and the capacity to respond to it, no system could survive for long, except by accident."[68]

Footnotes to Chapter Three

1. Masao Nomura (ed.), *Hoso Fuunroku* (The Vicissitudes of the Legal Professionals), Tokyo: Asahi Shimbunsha, 1966, Vol. 2, p. 216.

2. Roundtable discussion, "Saikosai no purakutisu ni tsuite" (The Supreme Court practices), in *Ho no Shihai* No. 40, September 1979, p. 61.

3. According to *Shiho Taikan* (Judicial Almanac), Hosokai, 1967, the judicial backgrounds of these twenty-six *chosakan* are: six from the Tokyo district court, two from the Tokyo high court, seven from seven local district courts, two from two local high courts, three from three local summary courts, two from two family courts, and four from the Supreme Court general secretariat. See also Michael K. Young, "Amerika no rempo saikosaibansho: Ro kuraku to sono eikyo

o chushin nishite" (The United States Supreme Court: Law clerks and their impact), in *Amerika Ho*, Vol. 1, 1979, pp. 1–22.

4. Akio Date, "Saikosai chosakan, II" (The Supreme Court *chosakan* II), in *Hanrei Jiho*, No. 270, 1961, p. 2. Also, Takeo Shimada, "Chosakan saiban" (Trial by *chosakan*), in *Hanrei Taimuzu*, No. 201, 1967, p. 284.

5. *Hoso* No. 170, 1964, p. 13.

6. Saburo Iwamatsu, *Aru Saibankan no Ayumi* (An Autobiography of One Judge), Tokyo: Nihon Hyoronsha, 1967, pp. 260–261.

7. Sup. Ct., G.B.; October 31, 1956; 10 *Minshu* 1355.

8. Sup. Ct., G.B.; March 12, 1948; 2 *Keishu* 191.

9. Saburo Ienaga, "Saikosai wa shinsei no michi o ayume: Saikosai chokan no kotai ni atatte" (The Supreme Court should lead a reformed life: On the occasion of a change of the Chief Justice), in *Hogaku Semina* No. 56, November 1960, pp. 2–6.

10. Masao Nomura, *Op. Cit.*, Vol. 1, pp. 279–280.

11. David J. Danelski, "The influence of the chief justice in the decisional process," in Walter F. Murphy and C. Herman Pritchett (eds.), *Courts, Judges, and Politics: An Introduction to the Judicial Process*, New York: Random House, 1986 (4th ed.), pp. 568–577.

12. Shigeru Oda, "Saikosaibansho o chokushishite" (Looking straight at the Supreme Court), in *Jurisuto* No. 31, April 1953, p. 23.

13. Sup. Ct. G.B.; February 22, 1955; 102 *Saibanshu Keiji* 399.

14. Dan F. Henderson, *Op. Cit.*, p. 429.

15. Koji Tanabe, "The process of litigation: An experiment with the adversary system," in Arthur von Mehren, *Op. Cit.*, p. 102.

16. Giei Tabaru, *Saikosai Hanketsu no Uchigawa* (An Inside View of Supreme Court Decisions), Tokyo: Ichiryusha, 1965, pp. 22–79. For similar comments in civil cases, see Shigekichi Hasebe, "Hotei zakkan" (Miscellaneous comments on the courtroom), in 12 *Horitsu no Hiroba* 12, 1959, p. 28.

17. 11 *Minshu* 510.

18. Sup. Ct., G.B.; May 22, 1963; 17 *Keishu* 370.

19. Sup. Ct., G.B.; February 5, 1964; 18 *Minshu* 270.

20. Sup. Ct., G.B.; December 16, 1959; 13 *Keishu* 3225; or John M. Maki (ed.), *Court and Constitution: Selected Supreme Court Decisions, 1948-60*, Seattle, Wash.: University of Washington Press, 1964, pp. 318–319.

21. John M. Maki, *Ibid.*, p. 329.

22. Sup. Ct., G.B.; April 30, 1975; 29 *Minshu* 572.

23. Sup. Ct., G.B.; April 4, 1976; 30 *Minshu* 223.

24. Nobuyoshi Ashibe, *Kempo Sosho no Riron* (The Theory of Constitutional Litigation), Tokyo: Yuhikaku, 1973, p. 203.

25. Tsugio Nakano, "Nishidoitsu niokeru ikenhanketsu no hoho" (Judicial review in West Germany), in Kazuo Ogawa *et al.* (eds.), *Koho no Riron*, 1976, Part I, p. 105 *et. seq.*

26. Nobuyoshi Ashibe, "Kempo saiban no mondaiten" (Issues of the constitutional trial), in 38 *Horitsu Jiho* 1, 1966, p. 17.

27. Sup. Ct., G.B.; January 26, 1955; 9 *Keishu* 92.

28. The Public Bathhouse Code, Article 2, as revised in 1950, reads as follows: A person who plans to operate a public bathhouse shall pay fees as stipulated in an ordinance, and secure a permit from the prefectural governor. . . . A prefectural governor may refuse to grant such permit when the site or facility of a public bathhouse is inadequate from the standpoint of public health or when such a site lacks a proper location. . . . The governor shall notify the permit applicant in writing the reasons for denial. . . . Each prefecture shall decide, in the form of ordinance standards, proper locations.

29. Kazushi Kojima, "Shokugyo sentaku no jiyu no seigen" (The restriction of the freedom of occupation), in Jurisuto (ed.), *Kempo Hanrei Hyakusen* (100 Selected Constitutional Cases), 1963, pp. 55–56.

30. Sup. Ct., G.B.; April 30, 1975; 29 *Keishu* 572.

31. Sup. Ct., G.B.; September 10, 1958; 12 *Minshu* 1969.

32. Nobuyoshi Ashibe, *Op. Cit.*, "Kempo saiban no mondaiten," p. 19.

33. *Hasegawa et al v. Japan;* Sup. Ct., G.B.; April 2, 1969; 23 *Keishu* 305.

34. Fukuoka Dist. Ct.; August 28, 1969; 23 *Keishu* 1514. In this case the district court ordered the RKB Mainichi Broadcasting Company to surrender its films as evidence in the criminal trial against Toshiaki Maeda and 870 other defendants. For its appellate decision, see Sup. Ct., G.B.; November 26, 1969; 23 *Keishu* 1490.

35. Kazuo Hirotsu, *Matsukawa Jiken to Saiban: Kensatsukan no Ronri* (The Matsukawa Incident and the Trial: The Prosecutors' Arguments), Tokyo: Iwanami Shoten, 1964.

36. Jurisuto (ed.), *Saiban Hihan* (Criticism of Trials), Tokyo: Yuhikaku, 1957, and also Saburo Ienaga, *Saiban Hihan* (Criticism of Trials), Tokyo: Nihon Hyoronsha, 1959, as well as Ken Hino, *Sabakareru Nihon no Saiban: Saiban wa Dokomade Shinrai Dekiruka* (Japan's Courts under Trial: How Much Can We Trust Trials?), Tokyo: Eru Shuppansha, 1970.

37. *Japan v. Ueda et al,* Sup. Ct., G.B.; December 16, 1981; 35 *Minshu* 1369.

38. Roundtable discussion, "Saikosai no purakutisu ni tsuite," *Op. Cit.*, No. 40, 1979, p. 79.

39. Sup. Ct., G.B.; October 12, 1955; 109 *Saibanshu Keiji* 2159.

40. Sup. Ct., G.B.; December 23, 1955; 111 *Saibanshu Keiji* 755.

41. *Iida et al. v. Japan;* Sup. Ct.. G.B.; February 22, 1955; 9 *Keishu* 1189. In *Kanemaru et al. v. Japan,* (Sup. Ct., G.B.; November 10, 1948; 5 *Saibanshu Keiji* 229) and *Otsuka v. Japan,* (Sup. Ct., G.B.; October 25, 1950; 19 *Saibanshu Keiji* 951). It is not clear whether decisions were made on each issue or on the conclusion of each case. *Yagi v. Japan* (Sup. Ct., G.B.; July 4, 1956; 114 *Saibanshu Keiji* 67) raised two different ways of voting, leading to two different conclusions.

42. Criminal Code, Articles 125, 126, and 127 read as follows: Article 125—(1) A person who damages or destroys a track or signal

of a railway or otherwise causes danger to the movement of a train or electric car, shall be punished with penal servitude for a limited period of not less than two years; (2) The same shall apply to a person who damages or destroys a light house or buoy or who otherwise causes damage to the movement of vessels; Article 126—(1) A person who upsets or destroys a train or electric car with passengers shall be punished with penal servitude for life or not less than three years; (2) The same shall apply to a person who capsizes or destroys a vessel with passengers; (3) A person who by committing a crime mentioned in the preceding two sections causes the death of another, shall be punished with death or penal servitude for life; Article 127—A person who commits the crime mentioned in Article 125 and thereby upsets or destroys a train or electric car or capsizes or destroys a vessel, shall be dealt with in the same way as provided for in the preceding Article.

43. Sup. Ct., G.B.; October 31, 1956; 10 *Minshu* 1355.

44. Kazuo Tanaka, "Mittsu ijyo no iken no tairitsu: Saikosai no hyoketsu no hoho" (Conflict of more than three opinions of the Court: Decision-making methods at the Supreme Court), in 29 *Horitsu Jiho* 6, 1957, p. 731.

45. Court Code, Article 77 reads as follows: (1) Except in cases where the Supreme Court has enacted special regulations in relation to a Supreme Court decision, decisions shall be rendered by a majority of opinions; (2) If in cases where decisions are to be rendered by majority opinion, there are three or more different opinions in respect of the following matters, none of which obtains the absolute majority, the decision shall be rendered in accordance with the opinion mentioned below; (a) In respect of an amount, the number of opinions in favor of the largest amount shall be added to the number of opinions in favor of the next largest amount, and so on until an absolute majority is attained; The amount of the majority opinion shall be that of the opinion in favor of the smallest amount which is held within the majority group; (b) In criminal cases, the number of opinions most unfavorable to the accused shall be added to the number of opinions next most unfavorable, and so on until an absolute majority is attained; The majority opinion there shall be that of the opinion most favorable to the accused which is held within the majority group.

46. *Sakagami v. Japan;* Sup. Ct., G.B.; July 22, 1953; 7 *Keishu* 1562. In a similar case (*Ozaki v. Japan;* Sup. Ct., G.B.; March 15, 1950; 4 *Keishu* 335) neither opinion of the Court nor any of the

comments on the case mentioned that the justices were divided into four groups and that no group received the majority vote.

47. Ibid., *Sakagami v. Japan*, p. 1596.

48. Sup. Ct., G.B.; February 223, 1955; 9 *Keishu* 344.

49. Takeyoshi Kawashima, "Individualism in decision making in the Supreme Court of Japan," in Glendon A. Schubert and David J. Danelski (eds.), *Comparative Judicial Behavior; Cross-Cultural Studies of Political Decision Making in the East and West*, New York: Oxford University Press, 1969, p. 108.

50. Yutaka Tezuka, "Yokota Hideo: Nihon no meisaibankan (2)" (Hideo Yokota: Distinguished judge in Japan), in *Hogaku Semina* No. 35, February 1959, pp. 58–61.

51. Justice Tsuyoshi Mano stated that he had drafted the opinion of the Court in both *Yoshiwara v. Japan* (Sup. Ct., G.B.; June 30, 1948; 2 *Keishu* 777) and *Kawashima v. Japan* (Sup. Ct., G.B.; June 23, 1948; 2 *Keishu* 715.) Similarly, Justice Tamotsu Shima identified himself as a drafter of the opinion of the Court in *Takiguchi v. Japan* (Sup. Ct., G.B.; June 23, 1948; 2 *Keishu* 722).

52. Sup. Ct., G.B.; December 24, 1952; 6 *Keishu* 1346.

53. Sup. Ct., 2nd P.B.; March 28, 1952; 6 *Keishu* 526.

54. Sup. Ct., G.B.; December 16, 1959; 13 *Keishu* 3225.

55. Tokyo Dist. Ct.; March 3, 1961; *Hanrei Jiho* No. 255, 1961, p. 7.

56. Kawashima, *Op. Cit.*, *Kagaku to shiteno Horitsugaku*, pp. 205–209.

57. Koichi Bai, *Op. Cit.*, No. 3, pp. 56–61; No. 4, pp. 86–95; No. 10, pp. 95–101; No. 11, pp. 38–43.

58. *Tonai Village, Nagano Prefecture v. Japan*, (Gr. Ct. Cass.; March 16, 1915) as quoted in Michitaka Kaino, "Hanrei kenkyu no mokuteki" (The objectives of the study of judicial precedents), in 34 *Horitsu Jiho* 1, 1962, pp. 12–13.

59. Tokyo Dist. Ct.; April 25, 1957; 8 *Gyosai Reishu* 754.

60. Tokyo H. Ct.; October 31, 1957; 8 *Gyosai Reishu* 1903.

61. Osaka Dist. Ct.; October 16, 1957; 8 *Gyosai Reishu* 1900.

62. Osaka H. Ct.; December 12, 1957; 8 *Gyosai Reishu* 2281.

63. Sup. Ct., G.B.; November 28, 1962; 16 *Keishu* 1953.

64. Roundtable discussion, "Musabetsu Bosshu no iken hanketsu ni tsuite" (The decision holding an indiscriminatory confiscation unconstitutional), in *Jurisuto* No. 268, 1963, p. 10 *et. seq*.

65. *Ibid.*, p. 12, p. 14.

66. Sup. Ct., G.B.; April 4, 1976; 30 *Minshu* 223.

67. Sup. Ct., G.B.; July 5, 1967; 21 *Keishu* 748.

68. David Easton, *A Systems Analysis of Political Life*, New York: Wiley, 1965, p. 32.

CHAPTER 4

How the Supreme Court Decided the Popolo Players Case

What makes a dispute a constitutional issue? In the absence of constitutional litigations under the Meiji constitution, the Japanese judiciary has had to face many new procedural questions deciding whether alleged constitutional disputes really raise issues prescribed in the Constitution of 1947. A study of constitutional litigation requires special attention to the question of fact and law of a case. It is difficult to make a constitutional question out of some alleged factual relations of a case. Constitutional policies are often abstract and general, and require value judgments of a highly political nature. This chapter traces a typical case of judicial decision making in constitutional disputes by undertaking a doctrinal analysis of the constitutional right to academic freedom (Article 23 of the Constitution).

A criminal proceeding of *Tokyo High Prosecutor v. Senda* (1953),[1] more commonly referred to as the *Popolo [or People's] Players* case, raised the conflict between university autonomy and academic freedom of university students on the one hand and national security on the other. The final resolution of disputes in favor of police power as exercised on a university campus will reveal the multiple nature of judicial fact-finding and legal interpretation. It also alludes to different judicial value orientations toward this newly acquired freedom. This chapter traces the beginning of the incident, Diet hearings, the lower courts' proceedings, the Supreme Court review, public reactions, and finally a retrial by the Tokyo district court. We shall also examine the precedental value of the Popolo Players decision in relation to other cases that arose later as well as the impact of the case upon the changing academic environment in Japan.

1. Academic Freedom and University Autonomy in Japan

Academic freedom was not only absent in the provisions of the Meiji constitution, but was also threatened by actual or attempted interferences by the government. Censorship of academic publications and indoctrination of the "essence of national polity" as defined by the government, were rigorously practiced. In 1935 the government banned the sale and distribution of the writings of Tatsukichi Minobe who expounded the view that the Emperor was not a divine ruler but merely a governmental organ. University autonomy was not recognized either. Teachers of national universities were treated as public employees whom the Emperor could dismiss freely on the advice of the state minister, and the efforts to maintain university autonomy on personnel matters were rendered very precarious under the authoritarian military government in the 1930s and early 1940s. For example, in 1933 the government forced the resignation of Koshin Takigawa of Kyoto University for his liberal academic views against the university's protest.

Postwar Japan has developed the world's second largest higher education system. The newly acquired constitutional right to academic freedom and its corollary, university autonomy, have provided academicians in Japan with an unprecedented degree of academic activities.

Academic freedom was among the people's rights incorporated in the 1947 Constitution at the insistence of the allied occupation authorities. In the United States there have been a wide variety of court decisions ranging from curriculum control, fitness tests for teachers, legislative investigations of teaching and teachers, the teacher as a citizen, students' claims for academic freedom, off-campus speakers, and the use of college buildings for discussions of controversial issues, many of which have involved the issue of academic freedom and university autonomy.[2]

In Japan the scope and extent of disputes involving academic freedom have been rather limited, primarily due to the relatively short history of this freedom. Whereas the Supreme Court in the Popolo Players case took the position that academic freedom is guaranteed to the general public, some leading scholars disagree. According to Toshiyoshi Miyazawa,[3] the freedom of thought and conscience and the freedom of expression are among the civil liberties which every citizen can enjoy, but the freedom to hold academic opinions based on academic research, to express academic opinions, criticize the existing orthodoxy, and especially to teach academic knowledge is unique to the professionals of higher learning, and not available to ordinary persons.

According to Robert MacIver, academic freedom is a professional, functional, and institutional freedom. First, academic freedom is a professional claim coming out of the nature and needs of the professional engaged in a continuous search for a more objective, comprehensive, and higher level of knowledge. Research and teaching require an environment in which academic inquiry of various theories can be freely pursued and appreciated. Academicians need the freedom to "investigate, to draw a conclusion and to impart knowledge,"[4] without assuming any freedom from duty under particular circumstances to bring their behavior in line with any professional orthodoxy. Furthermore, their competence must be judged by their peers, and then should not be sanctioned nor dismissed for causes not related to competence in their field, assuming they have met academic responsibilities. At the same time, their competency is in a particular and specific field, and outside of it they may be no more able than any other layman.

Second, academic freedom serves the societal function of

promoting the pursuit and communication of academic knowledge. Interference with the natural sciences, for instance, would be harmful not only to academic work but also to the public interest which depends on the free search for societal utilization of academic findings. Thus, institutions of higher learning function not only to further the interests of either the individual teacher or the institution but also to promote the common good in a society.

Third, academic freedom is a claim made by the institution of independent thought and higher learning. The School Education Code in Japan seeks the basis of academic freedom and university autonomy in the essential nature of the university as a center of arts and science where truth is pursued and higher learning and technical arts are studied and taught (Article 52).

The university whose distinctive nature lies in its function to search for and to communicate knowledge requires that autonomy be left to the university to run its internal matters. University autonomy becomes a corollary to academic freedom toward the goal of attaining research, study, and education as well as human growth of both students and professors. Without university autonomy academic freedom cannot be guaranteed. The Educational Public Employees Special Code in Japan provides for university autonomy in selecting the university president and faculty members, managing university facilities and finances, and supervising students (Articles 5, 6, 9, and 10).

Academic freedom can exist only in a community that values and respects this institutional privilege. The notion of academic freedom dates back to eighteenth-century Europe where colleges and universities, first established by the church, gradually came under the protective influence of the state. However, at the same time, the state began interfering with academic institutions. Since then academic freedom has been conditioned by society, public authorities, and public opinion. The scope and extent of such claim for privilege are determined by both milieu and subject matter. In Germany academic freedom had its greatest following in the nineteenth century, and came under severe attack from radical groups in the 1920s and 1930s. In *Adler v. Board of Education (342 US 485; 1952)*, which was decided at the height of McCarthyism, Justice William Douglas, in his condemnation of the New York Feinberg Law,[5] argued that the setting up of a system of spying and surveillance over teachers cannot go hand in hand with academic freedom.

Since academic freedom does not extend itself outside of the institutional framework, a professor or researcher has the same liberty as others and no more claim to be heard outside of it. Furthermore, academic freedom is not an absolute right but a qualified one, subject to the restriction of public welfare. For example, the freedom to teach is restricted by an obligation to be faithful to the Basic Law in West Germany. Likewise, the Fundamental Code of Education in Japan requires that education be conducted with responsibility carried directly to the entire people (Article 10, Paragraph 1). Academic freedom and university autonomy are restricted to such an extent that they would be compatible with the acts and actions taken by the state and society for public welfare.

Some university professors have been ideologically opposed to the LDP-controlled government and its policies, and feel that the government has increasingly been trying to institute a conservative or even reactionary type of thought control through school education. Article 102 of the National Public Employees Code and Article 14–7 of the Personnel Authority Regulation prohibit national public employees from engaging in political activities. This prohibition was not intended to be actually applied to university professors at the time of legislation. However, on May 15, 1958, the vice-minister of education issued a memorandum informing presidents of universities and colleges throughout the country that those professors of national universities who were opposed to the teaching evaluation system might be engaged in political activity proscribed by these two statutes. This opinion of the ministry was reaffirmed more recently by the government during the Diet interpellation.

Against this background the ministry of education's textbook review system, based on the statutory authority to supervise and approve textbook manuscripts for primary and secondary high schools, was challenged in 1970 as an unwarranted restriction of academic freedom and the freedom of expression. Saburo Ienaga, Marxist-oriented professor of history at the Tokyo Metropolitan University of Education, first published his senior high school textbook, *Shin Nihonshi* (New History of Japan) in 1953.

He was ordered by the ministry of education to revise thirty-four portions of his 1966 edition. Of the required revisions Ienaga protested six portions which, according to the ministry, could have been condensed to the following three points. 1) Whereas he contended that all early mythological writings were used by the imperial ruler primarily as a means to legitimize his control of the newly unified Japan, Ienaga countered that the ministry's criticisms were so vague about the unhistorical nature of myths as to revive the prewar type of reverence for the Emperor; 2) Ienaga captioned illustrations suggesting only workers and farmers contributed to Japan's history. 3) Whereas Ienaga alluded that the Russo-Japanese Non-Aggression Pact in 1941 was designed for Japan to prepare aggression southward, the ministry instructed an inclusion of the additional phrase "after overture from the Soviet Union." The ministry denied that requiring revisions would violate any constitutional rights inasmuch as the ministry did not object to anyone writing and publishing a book per se. Ienaga responded that the freedom of a scholar to write and publish a textbook, his freedom of expression, educational rights (Article 26), and the procedural due process (Article 31) were violated by the textbook certification system.

The Tokyo district court[6] sustained Ienaga's contentions and held that textbook review was not itself unconstitutional, but that its operation became unconstitutional when, as in this case, the ministry reviewed the substantive contents of a textbook and interfered with the freedom of author and publisher. The Supreme Court,[7] however, reversed the Tokyo high court decision which had upheld the district court ruling. In remanding the case, the Court ruled that Ienaga lost his legal interest and a standing to sue inasmuch as old certification guidelines had been revised by the ministry of education and that the minister's disposition of his manuscript could not be reviewed on the basis of old guidelines.

As long as the present level of intellectual freedom is allowed to continue, Japanese academicians will enjoy one of the most liberal academic environments in the world. However, the relative absence of court cases involving the academic freedom of university professors is contrasted with a series of events raising the issue of the academic freedom and autonomous activities of university students.

2. The Popolo Players Incident and the Lower Courts

Tokyo Public Prosecutor v. Senda was the first court case to raise the question of academic freedom and autonomous activities of university students. According to the fact cited in the indictment, on February 20, 1952, a few weeks before the end of the allied occupation a play was performed by the Tokyo University theatrical group known as the Popolo Players in a classroom on the university campus. Kenzo Senda, a senior economics major at the university, along with Shumpei Fukui and several other students, detected around 7:30 p.m. the presence in the audience of several plainclothesmen. He proceeded to hold Yoshiteru Shiba, a policeman from the Motofuji police substation, and punched him in the stomach. He then reached into the policeman's inside pocket and, in the process, ripped a button off his overcoat. The accused also held Takashi Kayano, another policeman, by both hands, reached into the policeman's inside pocket, and took a police notebook which had been tied by a string to a buttonhole of his overcoat. The prosecutors charged Senda with the violation of the provision of Article 1, Paragraph 1 of the Code Penalizing Violent Act.[8] Fukui was similarly charged with a criminal act.

According to one eyewitness account,[9] the following day tens of policemen were dispatched to the university campus to arrest the accused. They rushed onto the campus and spotted one student, later identified as Senda, walking in front of the auditorium building. They then caught up with the accused and threw him on the ground by applying *judo* techniques. They dragged him away in handcuffs, holding him upside down, and hauled him into a police van parked outside the main gate of the campus.

This incident was widely reported by the press and stirred up public debate. On March 4, 1952, the legal and education committees of the House of Councillors held a joint hearing which lasted nearly nine hours. First, Chairman Ono gave a lengthy opening statement:[10]

> Recently we hear the criticism that some students have neglected their work to acquire academic knowledge and cultivate their personalities and have been engaged in radical movements under the name of academic freedom; we also hear the criticism that the police have exceeded their authority in maintaining peace and order, and have violated civil rights and freedom. . . . Under the circumstances, the people are keenly sensitive to the recent frictions between the police and students, especially the present incident which took place at Tokyo University, one of the highest institutions of learning in the country. This joint hearing is designed to clarify the demarcation between academic freedom and police activities on campus so that we might be able to better cope with this type of incident in the future.

Then Vice-Minister of Education Kiyosuke Inada circulated among the committee members the memorandum which he had issued on July 25, 1950, and gave the following testimony. The Tokyo metropolitan ordinance was put into effect on July 3, 1950, regulating assemblies, collective marches, and demonstrations. Subsequently, the Tokyo metropolitan police and the vice-minister of education discussed interpretations and applications of the ordinance on a campus. They agreed that a university president would be primarily responsible for these activities on his campus, and that only upon the request from the university would the police step in. Then he notified the governor and various universities of this agreement to avoid unnecessary disputes.

University witnesses were headed by Tokyo University President Yanaihara and included Professor Otaka, dean of students, and representatives of the university student association. President Yanaihara stressed that this incident touched on the very foundation of academic freedom. Asked by Councillor Goro Hani whether the 1950 memorandum from the vice-minister of education represented a long established universal tradition of achieving the university mission of learning, research, and teaching, Yanaihara answered affirmatively and stressed that if the agreement between police and the education ministry were withdrawn, thereby allowing police intervention on campus, a university would no longer be able to function effectively. While conceding that police may be mobilized in case of an emergency without university request, he reiterated the importance of leaving the primary function of maintaining campus order with a university president. He also testified that most universities were capable of controlling student activities on campus and that there was no emergency which would have necessitated police presence on the day of the Popolo Players performance.

The hearing revealed very extensive police activities on the university campus. The police notebook produced at the hearing contained a summary of personal histories, ideological backgrounds, political and labor union affiliations, and the activities of teachers, researchers, and students. For instance, it listed the backgrounds of two professors and researchers of the Tokyo University Oriental Culture Research Institute, the result of the university presidential election, and the details of the farewell party given in honor of outgoing university president Nambara. According to the testimony of Yanaihara, since the new police chief's inauguration, the number of plainclothesmen on campus, especially around campus bulletin boards and classrooms, increased, thereby considerably irritating many students. Indeed, the intensive police surveillance activities were described vividly in the police notebook, in diary form, as follows: "December 18 (Tuesday), fine weather, I was on duty at Tokyo University from 8 a.m. to midnight; I watched the room of the central committee of the student association; later I followed the man who came out of the room and entered a noodle stand near the main campus gate." The presence of police on the university campus was verified by Noguchi, chief of the Motofuji police substation, who testified that the substation was staffed by one chief, one deputy chief, and six patrolmen and that police were always on duty on the Tokyo University campus on two twelve-hour shifts. Then, Eiichi Tanaka, head of the Tokyo metropolitan police, testified that the police conducted surveillance of students and professors on the strength of orders from the occupation authorities and that the present incident at Tokyo University created very serious security problems on the university campus.

When Councillor Yoshida questioned him about police activities on campus without university request, Tanaka replied that many universities lacked the capability to control student violence and that the federation of students' self-government associations (zengakuren), the federation of metropolitan students (togakuren), and the Tokyo University cell of the Japan Communist Party had circulated on the Tokyo University campus a variety of pamphlets, some of which may have violated the organizational control ordinance: it was the duty of the police to arrest an offender on the spot if he or she was distributing such fliers or to keep them from being circulated. Noguchi introduced the flier which he had confiscated on December 13, 1951, as illustrative of one which advocated violent revolution in contravention of the ordinance. It read in part as follows:[11]

> The workers began sharpening their daggers! It is wrong to think that they (enemy) can accomplish the liberation of Japan and democratic changes by peaceful means. Japan's militarization is now near completion. John Foster Dulles, war merchant, came here to make a deal with Prime Minister Shigeru Yoshida with some two hundred military bases and millions of dollars in bloody hands. The National Police Reserve in the outskirts of Tokyo are undergoing training to defend these bases. Eight thousand elite troops are stationed in the northeastern part of Tokyo to defend the metropolis and the grain storage area; they have been receiving an intensive training to suppress workers.

As far as the backgrounds of this incident were concerned, the intensified cold war between the East and West had a great impact on Japan. The communist takeover of China in 1949 and the outbreak of the Korean War in 1950 deepened the chasm that had existed between the conservative government and radical leftists. On the one hand, the conservative government tried to strengthen the national defense by concluding in 1951 the security treaty with the United States and tightened its internal security by revising anti-subversive measures and the police code. On the other hand, student activists, union members, and other leftists intensified their strong opposition to these pro-American and reactionary policies.

Almost from the outset of the American occupation, there had been confrontations between the police and the leftists. In the early morning of August 17, 1946, a train of the national railways overturned near Matsukawa station, in the northern part of the mainland, killing three railroad workers. As a result, leftist local union members were indicted on suspicion of a conspiracy and sabotage resulting in manslaughter. After many years of court battles, the defendants were acquitted by the Supreme Court, but the truth about the incident was never clarified.[12] The Matsukawa incident was followed by two other similar incidents in 1949: derailment of an electric train at Mitaka station, on the outskirts of Tokyo, resulting in six deaths and twenty injuries among waiting passengers and the suspicious death of President Sadanori Shimoyama of the national railways corporation on a railroad track. In each case persons connected with leftist labor unions were charged with sabotage and conspiracy in manslaughter.

Between April and June 1952 organized labor waged strikes mobilizing three million members in opposition to the proposed special criminal code against subversive activities and the proposed revision of the labor code restrictive of labor activities. Meanwhile, the government purged leaders of labor and the Japan Communist Party while dissolving the Federation of North Koreans and the Federation of All Labor as being subversive organizations in contravention of the organization control ordinance. In the face of mounting opposition, the government managed to pass the Subversive Activities Prevention Code, the Special Criminal Code in 1952, and a new Police Code in 1954, all designed to centralize and strengthen domestic security measures. It had also concluded in 1957 the United States-Japan Security Treaty. Diet debates often culminated in fist fights between the ruling conservatives and the opposition parties, especially over two education bills and the new Police Code. Under the circumstances, students focused their activities on broad social issues and became extremely sensitive to police activities on their campuses. A major characteristic of the Popolo Players incident was that the students and university authorities were united against the police for the cause of defending academic freedom and university autonomy.

Senda was tried by the three-man bench (Judge Takanosuke Yamada presiding) of the fifteenth criminal division of the Tokyo district court. Much of the testimony given at Diet hearings was repeated, and indeed the minutes of it were adopted as evidence. Its decision, finding the accused innocent, was announced on May 11, 1954.[13] The Tokyo public prosecutor's office immediately appealed to the Tokyo high court which held hearings while discounting the minutes of the Diet committees, presumably on the grounds of unclear circumstances under which the minutes were taken. On May 8, 1956, the three-man bench of its eleventh criminal division (Judge Masayoshi Kureta presiding) dismissed the prosecutor's appeal.[14]

The prosecution contended from the beginning that when a play was oriented toward political and social purposes, and the public was able to gain admission by purchasing tickets, such a play could have hardly been called an ordinary type of student activity for serious academic study. The prosecution presented evidence to prove this point. First, the Popolo Players group, in a play based on the ongoing *Matsukawa* trial,[15] tried to express its contention that the government and the police fabricated the criminal prosecution of those persons connected with leftist unions on the suspicion of sabotage, resulting in the death of railroad workers. The prosecution contended that this play intended to promote leftist causes and exceeded the bounds of academic study. A Tokyo University student newspaper ran an article indicating that the Matsukawa incident would be employed as a basis of the play.

Second, the application for permission to use a classroom listed simply a performance of "Someday" (one stage, two curtains) and "Poem on the Dawn" (one curtain), and was even accompanied by a letter pledging not to use the classroom for any political purposes. Thus, the intention to use the classroom for the play based on the Matsukawa incident was concealed from the university authorities. Furthermore, prior to the performance, a monetary contribution was solicited in support of the defendants in the *Matsukawa* trial, and a report was given about the student clash with police at the Shibuya railroad station two days before. Third, the gathering for the performance by the Popolo Players was part of the Anti-Colonial Struggle Day events[16] and was not tied to any study of a theatrical play or drama by the students involved. In the opinion of the prosecution, the Constitution protects academic freedom only to the extent that gatherings which are conducted at a designated place like a classroom with the objective of presenting lectures or debates of research by professors and other research personnel. The audience for the Popolo Players show should be regarded as a public gathering.

Both the Tokyo district court and the high court stated that a university was not a place where students were given knowledge alone and that even if students did, from time to time, go to extremes in the process of study and learning, it was the essence of university education to respect the self-discipline, self-teaching, and self-governance of the students and to guide them accordingly. The lower courts stressed that it was an important aspect of academic freedom for a student to select a topic for his study from among a wide range of political and social phenomena and to conduct his inquiry on his own initiative on the basis of empirical trial and error. In the opinion of the lower courts, the play was approved by the university authorities through a regular procedure and the political neutrality, lawfulness, and propriety of the play cannot be doubted by citing such trivial matters as the misrepresentation in the application form for the use of a classroom, actual or intended fund raising for the defendants of the *Matsukawa* trial, or the report of the Shibuya incident. Even though some of the materials for the play were taken from actual public events of the time, the theatrical group remained an on-campus research group authorized by the university. Furthermore, there were no reasons not to have admitted a few outsiders, including the policemen in question who had bought admission tickets because admitting the public did not necessarily change the nature of the play from that of a regular on-campus gathering. When considered with the fact that the policemen did not come in order to watch the play, the mere fact that they bought admission tickets did not lend lawfulness to their presence, unless the occupation's directive authorizing such police activity had been ruled lawful.

Next, the prosecution cited Article 8, Paragraph 2 of the Fundamental Code of Education which stipulated that schools should refrain from political education or other political activities for or against any specific political party. The Federation of All Students and the Federation of Metropolitan University Students and other unauthorized organizations continued to use university facilities. The Tokyo University cell of the Japan Communist Party, which had once been dissolved, was circulating fliers suspected of violating the organizational control ordinance under the name of the Tokyo University cell reconstruction group. Kazuo Oba and Fumiharu Saito testified at the Tokyo district court that students frequently committed extremely unlawful political conduct as exemplified by the campus demonstration in October 1950, protesting the Red purge against communist members and, on the day of the play in question, a students' march to the Shibuya railroad station without a permit. Under the circumstances, it was the duty of the police to investigate university campus activities peacefully and secretly. They thought of contacting the university authorities in case the latter decided to take measures to dissolve the gathering. Therefore, as long as police activity was conducted purely from the standpoint of maintaining peace and order on campus, neither the motive, objective, nor the method of entry of policemen into the gathering were infringements on academic freedom or university autonomy. The interpretation and applications of the 1950 memorandum from the vice-minister of education have often been ambiguous. The memorandum was understood to prescribe standards under exceptional circumstances and cannot be applicable to all kinds of police activities on campus.

The lower courts judged that the vice-minister's memorandum was mandated by the provision of Article 6, Paragraphs 2 and 4 of the Code concerning the Execution of Duties of Police Officials and should have been regarded as a general standard for exercising police power on a university campus. Since police information gathering activities could constitute an intangible pressure on academic freedom, the police should have let the university authorities handle on-campus violence which might normally have come under the police jurisdiction, especially, if the alleged violence took place inside the classroom or research facility. Only when the university authorities considered that the alleged act was beyond their control, and requested police assistance, should the police have been allowed to exercise their power at the place designated by the university authorities. Almost daily ever since late July of 1950, plainclothesmen from the Motofuji police substation had been on campus, following and eavesdropping on students and teachers, investigating their backgrounds and ideologies while maintaining a general surveillance of activities of student organizations and their officials. Security Chief Fujiwara of the Motofuji police substation cited a few on-campus criminal acts, but there was little danger of gravely disturbing peace and order which would justify intensive investigations by the police for an extended period. The police entrance in the present instance was part of this on-going police surveillance which infringed upon university autonomy and violated legal orders, especially the provision of Article 6, Paragraph 3 of the Code concerning the Execution of Duties of Police Officials.[17]

The prosecution concluded its argument as follows: Even if it was conceded that academic freedom and university autonomy were being infringed upon, those freedoms had been already restored when Officer Shiba, detecting a disquieting move of students, was trying to leave the place peacefully and voluntarily; there was no longer any immediate danger that needed to be removed by arresting the accused. Nonetheless, the accused caught and prevented the policeman from leaving; then, with the help of other students, dragged him onto the stage and attempted to snatch his police notebook. His action touched off further threats of violence when the policeman was left exposed to other angry students for more than two hours. Even if the accused intended to put a stop to future police activity on the campus, his action was still excessive inasmuch as he could have attempted to prevent his reentry by nonviolent vigilance and persuasion or by contacting the university authorities, whose function it was, according to the memorandum of the vice-minister of education on May 16, 1952, to negotiate with the police. The memorandum strictly advised the students against any direct dealings with the police. Whereas the imminent danger to university autonomy might justify a substantially unlawful act of the accused, there was time to seek a legal remedy, and the defendant's action was neither unavoidable nor the only means available. Furthermore, while academic freedom and university autonomy remained abstract rights, an assault on the policemen became a real and concrete threat to human lives. Condoning such unlawful exercise of force would have disturbed a social order and created a threat to the freedom of the entire people. The accused neglected the responsibility of learning as a student and resorted to an act which exceeded the socially accepted limit. Consequently, his act would still be unlawful even on grounds of self-defense and would not fall under the special provision in Articles 35 through 37 of the Criminal Code, providing for nullification of an otherwise unlawful act. These arguments of the prosecution were accepted by the Supreme Court later on. In conclusion, the lower courts weighed the legal interests of both the accused student and the policemen as follows: The policemen's legal interests as individuals were endangered in the execution of their police duty, however unlawful such a police duty might have been; meanwhile, the constitutional right of university autonomy was impaired in the process of such police duties. The alleged violence which the accused committed against Officer Shiba may have been somewhat rough, but he was motivated to defend the university's autonomy and the academic freedom of students, as was his right as a university student. The defendant simply resorted to a preventive measure against the unlawful police act. Any university administrator would have resorted lawfully to such measures as grabbing the policeman by the hand and pulling him by the collar of his coat in order to get his police notebook, the very criminal act with which the accused was charged. When the interest of maintaining university autonomy, which the accused was trying to protect, was compared with the personal legal interest of the policeman who suffered violence inflicted by the accused, the former clearly exceeds the latter. For these reasons both the Tokyo district and high courts dismissed the prosecution and acquitted the defendant.

3. The Supreme Court Remands the Case

The prosecution appealed the decision of the Tokyo high court to the Supreme Court. In its appeal brief the prosecution cited decisions of Japanese courts as well as the Federal Constitutional Court of West Germany, and opinions of both Japanese and German scholars. According to the Supreme Court decision in *Sakuma v. Japan* (1949),[18] since it was a function of the state to defend the public interest, private citizens should not be permitted to defend public interests not imminently threatened, and in justifying the private citizen's defense or an emergency evacuation to protect public interests, the notion of imminent danger and of defensive means employed should be restrictively constructed. In *Kojima v. Japan* (1952)[19] the Supreme Court reprimanded violent self-help and stated that in the absence of imminent danger to his rental house, its owner should seek remedy from the state in having the unlawful occupant evicted, rather than inflicting violence on the tenant's business. Likewise, the prosecution, citing the Osaka high court ruling in *Morita et al v. Japan* (1952),[20] stated that a violent act by workers like confinement, injury, or obstruction of management, would have exceeded a proper limit of the constitutional rights of workers in labor disputes. Another Tokyo high court decision[21] was cited by the prosecution to justify police surveillance of eight Japanese communist leaders and the distribution of the Japan Communist Party paper, *Red Flag*. In 1951 local police of Niigata prefecture eavesdropped on one of the suspects under surveillance by installing a microphone in a neighboring room in his boarding house, with the permission of the boarding house proprietor. The Tokyo high court held that electronic surveillance was within necessary and reasonable limits for the purpose of investigation.

Finally, returning to the concept of justifiable defense, the prosecution cited Koshin Takigawa, a criminal law specialist, as stating that the concept of justifiable defense should not be construed to include a defense rendered by an individual on behalf of the state.[22] Edmund Mezger, and the Federal Constitutional Court[23] of West Germany were also cited to point out that an unlawful act taken to defend one of two opposing legal interests might be justified if the legal interest would be gravely and irreparably endangered were it not for the act being otherwise unlawful.

On July 10 and September 11, 1962, the Supreme Court, third petty bench, presided over by Justice Shuichi Ishizaka, held oral hearings. On October 9, 1962, the case was transferred to the grand bench to have the constitutional issues resolved. On March 13, 1963, the grand bench held an oral hearing for two hours, and finally, on May 22, 1963, announced its decision. Presiding Chief Justice Kisaburo Yokota allowed cameramen to take pictures for three minutes inside the courtroom and then read only the main text (holding) of the decision.

The grand bench rendered its decision unanimously, with a few concurring opinions. The opinion of the Court was rather brief and constructed in a syllogistic manner with both major and minor premises and a conclusion. First, the Court gave its interpretation of academic freedom provided for in Article 23 of the Constitution. According to the Court, academic freedom includes the freedom to pursue academic research and to announce the results of such study; academic freedom, thus interpreted, is broadly guaranteed to all the people, including university students. According to the same opinion, while the freedom of education and teaching are not necessarily included in academic freedom, since a university is a center of arts and sciences where truth is intensively pursued and higher learning and technical arts are studied and taught, professors and researchers of a university are guaranteed the freedom to teach the results of their specialized studies in lectures and seminars. The Court also recognized university autonomy in order to guarantee the freedom of learning in universities, especially with respect to personnel matters and the supervision of facilities and students.

Then the Court conceded that as a result of the academic freedom of professors and other researchers, university students are entitled to a greater degree of academic freedom than the general public, and can enjoy the use of the university facilities, autonomously administered to a certain extent by the university authorities.

After having interpreted the nature of the academic freedom of students, the Court set forth the following two major premises, offered its minor premises based on facts found by the court below, and rendered its judgment on each major premise. According to the first major premise, a student gathering cannot enjoy academic freedom and university autonomy if it is not truly for academic study or for the expression of the results of such. On the basis of the facts ascertained by the Tokyo high court, the grand bench made the following minor premises: 1) the Popolo Players' performance was undertaken as part of an Anti-Colonial Struggle Day program; 2) the plot of the play was based on the ongoing *Matsukawa* trial; 3) donations were solicited in support of the accused in the criminal trial; 4) a report was given during the performance on the Shibuya incident. The Court concluded that these acts constituted political and social activities and not academic study and presentation thereof.

According to the second major premise put forward by the

Court, a gathering should be regarded as a public gathering when it is not exclusively for students but is open to the general public. On this premise the Court set forth the minor premise based on the lower court's findings that among the audience at the play were outside people who had bought admission tickets and that the policemen also had purchased tickets and had entered the theater freely. Thus, the Court reached the conclusion that it was a public gathering and not for the purpose of academic study and presentation.

Finally, by combining the conclusions from the two premises, the Court rendered its final decision that the play and gathering in question did not enjoy the constitutional protection of academic freedom and autonomy and that the entry of policemen was not an infringement of either academic freedom or university autonomy. By ruling that both the Tokyo district court and the Tokyo high court erred in interpreting and applying Article 23 of the Constitution, the grand bench remanded the case to the Tokyo district court for retrial.

According to the joint concurring opinion of four justices (Toshio Irie, Ken'ichi Okuno, Sakunosuke Yamada, and Sakuro Saito), the present gathering was a peaceful one, and the policemen attended the play primarily to gather public security information. Therefore, it would have been difficult to flatly deny that freedom of assembly was not impaired, if not academic freedom or university autonomy. However, when the policemen suspended their police activities and were on their way out peacefully, whatever imminent danger might have impaired academic freedom and university autonomy ceased to exist, and there was no urgent and unavoidable reason for the defendant to inflict violence on the two policemen.

Justice Katsumi Tarumi's concurring opinion stated that the play did not fall under the protection of academic freedom even though it was staged by university students, because the provision of Article 8, Paragraph 2 of the Fundamental Code of Education, which provided in part that "the political knowledge necessary for intelligent citizenship shall be valued in education," was applicable not only to a university but also to a high school. A play performed by university students without the participation or guidance of a specialist in the field was no more a specialized study of art or science than theatrical performances put on by junior or senior high school students or even the general public.

Justice Shuichi Ishizaka's concurring opinion stated that the Tokyo district court failed to inquire whether the acts of violence against the two policemen were perpetrated by the accused himself, whether Shumpei Fukui and several others engaged in acts of violence similar to those in the indictment, and whether there existed among the accused, Fukui and others, an intent to act jointly. If matters of joint criminal responsibility were found, the court should have made clear the concrete factual relationship involved. In the absence of these fact-findings, Ishizaka criticized the district court which held that there was no evidence to prove that the accused intended to act jointly with others in the commission of the crime.

Finally, Justice Masatoshi Yokota concurred with a similar opinion that the court below did not make the thorough inquiries or judgments necessary to make clear the true nature of the gathering concerning the nature of the Popolo Players group, the purpose of the meeting, the way it was actually conducted, and how the university authorities understood their purpose and the proceedings of the gathering when permission was given. So, he, like Ishizaka, favored retrial by concluding that it was impossible to judge whether or not the entry of police into the gathering exceeded the permissible limits.

The Supreme Court decision met mostly negative reactions from intellectuals. Chief Justice Kisaburo Yokota, a former international law professor at Tokyo University, was especially criticized bitterly by academicians. According to an article carried in the *Asahi Journal*,[24] three university professors, Michitaka Kaino of Tokyo Metropolitan University, Hideo Odagiri of Hosei University, Hyoe Ouchi of Tokyo University, and literary critic Yoshio Nakano were against the Court decision while Tatsuo Morita, Chairman of the Japan Student Scholarship Association, and Masao Nomura, editorial member of the *Asahi Shimbun*, supported it.

According to Kaino, the Court was too legalistic and formalistic to be appreciative of educational functions and seemed to have condoned secret police action as not detrimental to academic freedom. Student activities often encompass a wide scope of social and political activities, and neither in the study of literature, history, nor economics can academic value judgments be made outside of the political and social contexts. It would be ill-advised to hastily draw a line between academic and political activities, and between open and closed gatherings. The gathering in this instance probably was open to the outside audience as well as the university audience, but the students were in charge of the performance. It would have been more in tune with the spirit of democracy to be tolerant of student activities, and to regard this event as a campus student gathering. In general, the scope of academic freedom and university autonomy should be determined not by any hard and fast legal standards, but by thoughtful consideration of the nature and objectives of the university. Since the general public, which enjoyed freedom of assembly, could have rejected hostile intruders, the students in this case should have been able to enjoy special kinds of autonomy greater than that accorded to the general public. As it was, the Supreme Court has completely removed students' self-governance from university autonomy in the present case.

According to Odagiri, the Court disregarded the time element of this event, which had taken place eleven years before under a crisis situation. The Court approached this case from the contemporary perspectives of peace and order, and made no reference to the existing social conditions under which the Japanese police, on the strength of occupation forces, organized a large-scale security and information gathering network under the pretext of tracking down the eight Japan Communist Party leaders who had gone underground.

It should be noted, however, that the same critics were also unsympathetic to the action of the accused, and condemned increasing student violence in general. Yet they stressed that the present decision left the distinction between academic and political activities of students so ambiguous as to be readily abused in favor of the police.

Only two out of six contributors to the *Asahi Journal* supported the Supreme Court decision in the present case. Nomura was sympathetic with the way the Supreme Court drew the line between political and social activities of students and truly academic activities. He cited the Fundamental Code of Education (Article 8, Paragraph 2) which prohibits political activities by a university. Likewise, Morita considered that the Court had rectified the confusion surrounding the concept of university autonomy. In his opinion university autonomy was a means to guarantee academic freedom and was not stipulated in the Constitution; the university authorities should have taken a firm stand when the social and political activities of students disrupted education, research, and other academic activities.

The retrial was conducted by the Tokyo district court. Senda was thirty-three years of age and a tea merchant in a city of Akita prefecture, in the northwestern part of Japan, when the decision was announced on June 26, 1965, thirteen years after the incident by the third criminal division presided over by Judge Yasumura. The retrial mainly centered around the reexamination of the facts contested by the parties. In the opinion of the court, the question of whether the gathering had been a political and social activity or an academic gathering depended on the existence of the following facts: 1) the play was part of the Anti-Colonial Struggle Day events; 2) the play was based on the Matsukawa incident; 3) funds were solicited in support of the defendants in the *Matsukawa* trial and a report was made on the Shibuya incident, both prior to the performance. Likewise, the question of whether or not the gathering was closed to the general public depended on the following facts: 1) people other than students, faculty members, and administrative staff of Tokyo University, purchased admission tickets for the play; 2) the policemen also bought their admission tickets.

In view of the provision of Article 4 of the Court Code which binds lower court judges to a judgment of a higher court in the same case, if all these facts were ascertained, the court reasoned, the judgment of the Supreme Court would bind the present retrial and would lead to the conclusion that the police infiltration into the audience was not an unlawful invasion of academic freedom or university autonomy.

Based on a rehearing and review of previous trial proceedings, the district court attached low credibility to two policemen's testimony because the police witnesses denied whatever evidence was unfavorable to the police, and supported whatever evidence would have been damaging to the accused. Despite inconsistencies and ambiguities of the police testimony, however, the court concluded that it would have been inappropriate to brush off the policemen's testimony as fabrication. Although the facts presented by the prosecutors were generally corroborated by the police testimony, the following facts appear less obvious and convincing. First, in connection with the police contention that the play was conducted as part of the Anti-Colonial Struggle Day events, the court was not able to find any sufficient evidence to prove that several other events were planned or carried out concurrently with the present theatrical performance. Second, the court found no evidence of the fund raising for the Matsukawa defendants, for the police testimony to this effect was largely their imagination, based on the reference made to another fund raising campaign during the speech made prior to the play. Third, it was ascertained that the report concerning the Shibuya incident was made without the prior knowledge of the sponsors of the play.

In summary, the court reconstructed the factual relations as follows: 1) the play was based on the Matsukawa incident; 2) even though the gathering was not conducted as part of the Anti-Colonial Struggle Day events, the sponsors made no protest against the university students' newspaper article which treated the gathering as a part of such events; 3) even though the report on the Shibuya incident was made irrespective of the intent of the sponsors of the play, they tried neither to stop it nor oppose it. The retrial court, however, differed from the earlier findings of the Tokyo district court and the Tokyo high court regarding conspiracy, and concluded that the accused conspired with his codefendant and other students inside the hall to inflict violence on the two policemen who unlawfully entered the university campus. In the opinion of the court, the defendants inflicted violence as part of a series of group violence, but nowhere in the written opinion did the court present evidence for this conclusion.[25]

Finally, the court ruled that the policemen's entrance onto the university campus impaired the freedom of assembly. Police activities which have the danger of impairing fundamental human rights should be restricted to the absolute minimum. Although some outsiders were admitted to the play, it was performed in a quiet and orderly manner, and did not lose the character of an on-campus assembly. If the police needed to collect campus security information, they should have contacted the university authorities and a number of more appropriate methods would have been available. Therefore, the intrusion by the police exceeded the limit imposed on the police activities and violated the students' freedom of assembly. Yet, even though police intruded without authority, the action of the accused, which clearly exceeded the legal allowance, would not have been considered a self-defense nor emergency evacuation from danger. In conclusion, the lower courts before and after remand all judged the police intrusion unlawful, but disagreed on the degree of legal interests impaired by such intrusion and the unlawfulness of the alleged student violence. Such a disagreement was a result of different judicial value judgments on whether or not there was any other appropriate method available to justify what the accused thought to be an unavoidable and urgent action against the police.

4. The Popolo Players Decision and *Stare Decisis*

Although there is no formal principle of *stare decisis* in Japan, Japanese judges always rely on it as a working principle of their decision making. Now the question is how the Popolo Players decision has influenced judicial decisions made later in similar cases. Following the Popolo Players incident two incidents took place, and in each trial a court was called on to adjudicate the conflict between academic freedom and university autonomy on the one hand, and the propriety of police activities on or around university campuses on the other. Nowhere in either case can one find any specific reference to the judicial precedents established in the Popolo Players case. Also, various judges in these later cases sought, although mainly by implication, a precedental value in different court judgments of the Popolo Players case, whether it be the initial judgments of the Tokyo district and high courts, the Supreme Court decision, or the retrial in the Tokyo district court. Each of these incidents will be analyzed through a reading of court decisions of *Japan v. Nakatsuji et al* (1962),[26] and *Japan v. Amano et al* (1961).[27]

To start with the *Nakatsuji* case, Hiroshi Ogawa, policeman in charge of public security at the Tennoji police station, learned from a university yearbook that Shoko Taogoshi and he had graduated from the same high school and that she was a treasurer of the student association of the Osaka University of Arts and Sciences at the Ikeda campus. Ogawa visited Taogoshi during a university festival and talked with her for about two hours while dining together. She later told her friends that Ogawa asked her out repeatedly; word of this eventually reached Ishihara, one of the three students involved in this case.

Meanwhile, it was disclosed through another policeman's notebook that the police had been engaged in intelligence-gathering activities through some students concerning the student association of this university. An incident occurred when Taogoshi, Ishihara, and other members of the student association were on their way to the Tennoji campus to discuss, among others, Officer Ogawa's meetings with Taogoshi and a policeman's notebook, obtained recently. Soon, Ogawa, leaving the Tennoji campus after an investigation of another police matter, ran into Taogoshi a short distance away from the main gate of the campus. He was followed immediately by Ishihara, surrounded by other students, and asked to explain his association with Taogoshi. When he refused to reply, he was pushed into a store along the sidewalk, and then was taken by force to the on-campus student meeting previously scheduled.

Three students, Nakatsuji, Inoue, and Ishihara, were charged with a violation of Article 1 of the Code Penalizing Violent Acts committed in conspiracy with other people. According to the prosecution, it was outside the campus main gate that the accused stopped Ogawa and interrogated him. In taking Ogawa to the student meeting, the accused pushed and pulled the policeman by the arms toward the main gate. The defense countered that Officer Ogawa violated the constitutional guarantee of university autonomy. The prosecution denied any imminent danger to university autonomy, and concluded that the action of the accused could not have escaped criminality on the grounds of justifiable defense or an emergency evacuation from danger.

In *Japan v. Nakatsuji et al* (1962), the Osaka district court found all three defendants innocent. According to the facts ascertained by the court, Nakatsuji did not join the two others in forcing the policeman into the store; Inoue and Ishihara did resort to violence as charged, but, their action was not a crime inasmuch as Officer Ogawa first violated university autonomy. In the opinion of the court, the police were gathering information on the student association duly approved by the university authorities, thereby intensifying the student vigilance against it. In the present case Officer Ogawa approached Taogoshi to gather information, and in so doing he violated both the university autonomy and the individual dignity of Taogoshi. The alleged violence took place in the short time span of roughly one minute, the court opinion continued, and the accused acted violently only as the last resort. Furthermore, the topic of Ogawa's relationship with Taogoshi was on the agenda of the meeting, and it was appropriate to seek his explanation of it in person at the meeting. The accused justifiably feared the future of intensified police activities on campus, and thought that they might never have the same opportunity to protest police action if they had had to postpone the confrontation of law enforcement officials with the coed until a later time or take an action through the university authorities. The court concluded that under the circumstances of reasonable urgency the accused did not violate social justice in their motive, objectives, and method of protecting university autonomy and were not guilty of the violence they inflicted on Officer Ogawa.

Upon appeal by the prosecution, the Osaka high court on May 19, 1966,[28] sustained the acquittal of the accused for lack of substantial criminal evidence, but, at the same time, denied the policeman's impairment of university autonomy. The court found that the criminal act committed by the accused was minor, and that Officer Ogawa was also to blame for his behavior that could easily offend students, his motive and method of information gathering notwithstanding. In view of the prevalent student group activities resulting in disturbance of the public safety, the court reasoned, Ogawa suspected that political and social activities of the student association of the Osaka University of Arts and Sciences might lead to unlawful acts, and started to collect information on the organization; furthermore, his meeting with Taogoshi did not amount to the impairment of her constitutional right to personal dignity.

It is generally believed that the Osaka district court in the principal case relied on the first and second instances decisions (1954 and 1956) in the Popolo Players case, but that the Osaka high court came to learn of the Supreme Court decision (1963) in the Popolo Players case and subsequently was influenced by the retrial decision (1965) of the Tokyo district court.

In *Japan v. Amano et al* which was decided after the *Nakatsuji* case, however, the Nagoya district court followed the reasoning of the Tokyo district court in the retrial of the Popolo Players case, whereas the Nagoya high court followed the opinion adopted by the lower courts in the initial trial of the Popolo Players case. According to the *Amano* case, the dean of students and a professor at Aichi University supplied the police with information regarding student activities on campus in 1951, and a student gave a campus newspaper and other documents to the investigation bureau of the ministry of justice. Then the student association asked the police to stop information gathering activities on campus.

Meanwhile, in the light of a rumor that spies intruded into the student and faculty dormitories, several students, including Amano, were posted as guards. Around midnight these guards spotted and stopped two policemen walking on campus carrying guns and clubs. Unable to get satisfactory answers regarding the policemen's presence on campus, they grabbed the policemen by the arms and chest, threatened the officers with their own clubs, bound their hands, and dragged them to one of the student dormitories. Later, the policemen were released, but only after having written apologies for their intrusion onto the university premises and having agreed to leave their clubs, guns, and police notebooks with the students.

The prosecution produced a pamphlet confiscated on campus which stated that the Aichi University nucleus self-defense force had been organized with the objective of attacking, threatening, and inflicting violence on the spies, and contended that this organization made systematic plans to carry out their anti-establishment struggles. The accused were charged with premeditated violence by executing the present police harassment according to this operation. The court dismissed this evidence as immaterial, but also rejected the defense contention that the policemen violated university autonomy. In the opinion of the court no search and arrest could have been made by the police on a university campus without the university approval except in a case of emergency, but information gathering activities of the police could be conducted on campus under certain circumstances subject to limitations by the dictates of university autonomy. The two policemen entered the university campus to pursue men who had been acting suspiciously, and accordingly, their activity did not impair university autonomy. Thus, the Nagoya district court in *Japan v. Amano et al* found that Amano and several other students obstructed police duty by unlawfully detaining and coercing the policemen, but acquitted them by applying Article 37, Paragraph 1, Proviso[29] of the Criminal Code, as their objective was proper and their act was a justifiable defense.

Both the prosecution and the defense appealed to the Nagoya high court which, in turn, sustained acquittal while holding the policemen in contravention of university autonomy.[30] First, the court reversed the findings of the district court that the policemen entered the campus in pursuit of men acting suspiciously, and that the accused obstructed their police duty. The court found no eyewitness or any other sufficient evidence to corroborate the policemen's testimony. Since the purpose of the police entry on campus could not be determined, the students' action could not be held to be an obstruction of a legitimate police duty. Although a university may not deny police entry on an ordinary type of criminal investigation, the police should not be left with the power to decide unilaterally such entry except with a search warrant issued by a judge or in a case of extreme emergency. The policemen in this case entered the campus to gather campus security information when the university authorities were unlikely to consent to such entry, and accordingly, they violated academic freedom and university autonomy.

Second, the court ascertained that the accused were under the illusion that the two policemen were spies and informants who were threatening university autonomy and that capturing the policemen on the spot and making them leave would prevent any further invasion of university autonomy. Thus premeditation on the side of the accused was dismissed on the grounds that the alleged act, although based on imagination, was reasonable against what they perceived to be unfair interference with university autonomy. While the accused exceeded their objectives by resorting to violence, their motives were justifiable. Besides, a large number of students involved in this violence were not indicted, and eighteen years had elapsed since the incident. Under these circumstances the court saw no need to penalize the accused, and acquitted them.

The prosecution in the *Nakatsuji* case and the defendants in the *Amano* case, despite their acquittal, appealed to the Supreme Court for review. Dismissing the prosecution appeal without oral hearing, the Supreme Court in the *Nakatsuji* case gave the opinion that the prosecution did not raise any constitutional issues and that the judicial precedent cited by the prosecution was incorrect and did not contradict nor supersede the Osaka high court decision in the *Nakatsuji* case.[31] Likewise, by dismissing the defense appeal in the *Amano* case on technical grounds, the Supreme Court sustained the

Nagoya high court ruling which had denied the accused a ground of self defense.[32] In both cases the Supreme Court was silent about the academic freedom of students and university autonomy as interpreted by the lower courts. In the absence of the Supreme Court ruling on Article 23 of the Constitution in these two cases, it is not easy to determine whether or not the Court has changed its views as expressed in the Popolo Players case, academic freedom, and students' autonomous activities. As far as judicial conclusions were concerned, the Popolo Players precedent did not determine the outcome of either the *Nakatsuji* decision or the *Amano* decision. Yet it was significant for the Supreme Court to uphold acquittal of the students accused in these two cases who were similarly charged with the act of criminal violence, as was Kenzo Senda in the Popolo Players case.

If the very restrictive view of the Supreme Court marked an early judicial attitude toward the academic freedom and autonomy of university students, the *Nakatsuji* and *Amano* decisions may reflect a more liberal view of the Court. Notice twelve years of time difference and also vastly different compositions of the Supreme Court between these two cases in 1973 and the Popolo Players case in 1961. The shift of the Court's judgment may partly result from a changing judicial perception of social environments surrounding university students in Japan. Some administrators of Japan's top universities came to express liberal views of the academic freedom and autonomy of university students by the end of the 1960s.

These and other changing academic environments and student activities will be described next to place the academic freedom cases in proper perspective.

5. Academic Freedom of Students in Changing Social Environments

The narrow judicial interpretation of academic freedom and students' autonomous activities is typified by the decision of the Supreme Court in the Popolo Players case (1963). The opinion of the Court that students' academic freedom and autonomy were more restricted than those of professors and other research personnel and not recognizable in relation to the police and other third parties[33] may be partly accounted for by the Japanese tradition in which students play a passive role in receiving education under the strict guidance of instructors, and also by the influence of the educational policies initiated by the American occupation authorities reflecting the lack of the German notion of *Lernfreiheit*.

The nineteenth century German universities enjoyed both *Lehrfreiheit* (the freedom to teach) and *Lernfreiheit* (the freedom to study) while American universities have accepted the former but not the latter, partly due to the different academic and social responsibilities of universities in the United States. The notion of *Lernfreiheit* has been as conspicuously absent in the Japanese universities as in their American counterparts.

The postwar higher education system in Japan has been characterized by a phenomenal increase in the size of the student body and a mass production type of education at universities. This has made the functions of a university much more complex than before. On the one hand, many university students have continued to feel the need of dependence and protection as was accorded them in their families and primary and secondary schools. They were often frustrated and dissatisfied with the existing university system which did not fulfill their expectations.

Students' autonomous activities were stringently delineated by the university authorities, or more precisely, by the faculty as the governing body of the university. The rationale was that the students were not yet quite responsible and mature adults capable of independent thoughts and activities, and needed to be protected from external interferences. There was no built-in machinery responsive to student input, not to mention the protection of their rights in many universities. Especially, there was little or no recourse against a reprimand, suspension, or expulsion of a student. In *Fukumori et al v. Showa Women's College* (1963),[34] in which a student was expelled from a private school in Tokyo because of her leftist radical ideology, the Tokyo district court held that while a private college was free to advocate conservative educational objectives, Article 19 of the Constitution required a tolerance of a student's freedom of thought and that expulsion of a student on the grounds of his or her convictions and beliefs would also amount to a discriminatory treatment in violation of Article 14 of the Constitution. However, upon appeal, the Tokyo high court[35] overruled the decision by conferring on the college a wider discretionary authority over its students.

The students acknowledged their professors' authority in their academic fields, but resented the present university administration which gave professors the authority on all matters of university governance. Furthermore, the pressure on professors' research and off-campus activities, the expansion and complexity of university administration, coupled with the budget reduction of undergraduate programs in favor of graduate programs, all resulted in a sense of neglect and even isolation by many students. In the absence of effective means with which to channel their grievances and demands, radical students demanded institutional guarantees for student rights. Their dissatisfaction and distrust was not confined to the university administration, but extended to the contradictory political and social systems. Radical students often resorted to violence as was reflected in worldwide student riots such as at Columbia University and the University of Paris. In the end, however, factionalization crippled their concerted efforts to present their demands and make effective collective decisions in relation to the university authorities, the police, and the rest of the Japanese society.

Student demonstrations have been common in Japan for decades, but the issue involving university autonomy and academic freedom began to take on changing dimensions at the end of the 1960s. First, the students' main interest shifted to encompass not only a wide scope of political issues like the Vietnam War, the revision of the United States-Japan Security Treaty, and the reversion of Okinawa from the United States, but also internal problems of university administration, ranging from tuition increases and curriculum reforms to an increased voice in overall university policy making and the proposed University Code.

Second, radical students shifted their attack against the

government and law enforcement officers and now confronted university authorities, who, in turn, often worked with police in order to protect university autonomy and property from student radical activities. Many people sympathized with some broadly supported student demands, but many issues were stirred in with the students' leftist ideologies. Furthermore, many radicals were more interested in attacking wider political issues than university reforms.

An unprecedented upheaval of Japan's university system reached its highest point in 1968 when sixty colleges were disrupted and put under siege by the "anti-*Yoyogi* group," composed of a few thousand students opposed to the *Yoyogi* group (Japan Federation of Democratic Youth) which was associated with the Japan Communist Party. Most celebrated of all was the student riot at the University of Tokyo. The Tokyo University branch of the nationwide Young Medical Doctors Association was formed primarily under the initiative of the class of 1966 medical interns, and went on strike after an abortive attempt to gain the right to collective bargaining with the faculty of medicine over the terms and conditions of their medical internships.

The negotiations were marked by an incident in which the head negotiator, the business director of the Tokyo University hospital, was detained by radical interns for a prolonged period. Unable to secure the interns' testimony on the incident, the faculty meeting of medicine, with the concurrence of the university president, expelled, suspended, or reprimanded seventeen of the striking interns. The students countered that they were penalized simply because they were on the blacklist of student activists and that the school, for lack of evidence attesting to their absence from the scene of violence, deduced their presence there. Contending that some of them were not involved in the alleged violence, they demanded retraction of their disposition and occupied the Yasuda auditorium building.

Thereupon, the deans, with the consent of the university president and council, gave the police carte blanche authority to take necessary measures to remove the occupying students from the campus. It was believed that during the two-and-a-half hours of skirmish, the 1,200 armed police riot squad took pictures and reviewed university records without any school officials present. Many students in literature, economics, journalism, law, and graduate schools affiliated with the All-Students Common Struggle Congress, joined the interns' strike, class boycott, and lockout, blaming the police mobilization on the university authorities. The president's statement on August 10, 1968, defending the police mobilization and the expulsion of the seventeen interns further enraged the students who took this as a unilateral bureaucratic action. Demanding equal treatment with faculty members, the students reoccupied the Yasuda auditorium building. Many young professors were sympathetic with the students' grievances, and a series of faculty meetings were held in vain to accommodate some of the radicals' demands while protecting university autonomy from undue police and political involvement. On January 19, 1969, when the auditorium was finally cleared of radical students at Tokyo University, the number of disrupted schools nationwide decreased to thirty-three.

Against this background, about 500 students were charged with violence arising from the January campus disorder at Tokyo University. Clearly to make the courtroom a political forum, they demanded that they be all tried in one group, and refused to come to the trial. Appeals from judges and the bar associations were to no avail, and the trials finally went on in the absence of the defendants. The Tokyo district court was notably reticent about its decisions against the students, but there were some convictions. Yet no new judicial policy emerged from this criminal trial regarding the academic freedom and autonomy of students.

Meanwhile, another incident took place in which a reporter of the *Yomiuri* press, critical of the radicals' actions, became a victim of violence while gathering news in the medical school library of Tokyo University. To arrest some twenty students charged with bodily assaults, the police entered the university campus once again, but this time without a prior consent of the university authorities. The crisis showed an upward curve again. President Okochi subsequently assumed full responsibility for police mobilizations on campus, withdrew the expulsion of the seventeen medical interns, and resigned. While striking students in literature courses were negotiating with the dean, they confined him for one week and threatened other negotiating faculty members with abusive language and violence resulting in the indefinite suspension of the students involved. This event was met by the radicals' charge of misrepresentation of the incident and the suppression of student activities.

A large majority of students shared the reform sentiment but were opposed to violent tactics. They were led by the Tokyo University student group called *Yoyogi* faction. Only the radicals were organized, and they became factionalized as student riots intensified. The Young Medical Doctors Association and the All Students Common Struggle Congress formed the anti-*Yoyogi* faction and clashed with the *Yoyogi* faction over tactics. The *Yoyogi* faction was opposed to the lockout of classrooms and refused to arm themselves, but soon changed their tactics and opposed the anti-*Yoyogi* faction by force. Each faction reinforced its strength by collaborating with similar student groups at other universities and colleges, and interfactional confrontations and armed clashes were so intense that they overshadowed the presence of police and university authorities. "Somewhat paradoxically, the ultra-radical violence may have constricted the hitherto free atmosphere of Japanese student politics, while strengthening the hand of the radicals' enemies, the shrewdly moderate communists, the Japan Federation of Democratic Youth, and the rightist elements."[36] The Tokyo metropolitan police warned that it might enter a university campus without a request from the university in case of clashes between rival student groups in order to take necessary measures for the preservation of campus order. This was followed by a direct intervention by the ministry of education for a rapid solution of the crisis causing suspended commencement ceremonies and entrance examinations at the university.

The minister of education, speaking before the meeting of the presidents of the national universities, stressed the need to remove violence from university campuses, and normalize university education and research activities, and warned the presidents not to be hesitant about permitting police intervention. Acting President Ichiro Kato subsequently tried to mediate between warring student factions by proposing interfactional conferences, but to no avail.

In a statement issued in December 1968, Kato acknowledged for the first time that the notion of university autonomy long accepted as the autonomy of the faculty as governing body, needed to be reexamined in realization of the fact that students were no longer in a passive position of being educated but had their own demands as integral members of the university community.[37] Policy making in each of a dozen academic departments and research centers at Tokyo University had long centered around the faculty meeting. They formulated academic programs, selected students for admission, determined graduation requirements, and hired faculty members. Custom and tradition had strictly forbidden the university president, other administrators, and the university council, which was the highest decision-making body composed of representatives from each department, research center, and the library, to interfere with the faculty meeting's policy making.

Acting President Kato's policy statement was followed by the report of the Tokyo University reform preparatory commission on the role and rights of the students, issued on April 7, 1969.[38] This report set a distance from the ministry of education with regard to police mobilization and student participation in university governance. On the whole, it urged a major reform to increase the students' role and rights, but it also urged the students to become more responsible and mature members of a university community and exercise their freedom of thought and expression in such a way as not to impair similar freedoms of other members of the university community.

A failure of university authorities to deal effectively with radicalized student movements led to what many academicians came to regard as "a worrisome trend toward greater government involvement in university affairs." Against strong opposition from various quarters, the LDP-dominated Diet passed on August 3, 1969, the University Management Emergency Measure Code, giving the minister of education the temporary power to close schools which did not control campus disorders. This law became effective on August 17, 1969, and was to expire in five years, but it was extended without much debate in 1974.

By January 1970 much of the nationwide student violence had subsided. One facet of the restoration of college functions manifested itself in the decision of the Okayama district court in *Moriyasu et al v. President, Okayama University* (1969),[39] which held that it did not necessarily violate Articles 21 or 23 of the Constitution for a college to restrict speech and other forms of expression by students in order to restore the normal functioning of a college, but that a prohibition of the use of a microphone on a college campus amounted to a prior and unqualified restraint of free speech and expression, even though special conditions might be set for such use. The functions of academic research and education requiring tolerance of academic theories, ideas, or creeds provide a philosophical basis for political neutrality of a university.

As we saw, the prohibition of political activities by a university was reflected in the provision of Article 8, Paragraph 2 of the Fundamental Code of Education.[40] The political neutrality of a university was thought to bind teachers, university staff, students, and any formal campus organizations like a student association with compulsory membership. In many Japanese universities they were all traditionally discouraged from engaging in any political activities on campus. But political neutrality may be maintained by giving an equal chance to express political and social beliefs, instead of denying the chance to express them. While it is necessary to require political neutrality of a student association with compulsory membership lest it should impair the rights and freedom of its individual members, political neutrality is not required of a student group that a student joins of his or her own free will. The necessity of political education is acknowledged in Article 8, Paragraph 1 of the same law.[41] A real difficulty has been to balance these two dictates between the political neutrality of and political education by a university.

Given these changing environments surrounding academic

freedom of students, the judicial policy established in the Popolo Players case had very limited impact upon later cases. Each judicial decision was rather conditioned by a judicial perception and evaluation of the prevalent sociopolitical climate of a given moment.

Footnotes to Chapter Four

1. Sup. Ct., G.B.; May 22, 1963; 17 *Keishu* 370.

2. See, for instance, *Malloux v. Kiley*, 323 F. Supp. 1387 (D. Mass., 1971) and *Parducci v. Rutland*, 316 F. Supp. 352 (M.D. Ala. 1970).

3. Toshiyoshi Miyazawa, *Horitsugaku Zenshu 4: Kempo II: Kihonteki Jinken* (A Compendium of the Legal Study 4: Constitution II: Fundamental Human Rights), Tokyo: Yuhikaku, 1971 (new ed.), p. 396.

4. Robert M. MacIver, *Academic Freedom in Our Time*, New York: Columbia University Press, 1955, pp. 9–10.

5. Feinberg Law of 1949 dealt with elimination of subversive persons from the public school system. It was repealed in 1958, and the subject matter is now covered by Civil Service Law.

6. *Ienaga v. Minister of Education;* Tokyo Dist. Ct.; July 17, 1970; 21 *Gyosai Reishu* 1: also *Hanrei Jiho* No. 604, 1970, p. 35.

7. Sup. Ct., 1st. P.B.; April 8, 1982; 36 *Minshu* 594. A related civil case suing for damages was instituted by Ienaga in 1965, but was not decided until 1974. See Lawrence W. Beer, "Education, politics and freedom of expression in Japan: The Ienaga textbook review cases," in *Law in Japan: An Annual*, Vol. 7, 1975, pp. 67–90.

8. The Code Penalizing Violent Acts, Article 1, Paragraph 1 reads as follows: A person who commits in collaboration with other persons crimes stipulated in Article 208, Paragraph 1 of the Criminal Code or in Article 261 by show of force of group or multitude of people, either real or imaginary, or by a show of weapons shall be subject to not more than three years of imprisonment with hard labor or not more than fines of 500 yen.

9. Shigeki Endo and Yozo Watanabe, *Poporo Jiken: Kuroi Techo wa Kataru* (The Popolo Players Case: The Black Notebook Reveals), Tokyo: Shinko Shuppansha, 1964, p. 134.

10. Yasusaburo Hoshino, "Poporo gekidan jiken saikosai hanketsu ni omou: Gakuen no jichi to keisatsuken no genkai" (The Supreme Court decision on the Popolo Players case: The limit of academic autonomy and police power), in *Hogaku Semina* No. 88, July 1963, p. 10.

11. *Ibid.*, p. 11.

12. Chalmers Johnson, *Conspiracy at Matsukawa* (Berkeley, Cal.: University of California Press, 1972) offers the best accounts of this incident and trial in English. See also Kazuo Hirotsu, *Matsukawa Jiken to Saiban: Kensatsukan no Ronri* (The Matsukawa Incident and Trial: The Prosecutor's Logic), Tokyo: Iwanami, 1964.

13. Tokyo Dist. Ct.; May 11, 1954; 17 *Keishu* 428 *et. seq.*

14. Tokyo H. Ct.; May 8, 1956; 17 *Keishu* 445 *et. seq.*

15. The Matsukawa trial; Sendai H. Ct.; December 22, 1953; 13 *Keishu* 2111.

16. Tokyo University student newspaper confiscated on the campus, explains that February 21 was designated as an anti-colonial struggle day by the World Democratic Youth League in its second convention in Calcutta, India, in commemoration of the anti-British movement which the Indian navy had started in Bombay on February 21, 1946, touching off similar uprisings by students, farmers, and workers.

17. The Police Duties Code, Article 6, Paragraph 3 reads that a policeman shall not interfere without reason with the legitimate works of a person when he enters his premises in accordance with Paragraph 2 above.

18. Sup. Ct., 1st. P.B.; August 18, 1949; 3 *Keishu* 1465.

19. Sup. Ct., 2nd. P.B.; March 4, 1952; 6 *Keishu* 345.

20. Osaka H. Ct., 5th Cri. Div.; February 24, 1952; 3 *Kotosaibansho Keiji Saiban Tokuho* 224.

21. Case No. S27-ku-76; Tokyo H. Ct., 11th Cri. Div.; July 17, 1953.

22. Koshin Takigawa, 2 *Keiho Zasshi* 1, 1951, p. 212.

23. Case No. 72; West German Federal Constitutional Court; March 11, 1927; 61 *BVerfGE* 242 et. seq.

24. "Poporo jiken saikosai hanketsu eno iken" (Opinions on the Supreme Court decision in the Popolo Players case), in 5 *Asahi Janaru* 23, 1963, pp. 12–21.

25. Shin'ichi Takayanagi, "Poporo sashimodoshishin hanketsu ni tsuite" (The retrial of the Popolo Players case after remand), in 37 *Horitsu Jiho* 11, 1965, pp. 46–57.

26. *Japan v. Nakatsuji et al*; Osaka Dist. Ct.; May 23, 1962; 4 *Kakyu Keishu* 455, or *Hanrei Jiho* No. 307, 1962, p. 4.

27. *Japan v. Amano et al*; Nagoya Dist. Ct.; August 14, 1961; 3 *Kakyu Keishu* 750.

28. Osaka H. Ct.; May 19, 1966; 8 *Kakyu Keishu* 686, or *Hanrei Jiho* No. 457, 1966, p. 14.

29. Article 37, Paragraph 1, Proviso of the Criminal Code reads that unavoidable acts done in order to avert a present danger to the life, person, liberty, or property of oneself or another person are not punishable, only in case the injury occasioned by such acts does not exceed the degree of injury to be averted.

30. Nagoya H. Ct.; August 25, 1970; 2 *Keiji Saiban Geppo* 789.

31. *Japan v. Nakatsuji et al*; Sup. Ct., 1st. P.B.; March 20, 1973; *Hanrei Jiho* No. 701, 1973, p. 25.

32. *Amano et al v. Japan*; Sup. Ct., 1st. P.B.; April 26, 1973; *Hanrei Jiho* No. 703, 1973, p. 107.

33. Sup. Ct., G.B.; May 22, 1963; 17 *Keishu* 370.

34. Tokyo Dist. Ct.; November 20, 1963; *Hanrei Jiho* No. 353, p. 9.

35. Tokyo H. Ct.; April 10, 1967; 18 *Gyosai Reishu* 389.

36. Lawrence W. Beer, "Japan 1969: 'My homeism' and political struggle," in 10 *Asian Survey* 1, January 1970, p. 46.

37. Tokyo University Strife Documents Research Association (ed.), *Todai Funso no Kiroku* (The Records of the Tokyo University Strife), Tokyo: Nihon Hyoronsha, 1969.

38. The *Asahi Shimbun*, April 8, 1969. Excerpts from "the report of Tokyo University reform investigatory committee" (Todai kaikaku jumbi chosakai hokoku).

39. Okayama Dist. Ct.; October 2, 1969; *Hanrei Jiho* No. 570, 1969, p. 26.

40. The Basic Code of Education, Article 8, Paragraph 2 reads that schools designated in law shall not engage in political education or other forms of political activities for or against any particular political parties.

41. The Basic Code of Education, Article 8, Paragraph 1 reads that political knowledge that is necessary for citizens of sound judgment shall be respected educationally.

Chapter 5

The Self-Restrained Supreme Court

The 1947 Constitution functions as the highest and the organic law of the country. It dictates that any law and regulations that violate the Constitution be declared null and void, and that the separation of powers and the division of powers be delineated respectively. It is through the power of judicial review that this constitutional function is to be carried out. In fact the Supreme Court has voided from time to time public acts and actions on various grounds. If it is a judicial tendency to uphold the constitutionality of public acts and actions wherever possible, historical antecedents in Japan tend to promote judicial restraint. Thus, a review of judicial power, judicial independence, and the political environment of judicial decision making all tend to promote a self-restrained judicial culture in Japan. This chapter analyzes judicial activism and restraint in terms of constitutionality, and addresses itself to the question of how the Supreme Court has exercised its power of judicial review in relation to Diet, the Cabinet, the bureaucracy, and local governments.

The major legislative codes of Japan are grouped in the public law, the private law, the criminal law, socioeconomic laws, and treaties. The public law includes the Diet Code, the Court Code, the Administrative Organization Code, the Administrative Relief Code, the Finance Code, the Police Defense Code, the Environmental Protection Code, and the Education Code. The private law covers the Civil Code, the

Commercial Code, and the Code of Civil Procedure. The criminal law encompasses the Criminal Code, the Code of Criminal Procedure, and the Correction and Rehabilitation Code. Finally, socioeconomic laws range from various social codes and economic codes to the Intangible Property Code.

Policy makers in the political branches consist of Diet, the Cabinet, ministries and administrative agencies, and analogous offices of prefectural and other local governments. As the court of last resort, the Supreme Court is charged with the responsibility of determining the constitutionality of any law, order, regulation, or official act performed by these policy makers.

If the Supreme Court is the court of last resort (Article 81), the Diet is the highest organ of state power and the sole lawmaking organ of the state (Article 41), and the Cabinet is the highest executive organ (Article 65). Judicial review of the Supreme Court is balanced by the power of the Cabinet to appoint Supreme Court justices (Article 79) and the power of Diet to impeach judges (Article 64). Moreover, the parliamentary system in Japan has considerably diluted the separation of powers, particularly within the political branches of government. The Prime Minister and Cabinet members represent the majority party in the House of Representatives, and their authority to recommend legislation has allowed considerable participation by the executive branch in the legislative process. The executive involvement in policy making has also weakened the Diet's control over revenue and expenditure as well as appointments of high-ranking officials and ratification of treaties. At the same time, it has decreased the authority and prestige of the Cabinet as a formal institution. Policy making often involves major political parties, particularly the LDP which has controlled both Diet and the Cabinet since 1955. Here, a political function of the Constitution is to delineate legal boundaries and regulations within which these various political forces interact in making and implementing public policies. The judiciary is then charged with this constitutional function by examining the conformity to constitutional norms of these political forces ranging from Diet to labor unions. In view of the widely held view[1] that the Supreme Court often subserviently follows policy decisions of the conservative LDP-dominated government, this chapter will analyze the propensity with which the Supreme Court has upheld acts and actions of the political branches of government.

The judicial activism of the United States Supreme Court is well known. Starting with the Marshall Court, the United States Supreme Court has declared a number of public acts and actions unconstitutional, thus playing an active political role in making a wide range of sociopolitical and socioeconomic policies. Likewise, the Federal Constitutional Court in West Germany has disposed of many disputes involving the alleged unconstitutionality of delegated legislation, federalism, and equality under law. It was the American Supreme Court and its experiences that had a significant impact on establishing the Supreme Court of Japan and constitutional courts in West Germany, Italy, and Austria. The idea of adjudicating constitutional disputes was absent in these countries, including Japan, which had suffered the fascist abuse of power. The European countries after World War II established constitutional democracy and the rule of law, and empowered the special constitutional courts to guard against an infringement of their constitutions by simple legislative and administrative actions. Some dimensions of judicial ideologies manifest themselves in the constitutional questions of the separation of powers, delegated legislation, and the relationship between the central and local governments.

While Japan has a unitary form of government with the central government dominating policy making, prefectural and local governments are accorded certain degrees of autonomy on matters pertaining to their localities (Articles 92 to 95 of the Constitution). From time to time judges are called on to adjudicate disputes between the central and local governments, or to determine the legality of acts and/or actions taken by a local government, thereby manifesting one dimension of their attitudes or value judgments. Likewise, judicial attitudes on proper relations among Diet, the Cabinet, and the Supreme Court, as well as the scope and extent of policy making by each branch, and the legality of bureaucratic sublegislation evoke other important dimensions of judicial ideologies.

While judicial activism and restraint can be analyzed at the level of individual judges, groups of judges, or an entire court, the present chapter will be confined to the level of the Supreme Court as a whole. It will analyze the conflict and harmony over constitutional issues between the Supreme Court, on the one hand, and policy makers in political branches of both national and local governments, on the other hand. Here judicial activism or judicial restraint is operationally defined in terms of a conflict or harmony between the Supreme Court and policy makers over constitutional issues, and not in terms of the judicial assertion or judicial abstention from litigation itself. Simply stated, the Supreme Court reveals judicial restraint when it sustains policy makers' actions as constitutional, and it manifests judicial activism when it declares and invalidates them as unconstitutional.

1. Judicial Restraint vis-a-vis the Diet and the Cabinet

A court exercises judicial restraint either: 1) when both the Supreme Court and other policy-making groups remain static, that is, the former continues to uphold the constitutionality of the acts of the latter whose policy remains unchanged; or 2) when both sides change their policies respectively but the resulting changes are either in the same direction or equal in rate. In either case the Supreme Court and political branches maintain harmony with regard to the constitutionality of public policies. The vast majority of decisions reflecting judicial restraint fall under the first type simply because neither the political branches of government nor the Supreme Court often changes its respective policies.

There have been only a few instances that fell under the second type of judicial restraint. One such case arose when Diet revised the Local Autonomy Code in 1952 and the Supreme Court upheld the change in the law. Whereas Article 93 of the Constitution requires the election by direct popular vote of a chief local executive officer, the members of local assemblies, and such other local officials as may be determined by law, the Supreme Court upheld a new legislative policy on the mayoral election of the special Tokyo ward (*ku*). Acquitting the accused assemblymen in *Japan v. Kobayashi et al* (1963),[2] involving bribery in connection with an election of a ward mayor conducted in the Shibuya ward assembly in Tokyo in 1963, the Tokyo district court reasoned that since the special ward in Tokyo was a constitutionally established autonomous unit, it violated Article 93, Paragraph 2 to abolish, by a mere revision of the Local Autonomy Code, the popular election of the ward mayor and that neither the ward assembly nor the accused assemblymen had the authority to nominate and elect the ward mayor as they did. Consequently the money which the accused received did not constitute the crime of bribery.

Upon a direct appeal against the district court, the Supreme Court reversed and remanded the decision below. Stressing peculiarities in the administrative districting of Tokyo wards, the Court sustained the public prosecution against the defendants accused of election campaign bribery. According to the majority opinion of the Court, a special ward was not regarded as a constitutionally recognized local public entity either at the time of the enactment of the Constitution nor at the time of the 1952 revision of the Local Autonomy Code. The revised Local Autonomy Code changed the selection of a special ward mayor from a direct popular election to a selection by ward assembly by which the assembly of a special ward, with the consent of the metropolitan governor, selects the ward mayor from among those who are over twenty-five years of age and in possession of the right to vote for assemblymen of the special ward. This change was confined to the legislative policy and did not contravene the constitutional provision of local autonomy. In essence, the Supreme Court upheld the Diet's new policy in the selection of a special ward mayor in Tokyo and gave its reasoning that since the special ward is not one of those local autonomous units established by Article 93 of the Constitution, a selection of a special ward mayor need not be by direct popular vote, as required by the same constitutional provision. Here the Court revealed the second type of judicial restraint.

What is known as state governance creates the first type of judicial restraint in that a court, in deferring its judgment on public acts and actions of a highly political nature to that of the political branches of government, sustains the constitutionality of their policies. Toshiyoshi Miyazawa[3] was the first to introduce from France the act of state doctrine to prewar Japan. However, what Miyazawa expounded from the French law was seldom looked upon as binding on judicial decision making, nor did it arouse much interest inasmuch as what might be called an act of state in France was mostly outside the purview of judicial power in Japan. Only with the strengthened judicial power under the new Constitution did the doctrine of state governance begin to acquire a new significance. The Japan Science Council, at its 1955 general meeting, debated this topic by comparing the act of state doctrine and political questions in Great Britain, France, and the United States.

One of the earliest judicial references to state governance was made by Justice Tsuyoshi Mano in his concurring opinion in *Tomabechi v. Japan* (1953).[4] In his opinion the propriety of dissolving the Diet was not subject to judicial review, but the manner and method of dissolution was justiciable. Mano proceeded to review the merits of the dispute, and found that neither did Diet pass a resolution to dissolve itself nor was there any sufficient reason for the Cabinet to invoke Article 69 of the Constitution, the sole source of the Cabinet's authority to dissolve Diet.

It was in *Japan v. Sakata et al* (1959),[5] otherwise known as the *Sunagawa* case, that state governance became a major factor for the first time in the judicial decision making of the Japanese Supreme Court. A minor riot took place when the Japanese government in 1957 tried to expand a runway at an American air base located at Sunagawa village, a suburb of Tokyo. Government engineers, who were surveying privately owned farm lands as an acquisition site, were confronted with demonstrators opposed to the proposed runway expansion. Seven of the rioters were arrested and charged with violation of the Special Criminal Code, which imposed a heavier penalty than the Misdemeanor Code would against an ordinary kind of trespass. Dismissing the prosecutors' contention that the issue was a non-justiciable act of state governance, the Tokyo district court reviewed the substance of the issues and invalidated the 1951 United States-Japan Security Treaty with its accompanying administrative agreement as being in contravention of, *inter alia*, the Preamble and Article 9 of the Constitution.

The review by the grand bench, however, resulted in the reversal of the district court ruling and a retrial of the acquitted defendants. In the opinion of the Court, the Security Treaty is of a highly political nature affecting national survival, and its constitutionality must be decided by the political branches. The Court ruled that the Security Treaty, the accompanying administrative agreement, and the stationing of U.S. armed forces in Japan in accordance with these bilateral agreements were within the intent of Article 9, Article 98, Paragraph 2, and the Preamble of the Constitution. Indeed, the Court concluded that the district court should not review this kind of issue unless there is a clearly obvious unconstitutionality or invalidity.

How far can and should a court undertake a formal review to determine whether or not a case raises the issue of state governance and what criteria are there to determine a "clearly obvious unconstitutionality or invalidity" which will allow a substantive review?

First of all, the opinion of the Court appears to seek in the doctrine of the separation of powers the rationale for the non-justiciability of state governance. Reflecting this line of reasoning, Justice Toshio Irie elaborates that the principle of the separation of powers as being practiced in Japan leaves some areas of policy making unassigned to any one of the three branches, such as the referendum, popular initiative and recall that are reserved to the people by the Constitution, and that political issues ought to be settled by the people themselves, or as a next best alternative, by the political branches of government.

Justice Irie, subscribing to the French doctrine of the act of state, includes in the category of non-justiciable issues not only those that are reserved to the people's own judgment but also the following autonomous matters of both the Cabinet and Diet:[6] 1) the organization of the Cabinet and Diet (*e.g.*, the appointment of a Prime Minister, the appointment and dismissal of other ministers of state, the qualification of Diet members, disciplinary procedures of members, and the selection of chairmen and vice-chairmen of standing committees); 2) the operation of the Cabinet and Diet (*e.g.*, the structure, decisions, agenda, and voting methods at Cabinet meetings, and Diet, advice and consent of the Cabinet, and appointment by the Prime Minister of acting ministers); 3) negotiations between the Cabinet and Diet (*e.g.*, convocation of Diet sessions, a dissolution of the House of Representatives, submission to Diet of bills and other forms of drafts, as well as the amendment and withdrawal); and 4) national security and policy (*e.g.*, diplomacy, defense or peace-keeping mobilization, and the proclamation of an emergency state of affairs).

Justices Hachiro Fujita and Toshio Irie supported the doctrine of non-justiciable state governance and were of the opinion that the structure and process of judicial decision making with all its complex adversary and evidential requirements and strict adherence to the rule of law would not be adequate for reviewing questions of state governance and that in the light of popular sovereignty and political accountability of the Cabinet and Diet, the judiciary should not review highly political issues.

For Justice Katsumi Tarumi, the majority group appears to have undertaken a substantive review of constitutionality to determine the need for substantive review. According to logic only by an examination of the content of treaties can a judgment be made on their constitutionality. While acknowledging the widely held scholarly opinions negating judicial review of treaties and other international agreements, Justices Fujita, Irie, Tarumi, and Ishizaka argued that the domestic effects of a treaty were generally subject to judicial review even if a court could not deny the validity of a treaty under international law.

Finally, Justices Tamotsu Shima, Daisuke Kawamura, and

Shuichi Ishizaka believed that the "spirit of pacifism and international cooperation" embodied in the Constitution or a general conformity to the Charter of the United Nations offers a general guideline for determining abuses of discretionary power given to the political branches of government. Both Irie and Fujita suspected that what the majority group regarded as being a "clearly obvious unconstitutionality or invalidity" was something which, by and large, existed only in name and not in reality. Justice Katsushige Kotani, one of the three dissenters, held that had judicial power been restricted by state governance, the provision of Article 81 of the Constitution would have undoubtedly removed such a limitation.

Disagreeing with the majority view which held that the potential gravity of Article 98 of the Constitution capable of nullifying public policies dictated judicial restraint on the state governance issue, Kotani stressed the importance of judicial intervention into the Cabinet and Diet which could cause a very grave danger to national security because of the very nature of state governance. Since there can be no "clearly unconstitutional" instance in reality, Kotani continued, excluding judicial review of important policies would surrender the constitutional ideal of judicial supremacy and the rule of law to the rule of force and arbitrary authority.

Some Japanese deny the doctrine of state governance inasmuch as they believe that the doctrine does not allow even a formal review.[7] In their opinion, only after subjecting state governance to judicial review can a suspected illegality of the action and "uncontrollable consequences" arising from judicial nullification of the action be determined. They also deny the contention that state governance should not be adjudicated lest the greater "evil" should result from the unconstitutionality of a public policy of high significance.

Representing a more moderate view, Justices Ken'ichi Okuno and Kiyoshi Takahashi distinguished between legal and political judgments, and so long as a case is reviewable in purely legal terms as is the instant case, the doctrine of the state governance should not be invoked. In fact, they proceeded to examine the Security Treaty and found it constitutional except for certain evaluations made by the administration and Diet concerning military capabilities and the international situation. In their own words, ". . . the Security Treaty has been concluded . . . in accordance with the provisions of Article 5(c) and Article 6(a) of the Treaty of Peace. On the premise that there is danger of armed attack on Japan 'because irresponsible militarism has not yet been driven from the world.' (In regard to this evaluation of the international situation, which states that there may be such 'danger,' because it is a so-called political question it cannot be subject to review and judgment by the courts, . . .)"[8] Even where judicial review is excluded, they continue, the grounds should not be state governance per se but judicial incompetence to review certain parts of the case lest the court should step into political thickets. They are concerned about the implication of the opinion of the Court which may, in the long run, put restraint on judicial review by broadening such non-justiciable acts as reviews of international treaties and domestic legislation based thereon.

The Supreme Court has adhered to judicial restraint as exercised in the *Sunagawa* case, and its judicial policy on it has acquired a great deal of precedental value for later cases. Those residents at Sunagawa who were still opposed to the proposed expansion of the American air base brought suit seeking the revocation of a permit to expropriate their lands. However, the Tokyo district court, in *Aoki et al v. Prime Minister et al* (1967)[9] refused to review the propriety of the deliberative process in Diet concerning the 1960 Security Treaty by stating that as long as a treaty was properly deliberated, approved, and proclaimed by Diet, the court could only acknowledge that the treaty had received a proper and lawful legislative treatment.

Likewise, in *Matsumoto et al v. Japan* (1965)[10] where Matsumoto and two other plaintiffs sought to have the American air base removed from their lands which they had leased to the government during the occupation, the Fukuoka district court invalidated the lease of the disputed lands and gave the opinion that Article 9 of the Constitution would prohibit the use of private land for the purpose of providing the United States forces with military installations. However, this ruling was reversed by the Fukuoka high court which reiterated almost verbatim the opinion of the Supreme Court in the *Sunagawa* case.

The third petty bench of the Supreme Court, which included Justice Ishizaka, who had participated in the *Sunagawa* case, and four new Justices, Kakiwa Gokijyo, Kisaburo Yokota, Goroku Kashiwabara, and Jiro Tanaka, sustained the ruling of the high court on the strength of the state governance doctrine. In their views, the organization, function, and decision-making process of a court would not lend themselves to an adequate judgment of a highly political issue like this; involvement by a court into political conflicts would result in the politicization of the judiciary and a threat to judicial neutrality. Finally, in the opinion of the Court, causing the removal of the United States air base installations from the plaintiffs' lands would amount to an abuse of their rights inasmuch as the damage to the national security resulting from such a removal would be disproportionately larger than the loss presently suffered by the property owners.

The *Sunagawa* ruling was also followed by the Supreme Court grand bench itself in *Sakane et al v. Japan* (1969) involving the alleged conspiracy to incite judicial employees to rally in opposition to the proposed 1960 Security Treaty. The Court made it very clear that the treaty "cannot be held to violate Article 9, Article 98, Paragraph 2 and the Preamble of the Constitution on its face."[11]

The dictum that state governance, being of such a highly political nature, is so closely related to the fundamentals of national policy as to preclude judicial review, was invoked in *Tomabechi v. Japan* (1960)[12] in the context of Cabinet action. Representative Gizo Tomabechi sought, for the second time, judicial judgment declaring that the 1952 dissolution of the Lower House in which he was a member was unconstitutional and invalid and that he was entitled to reinstatement and a back pay of 285,000 yen. Alleging that this dissolution was unconstitutional and void, Tomabechi contended that whereas dissolution can be made only as provided in the Constitution, (Article 69), dissolution in this instance was carried out under Article 7 of the Constitution, and that dissolution procedure under Article 7 required advice and consent of the Cabinet, both of which were missing in this case. In response to this, the state argued first that dissolution of Diet is a non-justiciable type of state governance and second, even assuming for the moment that courts do have such a power, this dissolution was done with the advice and approval of the Cabinet and did not violate the Constitution.

By dismissing the state governance doctrine advanced by the state, the Tokyo district court conducted a substantive review of the disputed dissolution and declared it unconstitutional and invalid as lacking the constitutional requirement of consent and advice by the Cabinet. Upon appeal, the Tokyo high court sustained the view that a court did have the competence to judge the constitutionality of the House dissolution inasmuch as the dissolution affected Tomabechi's personal rights directly. At the same time, it reached the conclusion that the Cabinet should be considered to have rendered a proper form of advice and consent prior to the dissolution, since only Cabinet members are in the position to know whether or not there was a decision to dissolve the House and give advice and consent to the Emperor.

The same members of the Supreme Court grand bench which had decided the *Sunagawa* case overruled the high court decision in the principal case. In the opinion of the Court the district court exceeded its competence when it examined the government's action in applying constitutional requirements of advice and consent to the House dissolution. Four justices (Kotani, Okuno, D. Kawamura, and Ishizaka) upheld the constitutionality of the Diet dissolution only after having examined the substance of the case, whereas ten justices disposed of the appeal strictly as a non-justiciable type of dispute.

Unlike in the *Sunagawa* case, the Court as a whole did not undertake a substantive review of whether the district court was competent to pass judgment on the constitutionality of the issue. The opinion of the Court seems to base the doctrine not only on the principle of separation of powers, but also on the view that such an act of potentially grave consequences should not be nullified. The dissolution, according to the opinion of the Court, is of great significance both legally and politically because the dissolution forfeits a Diet member's status and stops the functioning of the House, however temporarily. Furthermore, the Cabinet dissolves the Diet whenever it seeks a public verdict on major policies or its own continued existence. It is advisable to exercise judicial restraint and tolerance on a highly political action which might be unlawful and void had it not been for state governance.

Justice Takahashi who had refused to apply the doctrine to the Security Treaty in the *Sunagawa* case apparently thought the dissolution of the House of Representatives to be a nonjusticiable type of issue in the present case. However, Okuno and Kotani wrote a concurring opinion which held that the dissolution would fall within the definition of "official act" in Article 81 of the Constitution and within the purview of judicial review provided it was susceptible to legal proceedings. For both justices, the individual's fundamental human rights should outweigh the doctrine of state governance; and inasmuch as the dissolution of the lower house clearly affects the right of its members, judicial review of it can be justified. Finally, Justices D. Kawamura and Ishizaka changed their opinions in the *Sunagawa* case and refused to concede nonjusticiable state governance in the *Tomabechi* case.

Challenged as unconstitutional in the *Sunagawa* case were the Cabinet's treaty-making powers and Diet's power to give advice and consent to the treaty. Likewise, in the 1960 *Tomabechi* case it was the action of the Cabinet that dissolved the House of Representatives that was challenged. However, in both instances the Supreme Court exercised judicial restraint on the grounds that a highly political issue was inseparably tied to the basics of national policy and should be entrusted to "the political departments like an Administration or Diet, . . . and ultimately to the decision of the people themselves."

Separate from the doctrine of state governance, discretionary powers of the political branches of government have also been determined by the Supreme Court as non-justiciable. There are some statutory grounds for the argument that the executive or legislative branch of the government has the "discretionary" power to decide its own internal matters. For example, provisions of Article 11 of the Special Code of Administrative Cases Procedure stipulate that an appeal lodged against administrative actions can be dismissed by a court when it judges the nullification of or changes in such actions which may be in contravention of laws, to be detrimental to the public welfare.

Likewise, the provision of Article 205 of the Public Office Election Code provides that when a suit is brought challenging the results of an election, the court is not allowed to judge invalid the results of an election even when a violation is committed unless there is a danger of affecting the election results. Furthermore, for former Chief Justice Kisaburo Yokota, the autonomous rights of Diet include the rights stipulated in Article 55 and Article 58, Paragraphs 1 and 2 of the Constitution as well as the internal police and peace maintenance power of Diet (Articles 114, 115, and 116 of the Diet Code).[13]

Yet, in the absence of any comprehensive enumeration, the scope and extent of autonomous powers of political branches have been decided on a case by case basis. In *Shimizu v. Governor of Osaka Metropolis* (1962),[14] otherwise known as the "taxpayer's suit," the Supreme Court unanimously held an actual legislative process in Diet to be a non-justiciable internal matter over which Diet has complete discretion. A new Police Code was enacted in 1954 to transform the city, town, and village police into the prefectural police system. The Osaka prefectural assembly approved an addition to the budget for fiscal year 1954, requested by the governor, which included a police expenditure to implement the new Police Code. Shimizu, a resident taxpayer of Osaka prefecture, lodged a complaint with the prefectural auditor's commission challenging the validity of the Police Code, but he was rejected on the grounds that the new Police Code was enacted in accordance with proper and normal legislative procedures; the prefectural assembly had properly approved of the budget; and it was within the governor's authority to administer the approved expenditures.

Upon an unsuccessful attempt, Shimizu filed a suit with the Osaka district court contending that the new Police Code was passed by the House of Councillors on June 7, 1954, and was put into effect even though the nineteenth session of Diet had closed on June 3, 1954. Thus, the Police Code was passed after the session had ended. Also, the following actions of the chairman violated the rules of the House of Representatives. The chairman was not seated at the rostrum when he announced on June 3 the extension of the session for another two days. He neither called the meeting to order nor distributed an agenda beforehand; he also failed to allow time for debate, voting, and announcing the results of the voting. The new Police Code in question, Shimizu concluded, violates the constitutional principle (Article 92) of local autonomy by depriving cities, towns, and villages of the function of operating their own police. The metropolitan legal counsel counterargued that a court did not have the power to review the House resolution to extend its own session and that since Article 243–2, Paragraph 4 of the Local Autonomy Code was available to a taxpayer challenging a local public officials' wrongdoing, he was not entitled to demand suspension or restriction of official duties resolved by the local assembly.

The Osaka district court, sustained by the Osaka high court, dismissed Shimizu's suit by stating that an alleged "unlawful expenditure" subject to judicial review under Article 243–2, Paragraph 4 of the Local Autonomy Code must be of such a kind that an auditor can request corrective measures against it and that the present suit is not subject to judicial review. Overruling the judgments below denying justiciability of a local assembly resolution, the Supreme Court undertook a substantive review of the legislative process of the Police Code and upheld its constitutionality. The Police Code is deemed to have been passed by the resolution of both Houses and to have been enforced in compliance with lawful procedure; the courts should respect the autonomy of the Houses and should not investigate any facts, as presented by the plaintiff, concerning the legislative procedure of the law, and should not pass any judgment upon the question of validity or invalidity. The Court conceded that once the Police Code had been enacted, a taxpayer could challenge in court a decision of a local government approving such expenditure.

A Diet member's conduct within the legislature is another area of the autonomous power of a legislature. In the face of the Diet's determination to exclude judicial power even by new legislation, the Supreme Court exercised judicial restraint in *Japan v. Nishio* (1949)[15] involving the alleged violation of the Political Contribution Code. The Tokyo prosecutors' office charged Suehiro Nishio, Diet member and secretary general of the Katayama Cabinet, with a violation of the Political Contribution Code when he failed to report a contribution of 500,000 yen in 1949. The Tokyo district court convicted the accused by dismissing his contention that the contribution was made to him in his capacity as an individual and was not subject to the regulation of law. Upon appeal, the Tokyo high court reversed the decision and acquitted him by accepting the defense contention. The Supreme Court further reversed his acquittal and dismissed the charge against Nishio.

By examining the legislative process of the Code concerning the Oath and Testimony Before Diet, the Court found that the code was enacted to investigate national government in each House and that the provision of Article 8 therein would require Diet itself to initiate prosecution against an alleged perjury and other misconduct committed by its own member. The Court also found that in the absence of a charge initiated either by the House of Representatives or its committees, the court below made an error by undertaking a substantive review of the alleged perjury only on the prosecutors' charge. Similarly, in *Japan v. Kono* (1949)[16] in which a political purgee, Ichiro Kono, was prosecuted for having given false testimony regarding his alleged political activities, the Supreme Court denied judicial competence in the absence of a Diet impeachment against him.

In summary, the Supreme Court has been much more restrained to both Diet and the Cabinet than to any other government organs. The doctrine of state governance or political autonomy has provided the Supreme Court with a judicial rationale for upholding constitutionality of actions taken by the political branches.

2. Judicial Restraint vis-a-vis the Administrative Agencies

The Cabinet as the chief executive branch is authorized to sublegislate within the guidelines of Diet.[17] Located below the Cabinet are the Prime Minister's office and such major ministries as justice, foreign affairs, finance, education, welfare, agriculture and forestry, international trade and industry, transportation, labor, postal service, construction, and local autonomy. Furthermore, important commissions under the jurisdiction of ministries include the fair trade commission and the national public safety commission (under the Prime Minister's office), the public safety review commission (under the justice ministry), the central labor commission, and the public enterprises labor commission (both under the labor ministry). Important agencies below ministries include the administrative management agency, the defense agency, the economic planning agency (all under the Prime Minister's office), the national tax agency (under the finance ministry), the food agency (under the agriculture and forestry ministry), patent agency and the small/medium enterprises agency (under the ministry of international trade and industry). Finally, at the prefectural and local levels can one find such administrative commissions like the board of education, the election control commission, the public safety commission, and the agricultural commission.

The ministries, commissions, and agencies, collectively referred to as administrative agencies, often exercise quasi-legislative powers in three distinctive ways. First, they make various orders to carry out not only the constitutional and legislative laws but also Cabinet and other ordinances. Second, they sublegislate details of legislative laws and executive ordinances. Third, they make administrative rules like notices and orders. In each instance, administrative acts necessary to carry out legislative policies may rest in part upon considerations not entirely susceptible of proof or disproof, and at times upon those considerations that cannot always be supplied by the legislature because of extraneous circumstances and subject matter. Thus, a statute confers upon administrative agencies discretion necessary for the exercise of the delegated power. Here an administrative agency is required not to exceed or act contrary to the scope and intent of the authorization delegated by Diet (Article 73, Paragraph 6 of the Constitution).

There are two kinds of discretion administrative agencies exercise in their quasi-legislative activities. First, administrative discretion exercised in levying taxes and licensing medical doctors, for example, enables administrators to interpret and apply the law and regulations. Second, discretion exercised in disciplining students of public schools and determining water rights, for example, is not spelled out in statutes, but is left to administrators who, in turn, take into account public interests and the intent of law. The difference between these two types of discretion is a matter of degree rather than kind, and the latter offers a wider latitude than the former.

Furthermore, they are both subject to judicial review. For example, upholding the action of the public safety commission which revoked the license of a taxicab driver with long records of traffic violations, who was being charged with having made an illegal U-turn, the Supreme Court in *Hiroshima Prefectural Public Safety Commission v. Umebayashi* (1964)[18] stated that the question of whether or not the driver's traffic violation constitutes grounds to revoke his license is stipulated in the statute and is not left to the discretion of the public safety commission but that the statute leaves to the commissioner the discretion to determine whether his illegal U-turn constitutes the grounds for revoking his driver's license.

When an administrative agency errs in exercising its discretion, statutory or otherwise, such an administrative action becomes unreasonable and improper, but not necessarily unlawful. In *Asahi v. Japan* (1967),[19] the Supreme Court was of the opinion that the authority to determine what constitutes the minimum standards of wholesome and cultural living is vested in the discretion of the minister of health and welfare and that his discretion does not immediately bring about the question of legality. An abuse of administrative discretion, however, could lead to an unlawful action, and a grieving party may resort to either administrative or judicial remedy or both. The pre-1945 practice that administrative review and remedies be exhausted before an administrative action is brought to the Administrative Court is no longer required. A grieving party may seek both administrative and judicial remedies simultaneously. However, it seems to be a settled practice for a grieving party to seek an administrative adjudication, wherever available, before filing a suit in court.

If judicial adjudication is a settlement by judges sitting in an ordinary court of law, administrative adjudication is a settlement by administrative agencies of disputes in concrete cases arising out of the execution of law and regulation. The latter is depersonalized, institutional decision making. A superior officer in an administrative agency usually renders judgment on the record gathered by his subordinate officer, and the man who makes the decision does not participate in the hearing of litigants or witnesses. This device is intended to afford more efficiency in the adjudication of administrative actions. Article 76, Paragraph 2 of the Constitution denies final judicial power to any organ or agency of the executive. The function of reviewing administrative actions is now placed solely within the jurisdiction of the ordinary court system. This is designed to place all such actions clearly under the rule of law, and offer judicial remedies to those whose legal interests are injured by unlawful administrative acts and actions.

Yet agencies such as special tribunals have grown as a condition accompanying the implementation of the new Constitution. The family court, having its origin in the United States, reveals substantial features of a special tribunal.[20] Similarly patterned after the American model, administrative commissions such as the national personnel authority, the national public safety commission, the fair trade commission, and the prefectural board of education were established by law with certain degrees of autonomy and political neutrality.

They exercise quasi-legislative and quasi-judicial functions while being responsible to the Cabinet for their actions.

The Administrative Complaint Review Code (*gyosei fufuku shinsa ho*) stipulates the procedure and processes of administrative adjudication and administrative remedies, while the Administrative Litigation Procedural Code (*gyosei sosho tetsuzuki ho*) provides for judicial review of administrative actions and administrative adjudication.

The former code provides for petition and complaint to be lodged with administrative agencies, and only in the following instances is mandated an administrative adjudication. First, highly technical, scientific, or specialized knowledge is required for a resolution of administrative disputes. Second, a uniform and standardized policy needs to be formulated to dispose of an administrative action which affects a large number of people, such as a mass dismissal of public employees. Third, a petition against an administrative act is to be reviewed by a third party administrative body. Even then, judicial review can be sought directly if no administrative remedy is forthcoming within three months from the time of filing a complaint, or if irreparable damage will be done unless an alleged administrative action is changed or revoked immediately, or if there is a legitimate reason not to request administrative review.

The Administrative Litigation Procedural Code provides for four types of judicial review of administrative actions which allegedly violate law, regulation, or public welfare. First, most typical is a suit seeking a revocation or change of an alleged act, lodged by a party whose legal interests are being injured by an administrative action, such as taxes unlawfully collected by the tax office. Second is litigation between two private parties over an administrative action. For example, an apartment house owner may file a suit against a local government seeking an additional amount above and beyond an unreasonably small monetary compensation for a room occupied by a patient with a contagious disease, which is ordered to be kept vacant during sanitation. Third, a person may file a suit seeking a correction of an administrative action which does not conform to law or regulation without showing any personal injury to himself. For example, a voter may file a suit against an election control commission to have an election result invalidated on the grounds of an unlawful election procedure. Fourth, a suit between two government organs over jurisdictional disputes is subject to judicial review. For example, a city assembly may sue a prefectural governor who, at the request of a city mayor, revoked a resolution of a city assembly.

The Japanese courts have relied on a trial *de novo* very heavily. Only after a trial *de novo*, for instance, did the Osaka district court uphold the discretionary authority of a police chief, to dismiss a subordinate officer in *Nakatsugawa v. Chief of the Osaka Prefectural Police* (1952).[21] Most judges have been reluctant to trust administrative experts even on highly technical matters in which administrative findings of facts are made by experts on the basis of evidence gathered at a hearing. There are only a few instances, therefore, where courts have relied on the substantial evidence rule, and conferred finality upon administrative fact-finding.

One of a few examples is Article 80 of the Anti-Monopoly Code which provides that facts determined by the fair trade commission are binding on the court when there exists a substantial evidence proving them. In *Japan Publishing Association v. Fair Trade Commission* (1953), the commission found that the publishing association had violated the Business Organization Code and ordered it to cease and desist from controlling paper allocation and other monopolistic activities. When the association brought this suit contending that the commission's findings were not supported by a substantial evidence rule, the Tokyo high court dismissed the suit by holding that "administrative findings of facts are not to be judicially disturbed if a record contains reasonable evidence to support such findings after a rational weighing of it against contradictory evidence."[22]

Likewise, the governor of Fukuoka prefecture, under the lobbying pressure of the health spa proprietors' association, instituted a policy not to permit any drilling of a new spa, except under special circumstances. Yet, in consultation with the technical advisory board, he issued a permit to a person who applied for a new drilling site after having failed to hit a good spot. Dismissing a suit by the health spa proprietors' association seeking retraction of the drilling permit, the Supreme Court in *International Buyer Designated-Hotel Daimaru Annex et al v. Governor, Fukuoka Prefecture* (1958) upheld the governor's action on the grounds of highly technical matters which required a wide administrative discretion by the executive agency.[23]

A dilemma arises in balancing administrative discretion with the rule of law and judicial supremacy. When the ambit of discretion narrows because of clearly applicable rules, safeguards are less necessary against administrative abuse, and it is also easier to have safeguards without impairing administrative performance. However, when policy discretions are wide and flexibility is required, safeguards like standardized and published procedures seem most needed. For instance, the Passport Code requires neither specific reasons for denying a passport nor the separation of administrative action and hearing in granting an appeal to the foreign minister. Overall, both statutory and case laws concerning administrative procedure have been slow to develop. Judges have been reluctant to make case laws where statutory provisions were ambiguous or even absent. After a trial *de novo*, judges tend to uphold administrative fact-findings and legal interpretation and application.

The following three trials *de novo* illustrate judicial reasonings behind the self-restrained Supreme Court in relation to administrative agencies. The first case illustrates the ministerial discretion exercised in denying passports to a group of Japanese who wanted to attend the national liberation ceremony of China in 1962. In the opinion of the Court in *Yoshida et al v. Japan* (1969)[24] the foreign minister took into due consideration pertinent facts such as personality, personal history, and occupations of the applicants and the purpose of their proposed trip. It was within the ministerial discretion of the foreign minister to conclude that the applicants' proposed trip to communist China would harm Japan's national interests in the light of basic differences between China's political aims and Japan's foreign policy goals, and the prevailing cold war between the East and the West.

The other two cases deal with discretionary powers of local administrative commissions. In *Kyoto City Board of Education v. Kitakoji et al* (1961),[25] the Court upheld the action of the local board of education as a necessary measure to settle quickly labor disputes when the board called its emergency meeting and decided to dismiss all those teachers who refused to follow the board's order to transfer to another school. In *Fujinuma v. Minami Kawauchi Village Mayor, Tochigi Prefecture* (1955),[26] a village mayor consulted with and notified village farmers of their allocation of rice to be delivered to the government. He did not notify the plaintiff, who had objected to his allocation many times in the past. The plaintiff filed a suit complaining about the discriminatory treatment by the village mayor, who later notified him of his allocation after discussing the matter with the local food provision adjustment commission but not with the plaintiff. In the opinion of the Court the village mayor, in the absence of the statutory provision on the matter, had the discretionary authority to decide the question of how and when the plaintiff should be notified of his rice delivery allocation.

All in all, the rule of law and judicial supremacy over administrative action has been firmly established in Japan since 1945. All administrative actions and administrative adjudications are subject to judicial review on matters of both facts and law. In this sense the Supreme Court does not automatically accord finality to administrative adjudications of administrative fact-finding and legal interpretation. Yet a review of the Supreme Court decisions during the first four decades indicates that the Court, as it actually reviewed administrative cases, has emerged very self-restrained in sustaining a wide latitude of administrative discretion on a wide range of public policies, pdiarticularly on highly technical ighly opomalitical issues.

At the same In timovement for a special tribunal centering around administrative adjudication does not seem in the forefront in Japan. Functions performed by special tribunals in other countries are fulfilled by an American-style system of administrative commission in Japan. In the absence of strong criticism of the structure, procedures, and efficiency of the regular courts on the side of the public who has had dealings with courts in special areas of law, a strongly felt need for special tribunals in other areas has been slight, and there is little urgency to the matter in Japan.

3. Judicial Restraint vis-a-vis Local Governments

Japan's political system is unitary, and the governing powers are vested primarily in the hands of the national government. The prefectural and local governments can exercise those powers that are delegated by the national government. Although Article 92 of the Constitution requires the Diet to make laws regulating organizations and operations of local governments in accordance with the principle of local autonomy, the local governments have been often subordinated to the central government and their sublegislative activities have been strictly regulated by the Local Autonomy Code. Yet, the Supreme Court has exercised judicial restraint by upholding a relatively wide autonomy and sublegislative activities of prefectural and local governments.[27]

With respect to the autonomous activities of a local assembly, the Supreme Court, in *Otaki et al v. Yamakita Village Assembly, Niigata Prefecture et al* (1960),[28] decided not to make a substantive review of the local assembly's temporary suspension of assemblymen, judging it an internal and autonomous matter. Where the plaintiffs in this case, village assemblymen, were opposed to a proposed ordinance change relocating a village hall, the majority assemblymen who favored such relocation passed a motion condemning the plaintiffs' disruption of the assembly's deliberation, suspended their attendance for three days, and approved the relocation of the village hall. Otaki and others immediately contested at a district court the assembly's actions on the grounds that the suspension violated the village assembly rules and also deprived them of their voting right over the present issue. The assembly gave its opinion that the plaintiffs had no legal standing to sue because of the lapse of the suspension time period. Appealing a district court ruling which supported the assembly's contention, the plaintiffs repeated the same argument that a local assemblyman, who is faced with punitive action under public law, should be protected by Articles 31 and 39 of the Constitution.

Dismissing the plaintiffs' appeal, the Supreme Court ruled that the suspension of attendance at assembly meetings is a matter lying outside judicial review and that judicial nullification of such suspension and the revised ordinance would be inappropriate. Justice Daisuke Kawamura was of the opinion that a local assembly's sanction against its own members is justiciable because it involves salary and other compensations of the affected member, but concurred with the majority which held that the plaintiffs' suit seeking merely a revocation of the assembly resolution failed to raise any personal and tangible injury and concrete remedy for it. Finally, in the concurring opinion of Justice Okuno, the assembly's action was an administrative sanction provided for in the Local Autonomy Code and the plaintiffs failed to file an administrative petition for judicial remedy available against such an administrative sanction.

The Supreme Court continued to uphold the power of local government in *Miyazaki et al v. Japan* (1967)[29] involving misconduct of Saga prefectural assemblymen by denying to local assemblymen such wide degrees of autonomy and privilege as possessed by Diet members. Where the accused, in protest against their chairman, obstructed assembly proceedings, a criminal proceeding was initiated against them, without the resolution of local assembly or formal charge by the assembly chairman. Upholding the prosecution against the accused, the Supreme Court was of the opinion that since a local assembly is granted the autonomy necessary to adequately perform its functions, its chairman may not have strictly followed an assembly rule, but performed his overall duties regarding assembly proceedings, and that the accused who inflicted violence or the threat of violence against the chairman in the performance of his duty should be held criminally liable for his misconduct.

Article 94 of the Constitution confers upon local governments the power to enact their own regulations within the law, and Article 95 therein requires Diet to legislate a special law, applicable to one locality, with the consent of the majority of the voters in the locality. In a number of instances the Supreme Court upheld sublegislations by local governments. *Matsumoto v. Japan* (1962)[30] illustrates judicial reasoning in support of such sublegislation. The city of Osaka enacted in 1950 an ordinance regulating and penalizing prostitution on the street in an effort to realize the objectives of maintaining public morality embodied in the Local Autonomy Code. The Diet passed the Prostitution Prevention Code in 1956, and put it into effect two years later. Although it superseded the 1950 city ordinance, the new law stated that unless otherwise stipulated herein, a commission of offense in violation of this law prior to the repeal of the ordinance would be disposed of in the same manner as before.

Matsumoto was charged with the violation in 1956 of the said city ordinance, convicted by the Osaka summary court, and fined 5,000 yen. The accused appealed the Osaka high court judgment, which had sustained the conviction, to the Supreme Court, contending that the imposition of a criminal penalty in the form of a city ordinance instead of a law violated due process (Article 31) of the Constitution. The Supreme Court gave the following reasons in dismissing the appeal. First, since the need to control prostitution varies between big cities and rural areas, it is more democratic and appropriate to leave some issues to be decided at the local level through the enactment of local regulations. Second, since the city ordinance sets forth punishment as delegated strictly and concretely by the Local Autonomy Code, the ordinance is not a "blanket" delegation of power, but rather a limited one strictly in accordance with the procedures established by law.

In general, the Court has reviewed very carefully any sublegislation which touches on civil rights and liberties. In *Kakunaga v. Sekiguchi* (1977)[31] the Court upheld a city government's expenditure incurred for undertaking a foundation ceremony of its city gymnasium, and dismissed the charge that such public expenditure would violate the constitutional principle of separation of religion and politics. According to the majority opinion, the foundation ceremony of city gymnasium, conducted in accordance with the *Shinto* manner, may have some bearing upon religion, but its purpose was to pray for the safety of the construction work and for a stable geological foundation; as such, the ceremony was a secular, social custom, as well as a ritual, and its intended effect was not to promote and assist the *Shinto* religion nor to suppress and interfere with other religions. Thus, it does not violate Article 20, Paragraph 3 of the Constitution for a city government to pay for the ceremony's expenses.

Five justices dissented by stating that the present foundation ceremony is clearly religious inasmuch as the priest conducted it in accordance with the manner unique to *Shintoism*. Such ceremony may have become largely a time-honored secular custom, but it is highly improper and unconstitutional from the standpoint of the separation of religion and politics for the municipal government to give administrative or financial assistance to the *Shinto* shrine.

In conclusion, an analysis of the grand bench decisions since the inception of the Supreme Court through 1980 reveals that the grand bench exercised judicial restraint in relation to the political branches concerning constitutional issues about half the time when it was divided, and over 90 percent of the time when it was unanimous. The grand bench showed judicial restraint in 86 split decisions (out of a total of 165), or 52 percent, on sociopolitical issues and in 19 divided decisions (out of a total of 40), or 48 percent, on socioeconomic issues. It was self-restrained in 159 unanimous decisions (out of a total of 173), or 92 percent, on sociopolitical issues, and in 86 unanimous decisions (out of a total of 87), or 99 percent, of socioeconomic issues. The relatively low degree of judicial restraint shown by the divided grand bench is mainly due to many decisions which involved the same constitutional issues over which the justices were divided. Since petty benches are supposed to follow the grand bench policies, the propensity of their restraint can be estimated to roughly correspond to that of the grand bench's restraint. Thus, in a large majority of decisions, there were no changes in the policies of either the Supreme Court or political branches; the Court dismissed appeals challenging acts and actions of the political decision makers.

Next, judicial activism of the Supreme Court will be examined in terms of its typology and propensity.

4. Three Types of Judicial Activism

There are three types of constitutional issues which give rise to an activist Supreme Court in relation to the political branches: 1) The Supreme Court follows its own judicial policy according to the working principle of *stare decisis* in spite of a policy change on the side of political branches; 2) both the Supreme Court and political branches change their policies respectively, but either in opposite directions or at an unequal rate of change; and 3) the Supreme Court changes its policy in spite of the status quo adhered to by the political branches. In each instance above, the Supreme Court comes into conflict with the political branch over a constitutional issue and results in judicial activism.

The first type of judicial activism manifests itself very rarely. It did happen when the Supreme Court struck down legislative policy changes as a violation of the constitutional freedom of occupation. In *Kakukichi Co. v. Governor, Hiroshima Prefecture* (1975),[32] the plaintiff applied for a new license to open a drug store in Fukuyama city, Hiroshima prefecture in 1963. While its application was pending in the governor's office, the Pharmaceutical Code of 1960 was amended in 1964 so as to empower the governor to deny a license if the location of the new drug store was too close to existing stores. In January 1964, the plaintiff was denied a license after having found the existence of many drug stores in the vicinity of the proposed site.

The Hiroshima district court first upheld the plaintiff's suit seeking revocation of the governor's action and held that the respondent erred in basing his judgment on the amended provisions which came into force after the application for the new license instead of the law which was in effect on the day of the application. Upon appeal, the Hiroshima high court reversed the district court's judgment on two accounts. First, the governor was correct in applying the law in effect at the time of his disposition, not the law at the time of the plaintiff's application. Second, the amendment to the law does not violate the freedom of occupation guaranteed in Article 22, Paragraph 2 of the Constitution because without such a regulation on the location of pharmacies, proper dispensation of medical supplies cannot be assured, and an excessive number of pharmacies might cause a dispensation of substandard drugs.

Upon appeal, the Supreme Court grand bench unanimously reversed the judgment below and held that the provision of the Pharmaceutical Code as amended and the Hiroshima prefectural ordinance were both in violation of the constitutional guarantee of the freedom of occupation. In the opinion of the Court, there was no evidence of prevalent abuse of dispensing substandard drugs so as to necessitate the application of geographical regulations to the licensing of new pharmacies. Granted the legislative intent to eliminate the maldistribution of pharmacies and to prevent public health hazards caused by substandard drugs, the Court concluded, the present restrictions on geographic locations of new pharmacies are neither reasonable nor necessary, and exceeded legislative discretion. Thus, the Court and Diet came in conflict with each other. Yet, Diet soon revised the unconstitutional portion of the law, thereby restoring harmony with the Court.

Similarly, in relation to the Cabinet and the local government, the Supreme Court has passed judgments on several occasions, narrowly constructing the scope and extent of the power of the executive as well as the local assembly.

One such occasion arose when the Aomori prefectural assembly in 1952 expelled its member, Giichiro Yoneuchiyama, on the ground that his remarks at a general assembly meeting violated the assembly's code of ethics. The Aomori district court first granted a temporary injunction against the expulsion order, and then after substantive review, declared that the local assembly exceeded its disciplinary power in expelling Yoneuchiyama. The court ruling was immediately followed by Prime Minister Yoshida's objection thereto.[33] Following the district court's judgment that the Prime Minister's objection was unsubstantial, the prefectural assembly filed a special appeal to the Supreme Court contending in part that a local assembly should be granted the same degree of autonomy to manage its own affairs as the Diet.

In *Yoneuchiyama v. Aomori Prefectural Assembly* (1953)[34] the Supreme Court, sustaining the judgment below by twelve to two, construed the provision of the Special Code for Administrative Litigation Procedure to require that the Prime Minister's objection be lodged before the district court issued its injunction. Justice Mano, in his concurring opinion, even held the provision in the Special Code to be in contravention of the principle of separation of powers. Denying the discretionary power of a local assembly to expel members, as in the present instance, Mano reasoned that the assembly, which makes ordinances and regulations, does not become a legislative organ any more than does the Supreme Court which makes rules and regulations, and the expulsion order which immediately affects rights and duties of injured members becomes subject to judicial review. Dissenting justices K. Tanaka and Kuriyama argued that except where an assembly's disciplinary action becomes unconstitutional, such as in violation of the equality clause, a local assembly is just as final an arbiter as the Diet in disciplining its own members for misconduct, and the propriety of an expulsion remains a political matter beyond judicial remedy.

The first type of activist Supreme Court is likely to emerge because of the time lag between changes in the composition of the Court and more rapid changes in the political branches of government. In the context of the Japanese government in which personnel and policies have remained essentially the same under the long reign of the LDP administration, the first type of activist Supreme Court seldom emerges. Major policy changes are likely to come only when opposition political parties succeed in reversing the LDP's razor-thin majority control in the Diet and institute significantly different policies, while the Supreme Court adheres to the precedents it has created during the LDP rule.

Next, turning to the second type of activist Supreme Court, it is little surprise that the Court and the political branches should seldom set forth policies that oppose each other or supplement each other but at an uneven rate. The Supreme Court decisions in two reapportionment cases and the subsequent corrective measures taken on the side of Diet are probably the only instances of this type of activist Court in Japan.

Koshiyama, a voter in Tokyo, brought suit in vain before the Tokyo high court after the 1962 election for the House of Councillors, challenging the validity of the election result which, in his opinion, grossly violated the constitutional principle of "one man, one vote." The Supreme Court, in dismissing the plaintiff's contention in *Koshiyama v. Chairman, Tokyo Election Control Commission* (1964),[35] ruled that apportionment in a national election had been left "to the discretionary authority of Diet" and that only in cases of extreme inequality "in the enjoyment of the elector's rights" could a court declare an election void in contravention of the equality clause in the Constitution. Inequality to the extent it exists today, the Court continues, is still only a problem of the propriety of legislation; the problem of unconstitutionality cannot be recognized.

On the question of whether or not malapportionment is even a subject for judicial review, Justice S. Saito wrote a concurring opinion which reflected judicial restraint more strongly than the rest of his colleagues. In his opinion a court should not render a judgment even in cases of gross malapportionment because confusion might arise out of different judgments between Diet and the Court in determining the extent of malapportionment. He also expressed strong doubt about the legality of a suit, as in the present case, seeking judicial nullification of an election.

Despite the fact that the Court dismissed Koshiyama's contention, the Diet went ahead and initiated a partial reapportionment in 1964 by adding five new electoral districts and nineteen new seats to five of the most underrepresented metropolitan areas. With this new policy a chance of major conflict between Diet and the Supreme Court seemed to have been averted on the issue of malapportionment.

Meanwhile, the Supreme Court changed by a narrow margin of eight to seven its policy in 1976 when it reviewed the appeal challenging the general election for the House of Representatives held on December 10, 1972, in the first electoral district of Chiba prefecture. In *Kurokawa v. Chiba Prefecture Election Control Commission* (1976)[36] the Court declared an election unconstitutional on the grounds that Article 13 of the Public Office Election Code, Accompanying Table I (prior to the 1975 revision) and Supplementary Rule (Articles 7 and 9) on Apportionment of Representatives in Each Election District violated constitutional provisions of Article 14, Paragraph 1, Article 15, Paragraphs 1 and 3, and Article 44, Proviso, all requiring political equality in an election. However, conceding that a judicial nullification of the election results would not correct any error already committed, the Court dismissed the portion of the appeal which sought nullification of the allegedly unlawful election result. Only Justice Amano favored dismissing the present suit entirely, because, as he saw it, there was no judicial remedy for malapportionment.

A series of events surrounding the *Koshiyama* decision, a subsequent move by the Diet, and the *Kurokawa* decision suggest that the Diet tried to correct malapportionment by redistricting and partially updating apportionments in some election districts; that the Supreme Court in the *Kurokawa* case demanded a more thorough practice of the "one man, one vote" principle; and that the Diet and the Supreme Court moved in the same direction of correcting malapportionment, but at different paces. Hence, the second type of judicial activism.

Next, the Supreme Court reveals a third type of judicial activism when it changes its policy in spite of the status quo maintained on the side of the political branches. Here the Court becomes a proponent of policy making while policy makers in the political branches of government stand pat. The Japanese Supreme Court, which has a little over four decades of constitutional policy-making history, has changed considerably fewer of its own policies when compared with the United

States Supreme Court which has over two hundred years of history behind it. Yet, there have been several instances in which the Japanese Supreme Court has acted as a catalyst by invalidating some statutory and administrative acts as being unconstitutional.

One of the earliest examples involved the Customs Code. In *Fujikawa et al v. Japan* (1955)[37] a seven-member majority of the Supreme Court ruled that a penalty against a crime committed in violation of the Customs Code in an area which at the time of the crime was still foreign territory, should not be construed to have been abolished on the ground that the area was later incorporated into Japanese territory and that the penalties had been abolished by a law after the crime. Six justices dissented by stating that "Government Ordinance 407 concerning the Temporary Measure in the application of Regulations Related National Taxes Following the Return of the Amami Archipelago" of December 24, 1953, incorporated this territory into Japan, abolishing a license required by the Customs Code to import and export to the region; that the provision of Article 76 of the Code Setting Forth the Penalties of Violation of the Customs Code lost its applicability; and that the accused should be acquitted by analogy to the abolition of penalty after conviction.

The *Fujikawa* precedent made by a one-vote margin was followed in seven other cases,[38] but was reversed in *Miyazaki v. Japan* (1957)[39] in which nine justices adopted the dissenting opinion of the *Fujikawa* case while six adhered to the majority opinion of the same case. Thus, in the *Fujikawa* case the Supreme Court upheld the law enforcement agency's action by convicting the accused. But in the *Miyazaki* case the Court came in conflict with the law enforcement body by acquitting the accused, thereby becoming an activist court of the third type. This change in precedent was a direct result of the new membership of the Court and not vote switching by any incumbent members. Iwamatsu, Motomura, Inoue, and Kuriyama, who all voted against the abolition of the penalty in the Customs Code, and Tanimura, who voted for such abolition, retired and were replaced by four liberals (D. Kawamura, Shimoiizaka, Okuno, and Tarumi) and one conservative (Takahashi). Fujita, M. Kawamura, Kobayashi, Kotani, Mano, Y. Saito, Shima, and Tanaka voted the same way in each case, respectively, while Ikeda and Irie who were absent in the *Fujikawa* case, voted conservatively in the *Miyazaki* case, all resulting in the reversal of the *Fujikawa* ruling by nine to six.

The third type of judicial activism is also found in a series of cases which dealt with the constitutional provisions of property rights (Article 29) and due process (Article 31), invoked in conjunction with a confiscation of ships and their cargoes used in smuggling. First, in *Omachi v. Japan* (1960),[40] in which some smuggled goods and a motorboat were confiscated in accordance with Article 83, Paragraph 1 of the old Customs Code, the Supreme Court dismissed, by the narrow margin of eight to seven, an appeal against the Fukuoka high court, Miyazaki branch. Upholding the constitutionality of the confiscation by the government, eight majority justices were of the opinion that the accused was not allowed to seek remedy by challenging the confiscation of a third party's property used in a crime. Especially, Justice Takagi stressed that confiscation in this instance serves the function of preventing future crimes and that since an innocent owner of the confiscated property could later seek a judicial remedy, the accused should not be allowed to claim innocence.

Five of the dissenting justices argued that it violates Article 31 of the Constitution to confiscate a boat belonging to a third party to a crime without giving him such protections as notice, a hearing, and claim of self-defense in a criminal proceeding. Daisuke Kawamura even went so far as to say that Article 83, Paragraph 1 of the old Customs Code itself violated Article 31 of the Constitution in allowing confiscation of a property possessed by the accused.

However, two years later the Supreme Court changed its own policy established in the *Omachi* case when it decided *Nakamura et al v. Japan* (1962).[41] The accused in this case attempted to smuggle contraband goods to South Korea in a motorboat, but failed to transfer the shipment to a fishing boat off the coast of Hakata (Fukuoka, Kyushu) because of stormy seas. The Fukuoka district court, sustained by the Fukuoka high court, convicted the accused for their attempted violation of the Customs Code, and confiscated the motorboat and cargo. However, since the cargo confiscated included that of a third party, the accused appealed to the Supreme Court contending that an unknown person to whom the cargo belonged was unaware of the commission of the alleged crime and yet had his property confiscated without redress. The fourteen-member grand bench reversed the *Omachi* precedent by the vote of nine to five. Nine justices agreed with the defense contention that the accused in possession of the third party's property to be confiscated can appeal to the Supreme Court, challenging the constitutionality thereof and that confiscating, on the strength of Article 118, Paragraph 1 of the Customs Code (corresponding to Article 83, Paragraph 1 of the old Customs Code), without safeguards, the property of a third party to a crime violated Articles 29 and 31 of the Constitution. Justice Okuno expressed his concern that an owner, who has more at stake than the accused, may not be able to seek remedy, civil or criminal, once the confiscation of his property is finalized.

After the *Omachi* decision, two liberals (Kotani and Shima) and two conservatives (Tanaka and Y. Saito) retired. Of the four new justices, K. Yokota, Gokijyo, and M. Yokota decided against such a confiscation while only Yamada adhered to the *Omachi* decision. Switching Tarumi's decision in the two cases also aided the proponent of the new policy on this issue. Five justices who were among the majority in the *Omachi* case became a minority group in the present case, and repeated the same arguments in the earlier case.

Thus the *Nakamura* decision rendered the Supreme Court an activist in relation to the Diet, but no sooner had conflict emerged between the Court and the Diet than the latter enacted on July 12, 1963, an emergency measure (Code 138) providing a third party whose property is being confiscated with notice, a hearing, and other safeguards in a criminal proceeding.

In view of this new legislation the Supreme Court began upholding once again the constitutionality of confiscation, while maintaining its vigilance. In *Tokunaga v. Japan* (1963)[42] the Supreme Court stressed that an appellate court, in reversing and remanding a first instance court decision, should instruct the latter to follow the new statutory requirements. Likewise, in *Yoshida v. Japan* (1965)[43] the Court ruled that the court below violated Articles 29 and 31 of the Constitution to order, in accordance with Article 197–4 of the Criminal Code (prior to revision in 1958),[44] a third party to a crime to pay the price of a bribe. Finding that the third party was questioned merely as a witness in the lower court's hearing and was denied the opportunity to defend his property right with due process, the Court denied the state the power to order a third party to a crime in a case in which he was judged to have received a bribe, to repay a sum equal to that of his bribe.

Finally, in *Japan v. Che et al* (1966)[45] the Court ruled that confiscation, without notice, hearing, or self defense, of property belonging to an unindicted co-owner violates Articles 29 and 31 of the Constitution. It is not clear from the reading of the *Nakamura* decision whether the Court declared unconstitutional the provision of Article 112, Paragraph 1 of the Customs Code itself,[46] the administrative action of confiscation, or both. Nonetheless, the Supreme Court sent a copy of its decision to the Diet as reference. Thereupon the Diet acted to remove what the Supreme Court considered to be an unconstitutional portion of the law, restoring harmony with the *Nakamura* decision.

If the *Nakamura* ruling left some ambiguity on the question of whether the Court declared unconstitutional a provision of the Customs Code, the administrative action of confiscation, or both, the Supreme Court was explicit in declaring Article 200 of the Criminal Code unconstitutional in the 1973 patricide cases.

The accused in *Fukuoka District Prosecutors' Office v. Yamato* (1950)[47] beat and killed his father and was subsequently charged with inflicting bodily injury on his father resulting in death. The Fukuoka district court found him guilty and sentenced him to three years at forced labor with a stay of execution for three years. The same court, however, found the provision of Article 205 of the Criminal Code, which imposed much severer punishments on those guilty of inflicting bodily harm on lineal ascendants than on others, unconstitutional in violaton of the constitutional principle of equality under law (Article 14).

Upon appeal, the Supreme Court grand bench reversed and remanded the verdict of the first instance court, upholding the constitutionality of Article 205 of the law. The thirteen-member majority (Tsukasaki, Hasegawa, Sawada, Shimoyama, Inoue, Kuriyama, Iwamatsu, Kotani, Shima, Y. Saito, Fujita, M. Kawamura and K. Tanaka) held that since the rationale underlying the provision incorporated the eternal natural law which attached special importance to the moral duties of the child toward his parents, ancestor worship, unity of loyalty, and filial piety which constituted the moral and social backbone of Japanese society, the deviation from such would be a travesty of the Japanese social fabric. Only Mano and Hozumi dissented. Justice Hozumi regarded punishing ascendant manslaughter by a heavier penalty as unreasonable and unnecessary. Tsuyoshi Mano was the only justice who declared the discriminatory provision to be a violation of the equality clause.

It took more than two decades for the Supreme Court to change the *Yamato* policy when it reviewed *Aizawa v. Japan* (1973).[48] The Utsunomiya district court (Tochigi prefecture)[49] in this case acquitted the accused, a daughter, who killed her father after having been forced to live with him as a common law wife. In the opinion of the district court, Article 200 of the Criminal Code, which imposes a severe penalty only upon a lineal descendant who kills a direct lineal ascendant by stressing the socially harmful and unethical nature of killing a lineal ascendant, unreasonably discriminates against lineal descendants. In contrast to a husband who kills his wife, or a lineal ascendant who kills a lineal descendant, the court continued, the provision puts the parent-child relationships above matrimonial ones. This discriminatory provision stems from the notion of the old family system based on the supremacy of parental (especially paternal) authority, and on the authority-obedience, hierarchical relationship between lineal ascendants and descendants, rather than on a status of legal equality between spouses and one between a parent and a child.

The court concluded that the provision in question is unreasonable and should be declared invalid.

Eight members of the Supreme Court, by this time having been composed of entirely new members, basically accepted the opinion of the district court that the intent of punishing lineal ascendant manslaughter by a penalty heavier than other types of manslaughter may be a reasonable discrimination, but that Article 200 of the Criminal Code by far exceeds the necessary limit to achieve this legislative objective by restricting the choice of such heavier penalty only to capital punishment or life imprisonment at hard labor. In comparison with Article 199 of the same law, dealing with manslaughter of all other types, the Court concluded, Article 200 is unreasonably harsh and violates Article 14, Paragraph 1 of the Constitution, and Article 199 should be, henceforth, applicable to the manslaughter of lineal ascendancy. Six concurring Justices (Ogawa, Sakamoto, Shimomura, Irokawa, Osumi, J. Tanaka) held that distinguishing the manslaughter of lineal ascendant from other types of manslaughter while penalizing the former more stiffly than the latter is against Article 14, Paragraph 1 of the Constitution.

Justice Shimoda, the sole dissenter, was of the opinion that a distinction between lineal ascendants and lineal descendants does not fall under a social distinction prohibited in Article 14, Paragraph 1 of the Constitution and that however discriminatory, Article 200 of the Criminal Code is not unconstitutional. The Supreme Court formally sent a copy of its decision to both the Cabinet and Diet, while announcing it in the government gazette of April 16, 1973.

The present Criminal Code was adopted in 1907 under the Meiji constitution. Much of the Criminal Code was revised in 1947 to better accord with the spirit of the new Constitution, but Article 200 was not touched then or later. Most leading Japanese constitutional lawyers hailed this landmark *Aizawa* decision, but feel with the concurring opinions that the majority might have gone further in bringing the Criminal Code into line with the constitutional principle of equality under the law. The entire Criminal Code was under deliberation for some years. The Criminal Code Revision Preparatory Committee deleted from its draft proposal the heavier penalty against patricide in line with the dissenting opinion of Justice Mano in the *Yamato* case, which now commands a majority among the Supreme Court justices, but the Diet has yet to delete either Article 200 or Article 205, Paragraph 2.

5. The Activist Supreme Court vis-a-vis the Administrative Agencies

As stated earlier, the Supreme Court has been reluctant to concede unreviewable administrative discretion and has been upholding administrative actions only after trials *de novo* in many instances. It was in relatively small numbers of cases that the Court has set aside administrative actions on the grounds of an abuse of discretion or an error in fact-finding, thereby becoming an activist Court.

Such was the case of *Governor of Mie Prefecture v. Nishiguchi* (1953),[50] in which the Supreme Court denied a local agricultural commission discretion to apply the owner-farmer establishment special measure, authorizing the government to purchase private land, agricultural or residential, in order to promote agricultural productivity and management. Where Nishiguchi, a prospective owner-farmer, applied to the agricultural commission for the purchase of residential land which he had originally leased for agricultural purposes, the Supreme Court ruled that while Article 15 of the said measure left to the local agricultural commission the discretion to recommend approval of certain land sales, the commission's task was to interpret and apply the law, and not to exercise free discretion to approve a purchase application, as in the present case, which would not serve the objective of the measure.

Also, in *Hayashi et al v. Governor, Aichi Prefecture et al* (1971)[51] the Supreme Court passed the judgment that a provision of the Government Ordinance to Enforce the Agricultural Land Code was an unconstitutional delegation of the legislative power to the minister of agriculture and forestry. Whereas the government bought the arable lands from Hayashi and others (plaintiffs) under the owner-farmer establishment special measure (Article 3, *inter alia*), which had been legislated provisionally for agricultural reforms, the agricultural minister, with the concurrence of the governor of Aichi prefecture, in 1953 redistricted the land for housing on the basis of Article 13, Paragraph 1, Proviso of the old City Planning Code. Some of the redistricted lands were used to build streets, a railroad station, a city square, and a park while other redistricted plots were sold for residential purposes. When the governor sold the plaintiffs' land in 1961 to a person who did not intend to engage in full-time farming, Hayashi and others petitioned in vain to the agricultural minister to nullify the governor's decision. Thereupon they filed a suit at Nagoya district court, contending that they had the first refusal to repossess the land thus disposed inasmuch as Article 80 of the Agricultural Land Code stipulates in part that the agricultural minister may sell the agricultural land or change the jurisdiction thereon, if he judges, in compliance with a government ordinance, that the land is unlikely to promote agricultural productivity or the creation of owner-farmers (Paragraph 1), and that the agricultural minister shall sell it back to its former owner (Paragraph 2).

Both the Nagoya district court and the Nagoya high court dismissed the suit and reasoned that the court did not have the power to order the minister to return the agricultural land to the plaintiffs, and that the plaintiffs were presumptuous in assuming that the provision of Article 80 of the Agricultural Land Code was applicable to their arable lands, because redistricting of the arable land for city planning did not necessarily lose the residential and agricultural values of the property. The plaintiffs then appealed to the Supreme Court, seeking first a judicial revocation of the agricultural minister's judgment and the governor's disposition of the redistricted lands, and, second, a judicial nullification of the transaction of their former lands.

While dismissing the appeal on the first point, the Court upheld the second point of the plaintiffs in that while Article 80, Paragraph 1 of the Agricultural Land Code delegated to the Agricultural Land Code Implementation Ordinance the authority to prescribe conditions for the sale of agricultural land, the latter ordinance, in Article 16, Item 4, exceeded the delegated authority by unduly restricting the agricultural minister's discretion granted by the law and accordingly violated Article 73, Item 6 of the Constitution. In the opinion of the Court, the Agricultural Land Code is designed to set conditions for the sale of arable lands by taking into account long range socioeconomic changes, and in the present case no urgent necessity existed to change into a high priority public use a land originally acquired for agricultural purposes. Furthermore, whereas Article 80, Paragraph 2 of the law obliges the government to return the agricultural land to its former owner when the land has lost its original function of establishing owner-farmers, the Agricultural Land Code Implementation Ordinance, in Article 16, Item 4, unduly restricts the statutory discretion of the minister only to the situation under which the arable land bought by the government for agricultural purposes is urgently needed to stabilize and promote public welfare. In reversing and remanding the decision below, the Supreme Court gave the plaintiffs the following relief: the plaintiffs may directly request the agricultural minister to return their agricultural land; if the minister fails to respond favorably, they may seek a judicial remedy in accordance with the Code of Civil Procedure; and if a governor has already sold it to a third party, the former owners may seek a judicial revocation of the transaction in accordance with the Procedural Code of Administrative Litigation.

Thereupon, Diet moved swiftly to amend the unconstitutional portion of the ordinance, thus restoring harmony with the Court. It may also be mentioned that Diet set former landlords' purchase prices so low that it invited wide criticism that the government was catering to the former landlords.

The Supreme Court also denied administrative discretion in a case which touched on the constitutional right of the freedom of occupation. In 1959 the Tokyo transportation bureau decided to increase the public transportation system including owner-driven taxicabs in order to meet an increasing transportation demand. The bureau prepared a questionnaire for use by officers in interviewing applicants for a commercial license who wanted to use their own cars as taxicabs. The plaintiff, who ran a small clothing store, applied for a commercial license, but was turned down for two reasons after a hearing. First, he lacked seven years of driving experience, which was required by law, and second, he was believed to have great difficulty in closing his present business and becoming a full-time cabdriver. Since the transportation minister did not respond to the plaintiff's petition to review his case, the plaintiff filed a suit with a court.

Sustaining the judgment of the district court, which conducted a trial *de novo* and which was upheld by a high court, the Supreme Court upheld the following fact: the bureau failed to instruct its hearing officers regarding the standards for granting the commercial license, and consequently, the hearing officer failed to ask pertinent questions to find out whether the plaintiff had at least seven years of driving experience, if he were allowed to count his driving experiences during his military service, and whether he had full intentions of becoming a full-time cabdriver once he secured a license. Also, the Road Transportation Code lacked any specific procedure, except for a hearing, that would insure a thorough review of the applicants' qualifications. In view of the fact that the present question of granting a commercial driver's license was directly linked to the constitutional right of the freedom of occupation, the bureau's failure to give applicants a chance to present their qualifications and evidence concerning their eligibility, and its failure to produce clearly defined guidelines in granting a commercial license, in conformity with the general provisions of the Road Transportation Code, resulted in an unfair procedure, rendering the present disposition arbitrary and unlawful.[52]

More than any other government agencies, the law enforcement authorities and its officers rendered the Supreme Court an activist one. The Court took extra care in protecting the constitutional rights of criminally accused persons, and, from time to time, rejected the law enforcement agency's actions. To name only a few examples, during the occupation period a series of Potsdam ordinances enacted by the Japanese government to implement the GHQ, SCAP directives, were effective above and beyond the Constitution. After the peace treaty and restoration of independence and sovereignty, however, the attorney general, the highest law enforcement officer, continued to invoke these ordinances by taking the view that they would not lose their effect until and unless abolished by new legislation passed after the commission of crime.

In 1961 the Supreme Court became an activist in relation to the attorney general when it held the Organization Control Ordinance, one of the Potsdam ordinances, unconstitutional and invalid when applied after the effective date (April 28, 1952) of the San Francisco Peace Treaty. Matsumoto, a central committee member of the Japan Communist Party, was ordered in 1950 by the attorney general to appear at his office in accordance with Article 10 of the Organization Control Ordinance. Upon failing to do so, he was criminally charged in 1953 after the effective date of the peace treaty, as prescribed by the said ordinance. The Tokyo district court acquitted the accused on grounds that punishing a person accused of having failed to comply with the attorney general's order compelling him to report to the latter's office for criminal investigation just as harshly as a person who violated those acts prohibited by the ordinance, would amount to a criminal investigation in contravention of Articles 31 and 33 of the Constitution. The Tokyo high court further dismissed the charge against him.

The Supreme Court in *Japan v. Matsumoto* (1961)[53] sustained the high court opinion that the criminal charge against the accused should be disposed of in a manner analogous to a case in which a penalty has been abolished by law enacted after the commission of the crime charged. For Justices Irie and Takagi, the provision of Article 10 of the ordinance is for administrative investigation, and should not be used, as in the instant case, to investigate an alleged criminal act. Only Ikeda and Ishizaka dissented by stating that a violation of the ordinance should be subject to the penal provisions of the ordinance, even after the expiration thereof.

Likewise, the Supreme Court overruled law enforcement agents and criminal investigating officers in *Okayama v. Japan* (1970).[54] The wife of the accused told police investigators that she had illegally bought a pistol, the weapon used in her husband's crime, without his knowledge. Her husband, the defendant, agreed with her statement and even told the investigators that he had told her to return the pistol to the place of purchase. The investigators then told the accused a lie. He asserted that the wife had confessed she conspired with him in the commission of the present crime, and urged him to confess his involvement. Led by the lie, the accused admitted his involvement. The same investigators proceeded to tell the wife that her husband had confessed his conspiracy with her. Reversing the Osaka high court ruling which sustained conviction, the Supreme Court judged that investigating officers apparently tricked the accused party into a confession of his crime, and that such a confession was inadmissible in court as evidence because it violated Article 38, Paragraph 2 of the Constitution.

The Court has denied administrative actions either as unconstitutional or unlawful primarily when an administrative order has directly infringed upon specific constitutional civil rights and liberties. In this area, at least, judicial review of administrative actions has been a great advance over the Meiji constitutional system in which an arbitrary exercise of administrative discretion often remained unchecked. Now administrative agencies must be sensitive to Supreme Court pronouncements on the scope and extent of their discretionary authority on many specific policy issues.

Upon a review of administrative actions, the courts can offer several remedies. Article 17 of the Constitution stipulates that every person may sue for redress as provided by law from the state or a public entity when damage has been suffered through the illegal act of any public official. One can also request just compensation for giving up private property for public use (Article 29, Paragraph 3). A court can also revoke an administrative action, or reverse an administrative adjudication thereof. It can pass a declaratory judgment that an administrative act is null and void or that a non-action on the part of an administrative agency is illegal. By a petitioner's plea or through its own authority, a court can also issue an injunction to avoid irreparable damages to be caused by an administrative action (Article 2 of the Administrative Dispute Contentious Special Code). However, a minister may object to such an injunction when he deems that a suspension of administrative action would cause grave harm to the public welfare (Article 10, Paragraph 2, main text) and this ministerial objection does not violate the provision of Article 76, Paragraph 3 of the Constitution,[55] which insures judicial independence.

In summary, an analysis of the grand bench decisions since the inception of the Supreme Court to 1980 indicates that the grand bench became an activist vis-a-vis the political branches over constitutional issues about half of the time when it was divided, and only some of the time when it was unanimous. Specifically, the grand bench was an activist in 79 divided decisions (out of a total of 166), or 46 percent, on sociopolitical issues, and in 21 divided decisions (out of a total of 41), or 51 percent, on socioeconomic issues. The grand bench, however, was activist in 14 unanimous decisions (out of a total of 174), or 8 percent, on sociopolitical issues, and only in one unanimous decision (out of a total of 89), or 1 percent, on socioeconomic issues.

Granted that many divided activist decisions involved rather limited kinds of the same constitutional issues, the statistics that nearly half of the divided grand bench decisions characterized the Court as activist vis-a-vis the political branches is significant enough to qualify the widely held view that the Supreme Court has blindly followed the policies and actions of the LDP-dominated government.

The Supreme Court decision in *Itabashi Ward Assembly, Tokyo v. Yamaguchi* (1960)[56] and a subsequent action taken by the Diet illustrate sensitivity to Supreme Court decisions on the side of the political branches even in the absence of actual conflict between the two. Where the Supreme Court rules or is likely to rule some legislative policies unconstitutional, the legislature may be quick to change the policies objectionable to the Court, thereby removing an actual or potential conflict with the Supreme Court. In an appeal involving an expulsion of a representative from a local assembly, the Supreme Court by a one-vote margin of eight to seven ruled that an expelled member would lose legal standing to seek reinstatement and a judicial revocation of a local assembly's resolution after the term of his office had expired. In 1962, however, the Diet added a new provision to the Administrative Litigation Code, thereby giving an expelled assemblyman legal standing to file a suit even after the expiration of his office term.

Hideo Wada[57] speculates that a dissenting opinion of seven justices who supported the expelled member's standing to sue in the *Yamaguchi* case might have given an added impetus to proponents of new legislation in Diet. Recall that following the *Nakamura* decision, the Diet passed an emergency code of 1963 providing for a prior notice and hearing before confiscation; likewise, the Diet swiftly acted to amend the unconstitutional portion of the Agricultural Land Code Enforcement Ordinance, thus restoring harmony with the Supreme Court.

6. Antecedents of Judicial Restraint

Next, the relationship between the judiciary and the political branches will be historically traced to probe the nature of judicial restraint in Japan.

The Meiji constitution provided for the proper qualification, tenure, and discipline of judges in accordance with the law (Article 58).[58] The constitutional guarantee for judicial independence was also stated in the Court Organization Code of 1890. Tenure for life was established, and then it was later changed to compulsory retirement at sixty-three years of age. Judges were selected for legal expertise, and their salaries were excluded from a general official cut in 1931. Their dismissal was possible only after criminal conviction or formal disciplinary action stipulated by law. These legislations reflected a great improvement over the Tokugawa practice, and contributed to generating the tradition in which Japanese judges could perform their duties relatively independent of political fluctuations in the subsequent era.

A review of judicial history, however, reveals instances of politically motivated onslaughts on judicial independence. The executive not only exerted undue pressure on judicial decision making in a courtroom but also attempted to replace judges for political reasons. Vice-Justice Minister Kikuomi

The Self-Restrained Supreme Court

Yokota, taking advantage of a newly appointed justice minister, attempted to force the resignation of ten elder judges to be replaced by those judges who were affiliated with Yokota's political party in 1898. This attempt was stopped by the new minister at the very last minute.[59] The famous test case of the *Otsu* trial (1891)[60] is often cited as exemplary of an effort to secure judicial independence under the Meiji constitution. This was a criminal trial of Japanese policeman Sanzo Tsuda who wounded the Russian crown prince Nicholas II with a sword in an assassination attempt at Otsu in 1891. The Japanese government, for diplomatic reasons, wanted the death penalty, but the Criminal Code provided only life imprisonment for an attempted murder unless the victim was a member of the Japanese imperial family. Chief Justice Ikken Kojima of the Great Court of Cassation refused to give in to political pressure and the five man criminal division of the Court sentenced Tsuda to life imprisonment in accordance with the law.

The wartime Prime Minister Hideki Tojo's attack[61] on liberal judges and his demand for their cooperation with the Japanese war effort eventually led to what Otto Kirchheimer would call political justice, in which a judge collaborated with or at least works for the interest of the regime of the day and attempted to suppress its opponents. There were some Japanese judges who tried to withstand the political pressure. Nagayoshi Hosono, chief judge of the Hiroshima Court of Appeals, in 1944 protested Tojo's speech that threatened judicial independence. Likewise, Shotaro Miyake of the Great Court of Cassation acquitted Godo Ozaki on June 27, 1944, of the prosecution's charge that Ozaki committed the crime of *lese majesty* during an election campaign speech he made on behalf of liberal candidate Daikichi Togawa when he compared the Meiji, Taisho, and Showa Emperors. Shuichi Ishizaka of Tokyo district court acquitted Professor Eijiro Kawai who was charged with the violation of the Publication Code. Hisashi Yoshida of the Great Court of Cassation nullified the March 1, 1945, election victory in the Kagoshima second district, claimed by Tojo's Imperial Rule Assistance Association. But, some judges probably could not have been expected to resist the military government's attempts to suppress anti-war liberal thoughts, or even such basic rights as the freedom of speech and religion.

Based on his findings that 4,119 of 4,208, or 98 percent, of all those prosecuted were formally placed on trial after a preliminary hearing between 1936 and 1940 while 1.1 percent of them were dismissed and 0.9 percent were dropped, Eigoro Aoki suspects that judges accepted testimony by the police and prosecution without much examination and proceeded to place their charges on trial.[62] Under such circumstances, judicial independence might have been a hollow principle, yet no recorded account offers any evidence of wholesale distorted trials. If there had been any, a miscarriage of justice would not have been so large as to lead to the total collapse of judicial independence.

During the allied occupation of Japan there was no judicial independence in the political sense, because GHQ,SCAP functioned outside the constitutional framework in the Japanese judicial decision making. Many orders and directives issued by GHQ,SCAP were binding above and beyond the Japanese Constitution. The judicial attempt to reinstate a former Cabinet member showed a peculiar feature of the Japanese judicial independence under the occupation. Rikizo Hirano, then minister of agriculture, was dismissed by Premier Tetsu Katayama because of his disagreement with the Cabinet. Hirano, who was also purged as a suspected war criminal, requested the Tokyo district court to rescind his dismissal from the Cabinet. The court in *Hirano v. Premier Katayama* (1948)[63] granted an injunction on February 2, 1948, but GHQ,SCAP ordered the retraction of this injunction on the grounds that the Japanese courts did not have a jurisdiction over such a purgee case. Three days later the Supreme Court, in compliance with the GHQ directive, ordered the district court to reverse the judgment. Former Justice Tamotsu Shima denies GHQ,SCAP's interference with other trials while others argue that GHQ,SCAP openly directed trials involving occupation policies.[64] An ever-present possibility of a court's decision being overruled by the occupation government made Japanese judges in the early period very uncertain and cautious.

Judicial independence under the present constitutional system is insured in a number of ways. The courts are independent of the ministry of justice. The judges are not removable except by public impeachment. No disciplinary action against judges may be taken by the executive (Article 78), and judicial salaries shall not be decreased during their terms of office (Article 79). Nevertheless, political involvement in trials have not been absent.

Diet was criticized for having interfered with judicial independence during an ongoing trial in 1948.[65] On April 6, 1948, Urawa poisoned and strangled to death her three children after she was abandoned by her husband and could not take the hardship of supporting her family. After an abortive suicide, she turned herself in to nearby police, upon which the public prosecutor charged her with manslaughter and sought a three-year imprisonment. The Urawa district court of Saitama prefecture sentenced her to a three-year imprisonment, but granted her a three-year stay of execution. When the prosecutor decided not to appeal, she was immediately released.

Then the House of Councillors' Legal Committee invoked the constitutional power (Article 62) to investigate government affairs and criticized the court's decision by arguing that the sentence was allegedly based on the feudalistic notion which viewed children as mere possessions of their parents. There was also an unproven assumption that the defendant's hardship drove her to an abortive suicide with her children. The committee held the court's sentencing unreasonably light. Against the protest by the Supreme Court, the committee defended this investigation of the ongoing case by stating that the power of investigating government affairs extended equally to all three branches of government and might demand the testimony of witnesses and a transcript of judicial proceedings. The reaction of Diet to the Urawa trial stirred up wide criticism from many quarters as political interference in judicial independence.

Judges have also been subject to criticism from both the prosecutor and defense counsel in criminal trials. On November 19, 1963, one hundred and three defense attorneys of the *Matsukawa* case (1950)[66] and the *Shiratori* case (1952)[67] filed in vain a petition which the Diet Judge Impeachment Committee sought the dismissal of Supreme Court Justice Masuo Shimoiizaka on the grounds of improper judicial conduct.[68] Likewise in 1966, prosecuting attorney Ichiro Osawa of the Osaka district prosecutor's office criticized at a press conference the lack of severity in a penalty imposed by two judges of the Osaka summary court in a traffic violation case. While the judicial conference of the Osaka district court held the criticism to be improper, it later transferred the two summary court judges. Thereupon, the Osaka Bar Association requested the Osaka district court and the prosecutor's office to insure the judicial independence of the two judges.[69]

The Meiji constitution did not have any notion of judicial review of overseeing the constitutionality of governmental acts or actions. Although the view was persuasively set forth by many people that a court was empowered to invalidate a law which conflicted with the Meiji constitution, both the Great Court of Cassation and the mainstream of lawyers refused to recognize judicial review of the law.

As recently as 1937 the Court ruled in *Sato et al v. Japan* (1937)[70] that it could not reject the application of a constitutionally dubious law as long as such a law met the formal requirements of legislative procedure. Hirobumi Ito, the first Prime Minister and an important framer of the Meiji constitution, argued along the line of the unitary imperial sovereign power that the judiciary was a part of the executive and might not review the constitutionality of actions taken by the legislature, which was ranked equal to the executive. Tatsukichi Minobe, a prominent public law scholar, based his case against the judicial review of law on the principle of separation of powers, as he understood it from the European legal experiences in the nineteenth century. Although the parliamentary-cabinet system in Japan has modified the "rigid compartmentalization" of the separation of powers by harmonizing the executive and legislative powers, Minobe concludes,[71] each branch of government should be left free to judge for itself its own constitutional competence and responsibilities. Furthermore, there was no centralized court system in Japan until 1875. Justice Minister Shimpei Ito's efforts toward judicial independence were first directed toward a separation of judicial function from the local administration rather than the political branches of the national government.

The judicial power of the Great Court of Cassation was restricted by political forces of the day as well. The provision of Article 57 of the Meiji constitution required the judicial courts to perform their duties "according to law in the name of the Emperor." Under this provision the privy council was entrusted with the function of providing the Emperor with the most authoritative interpretations of the constitution, laws, and imperial ordinances. Whenever the Diet requested the Emperor's judgment over disagreements between the two Houses of Diet, or between the Cabinet and Diet, the Cabinet was obliged to refer the matter to the privy council. Yet due to the lack of a clear separation between the government and the privy council, as exemplified by the overlapping membership between the two, the council's advisory opinions had a dubious binding force on the government. Also, because the privy council could meet only upon the Emperor's request and was not held responsible to Diet, it remained inactive and was by no means an effective institution to examine the government's legal interpretations. In reality, key policies were made by a handful of oligarchical leaders who invoked the Emperor's name mainly to legitimize their own decisions. In turn, judicial efforts to conform to the imperial will or the national polity often caused him to follow the oligarchical leaders.

Judicial control did not extend over administrative disputes, either. Article 61 of the Meiji constitution conferred on the administrative court the competency to deal with the rights allegedly infringed by the illegal measures of the administrative authorities. Yet adjudication by the administrative court was far from satisfactory. Influenced by German positivism, administrative codes were legislated in such a way as to confer upon bureaucrats rather restricted discretionary powers. Yet whatever administrative discretion existed gained finality in a wide range of matters, and administrative interpretation and application of law and regulation tended to overshadow those by the administrative court. An alleged misapplication of law by a public official was heard by successive levels including a competent minister, and then, if a judicial hearing was granted, a suit could be brought to the administrative court. However, the administrative court was not structured to handle a large number of cases. The Administrative Court Code restricted the jurisdiction of the court to only a limited list of narrowly and specifically enumerated claims, and a person adversely affected by an illegal administrative action could bring a charge only when a statute permitted him to do so.

Commenting on Article 61 of the Constitution, Hirobumi Ito[72] stated that individuals were free to petition the court but not to resort to any legal suit against an administrative action. On the average, less than three hundred administrative cases were filed annually between 1890 and 1930, and inadequate procedural safeguards in the proceedings of the administrative court often adversely affected the substantive rights of the injured individual. Whenever the administrative court turned to the Code of Civil Procedure to fill a procedural gap, it, too, was often ill-equipped to handle such a need. Finally, many administrative judges tended to be favorably disposed toward bureaucratic actions, and many complaints, including wages and other public law-related claims brought before it, were dismissed as being immaterial.

There were occasional jurisdictional disputes between the administrative court and the Great Court of Cassation, and two different decisions were sometimes rendered on virtually identical cases. Although no administrative court decisions were appealable to the judicial courts for review, some government actions in private law like contract and tort were challenged in separate suits before a judicial court. This created, in turn, the need for a uniform interpretation between the Great Court of Cassation and the administrative court on the same public policy problems. The administrative court in *Ouchi Village Mayor v. Aomori Prefecture, Obayashi District*

Forestry Bureau Chief (1914),[73] held irrevocable any mistake made by administrators in their assessment of boundary lines between public and private lands. The Great Court of Cassation, however, ruled in *Omiya et al v. Japan* (1917)[74] that such a wrong boundary could and should be corrected. Tatsukichi Minobe[75] attributed such conflicting decisions to the practice of the judicial court to determine the applicability of administrative laws in civil actions.

Whereas many scholars, including Minobe, favored substantive review of ordinances, the Great Court of Cassation initially limited judicial influence to the form of law and orders, and not the substance. In *Japan v. Shimada* (1913)[76] the Court, upholding an order for the police criminal investigation which led to the conviction of Shimada, gave the opinion that the term "law," as used in Article 23 of the constitution, included the order which was sublegislated to carry out the imperial rescript. After 1916 the Court began unmistakably to review the substance of ordinances and orders under challenge in criminal cases, and between 1900 and 1939 the Court reviewed and sustained government orders in sixteen cases.[77] Only in *Sato et al v. Japan* (1937)[78] did the Court invalidate the provision of Article 1 of the Foreign Exchange Control Ordinance prohibiting preparation for smuggling on the grounds that restrictions imposed therein exceeded the authorization delegated by Diet. Only a few civil cases involving ordinances were reviewed and upheld by the Court, and then no reference was made to any specific provisions of the Constitution.

The Commission on the Constitution was created in 1956 to investigate the background of the present Constitution and advise any need for constitutional revision. It debated judicial review more heatedly than any other aspect of the judiciary. The majority of the committee members felt that the present scope of judicial review should not be changed, while some members felt that the power of judicial review gives the Supreme Court too much of an edge over Diet. In the opinion of the opponents, it is contrary to the principle of democracy for the fifteen members of the Supreme Court, who are not chosen by the public, to pass a judgment on the constitutionality of a law enacted by the majority of the popularly elected Diet members. They also cited the MacArthur draft constitution which proposed that judicial review on matters other than fundamental human rights should not be final but might be overruled by a two-thirds majority vote of a unicameral Diet.

In short, precarious judicial independence and absence of judicial review in relation to political branches conditioned the judicial environment in prewar Japan. While judicial independence and judicial review are now firmly established, the judicial self-restraint remains pervasive in Japan, and some Supreme Court justices who were trained and worked under the old judicial system cannot be expected to behave otherwise. Furthermore, they feel strongly that the judiciary should not declare acts and actions of political branches unconstitutional and invalid unless it is absolutely necessary. This feeling is especially strong on constitutional policies which often require high levels of political discretion.

Where a given law or ordinance is amenable to more than one interpretation, a court tends to adopt an interpretation that would uphold its constitutionality. For example, according to the majority opinion in *Hasegawa et al. v. Japan* (1969),[79] the basic rights of labor are extended to local public employees as a rule, and if provisions of the Local Public Employees Code are interpreted to prohibit any and all kinds of labor disputes waged by local public employees and also penalize those who conspire, incite, and instigate these disputes, such a provision would violate Article 39 of the Constitution. However, legal provisions should be interpreted in harmony with the constitutional spirit as much as possible. Thus these provisions, despite their wording, should not necessarily be interpreted as unconstitutional.

Footnotes to Chapter Five

1. See, for instance, Hideo Wada, *Kempo to Saikosaibansho* (The Constitution and the Supreme Court), Tokyo: Gakuyo Shobo, 1975, p. 24; Nobuyoshi Ashibe, *Kempo Sosho no Gendaiteki Tenkai* (Contemporary Developments of Constitutional Litigation), Tokyo: Yuhikaku, 1981, p. 159.

2. Sup. Ct., G.B.; May 27, 1963; 17 *Keishu* 121.

3. Toshiyoshi Miyazawa, *Kempo to Saiban* (The Constitution and Trial), Tokyo: Yuhikaku, 1967, p. 73 *et. seq.*, and p. 99 *et. seq.*

4. Sup. Ct., G.B.; April 15, 1953; 7 *Minshu* 305.

5. Sup. Ct., G.B.; December 16, 1959; 13 *Keishu* 3225.

6. Toshio Irie, "Tochikoi" (State governance), in *Koho Kenkyu*, No. 113, 1955, p. 93.

7. For example, Tatsugoro Isozaki, *Tochikoisetsu Hihan* (The Criticism of the Doctrine of State Governance), Tokyo: Yuhikaku, 1965, especially pp. 72–141.

8. 13 *Keishu* 3283–3284.

9. Tokyo Dist. Ct.; December 12, 1967; *Hanrei Jiho* No. 504, 1968, p. 3.

10. Sup. Ct., 3rd. P.B.; March 9, 1965; 19 *Minshu* 233.

11. Sup. Ct., G.B.; April 2, 1969; 23 *Keishu* 685.

12. Sup. Ct., G.B.; June 8, 1960; 14 *Minshu* 1206.

13. Kisaburo Yokota, "Rippofu no jiritsuken to shihoken" (The autonomy of the legislature and judicial power), in *Jurisuto* No. 337, January 1, 1966, pp. 24–38. The provisions of the Diet Code mentioned here are as follows: Article 114—In order to maintain discipline in each House while the Diet is in session, the power of internal police shall be exercised by the president of each House in accordance with this Code and regulations prescribed by each House. . . . The same shall also apply during the recess; Article 115—Police officers which either House requires shall be dispatched by the Cabinet upon demand by the president and they shall be under the command of the president; Article 116—When a Diet member, during sessions of the Diet, contravenes this Code or rules of proceedings or otherwise disturbs the order or injures the dignity of the House, the president shall guard against or restrain such conduct, or cause the member to retract such utterances. . . . When the member fails to obey these orders, the president may prohibit the member's speech until the proceedings of the day are finished, or until, in the event the proceeding continues through the next day, the proceeding is over, or cause him to retire from the floor of the House.

14. Sup. Ct., G.B.; March 7, 1962; 16 *Minshu* 445.

15. Sup. Ct., G.B.; June 1, 1949; 3 *Keishu* 901.

16. Sup. Ct., G.B.; June 13, 1949; 3 *Keishu* 998.

17. The Liquor Tax Code delegated to an administrative agency the power to specify information which liquor dealers must record in their account books for the purpose of filing tax returns. In *Fujisawa v. Japan* (Sup. Ct., G.B.; July 9, 1958; 12 *Keishu* 2407) the Supreme Court sustained a director of the tax bureau who set forth information that a manufacturer or dealer of liquor and its ingredients must report concerning the manufacture, storage or sales thereof. Likewise, the Supreme Court in *Takiguchi v. Japan* (Sup. Ct., G.B.; January 23, 1948; 2 *Keishu* 722) sustained a penal provision in the Cabinet Ordinance Barring the Possession of Guns and Weapons, which is based on Imperial Ordinance No. 542 of 1945 Regarding the Order to Be Issued upon Acceptance of the Potsdam Declaration, which, in the opinion of the Court, had been effective under both the new and old constitutions. In *Yanagi v. Japan* (Sup. Ct., G.B.; February 1, 1950; 4 *Keishu* 73) the Court ruled that a law can delegate the power to establish penal provisions to a government ordinance, according to Article 73, Item 6, Proviso of the Constitution.

18. Sup. Ct., 1st. P.B.; June 6, 1964; 18 *Minshu* 745.

19. Sup. Ct. G.B.; May 24, 1967; 21 *Minshu* 1043.

20. Akira Mikazuki, "A comparative study of judicial systems" (trans. by Hiroshi Itoh and Eugene H. Lee), in *Law in Japan: An Annual*, Vol. 3, 1969, p. 15. The Court in *C.K. Lee v. Japan* (Sup. Ct., G.B.; May 30, 1956; 10 *Keishu* 756) is of the opinion that a family court is an ordinary court and is not a special tribunal prohibited by the Constitution and that the Juvenile Code conferring upon a family court jurisdiction over offenses in the Child Welfare Code does not violate Article 76, Paragraph 2, of the Constitution.

21. Osaka Dist. Ct.; May 9, 1952; 3 *Gyosai Reishu* 840. Upon appeal, the Supreme Court reversed the Osaka high court decision, which had sustained the district court, thereby upholding the disciplinary measure against the dismissed policeman. (Sup. Ct., 2nd. P.B.; May 10, 1957; 11 *Minshu* 699) *Osawa v. Director, Patent Bureau* (1953) is another example of trial *de novo* of administrative fact-finding (Sup. Ct., 2nd. P.B.; October 16, 1953; 4 *Gyosai Reishu* 2424). See also Nathaniel L. Nathanson and Yasuhiro Fujita, "The

right to fair hearing in Japanese administrative law," in 45 *Washington Law Review* 2, 1970, pp. 273–334.

22. Tokyo H. Ct.; August 29, 1953; 4 *Gyosai Reishu* 1898.

23. Sup. Ct., 3rd. P.B.; July 1, 1958; 12 *Minshu* 1612.

24. Sup. Ct., 2nd. P.B.; July 11, 1969; 23 *Minshu* 1470. Likewise, in *Matsumoto v. Minister of Foreign Affairs* (September 27, 1952; 3 *Gyosai Reishu* 1863) the Tokyo district court sustained the denial of a passport as a matter of diplomatic policy within ministerial discretion inasmuch as the foreign minister's judgment about the effect on the national interest of issuing a passport was not subject to judicial review. See also *Hoashi v. Japan* (Sup. Ct., G.B.; September 10, 1958; 12 *Minshu* 1969). However, in *Miyamoto v. Minister of Foreign Affairs* (April 28, 1960; 11 *Gyosai Reishu* 1217) the same court was of the opinion that the freedom to travel abroad should not be deprived merely because of one's beliefs, ideologies, or associations.

25. Sup. Ct., 1st. P.B.; April 27, 1961; 15 *Minshu* 928.

26. Sup. Ct., 2nd. P.B.; June 24, 1955; 9 *Minshu* 930.

27. In the absence of a constitutional definition of local autonomy as stipulated in Article 92, the Supreme Court grand bench in *Kudo et al v. Kamoshima Town et al* (July 20, 1959; 13 *Minshu* 1103) left to a legislature the power to establish such litigation systems as stipulated in the revised Local Autonomy Code. It also ruled that the absence of such a litigation system in the old Local Autonomy Code, prior to the July 1948 revision, does not violate Article 92 of the Constitution. In *Iwasaki v. Sato et al* (Sup. Ct., G.B.; March 14, 1962; 16 *Minshu* 537) the Court ruled that Article 251-2, Paragraph 1, of the Public Office Election Code, disqualifying a successful candidate for local public office due to an election law violation by his manager or treasurer, does not violate Articles 43 or 93 of the Constitution.

28. Sup. Ct., G.B.; October 19, 1960; 14 *Minshu* 2633.

29. Sup. Ct., G.B.; May 24, 1967; 21 *Keishu* 505.

30. Sup. Ct., G.B.; May 30, 1962; 16 *Keishu* 577.

31. Sup. Ct., G.B.; July 13, 1977; 31 *Minshu* 533.

32. Sup. Ct., G.B.; April 30, 1975; 29 *Minshu* 572.

33. Article 10, Paragraph 2, of the Special Code for Administrative Litigation Procedures reads that in the case of a suit brought based on Article 2 of this code, the courts may, when they recognize it to be urgently necessary to avoid uncompensable damages arising from an execution of dispositions, issue, upon a request by petition or on their own authority, an injunction in the form of a *kettei*-decision to stop the execution of disposition. But when it is deemed that such an injunction may have a grave effect upon the public welfare and also when the Prime Minister makes an objection to such an injunction, the courts may not do so.

34. Sup. Ct., G.B.; January 16, 1953; 7 *Minshu* 12. Similarly, the 1st. petty bench of the Supreme Court in *Sapporo City Assembly v. Maeda* (December 4, 1952; 7 *Saibanshu Minji* 595) held that the local assembly was not left entirely free to resolve such disciplinary actions as the expulsion of its own members.

35. Sup. Ct., G.B.; February 5, 1964; 18 *Minshu* 270. See Nobuyoshi Ashibe, "Malapportionment and equality under the law" (trans. by Rex Coleman), in *Law in Japan: An Annual*, Vol. 1, 1967, pp. 150–153.

36. Sup. Ct., G.B.; April 14, 1976; 30 *Minshu* 223.

37. Sup. Ct., G.B.; February 23, 1955; 102 *Saibanshu Keiji* 885.

38. Seven other cases are *Matsunaga et al v. Japan* (1955), *Yasaka et al v. Japan* (1955), *Shimano v. Japan* (1956), *Yagi v. Japan* (1956), *Japan v. Miyazaki et al* (1956), *Nakamura v. Japan* (1956), and *Hui v. Japan* (1956). Each justice was consistent in his voting behavior either for or against the accused(s) in each case.

39. Sup. Ct., G.B.; October 9, 1957; 11 *Keishu* 2497.

40. Sup. Ct., G.B.; October 19, 1960; 135 *Saibanshu Keiji* 565.

41. Sup. Ct., G.B.; November 28, 1962; 16 *Keishu* 1593.

42. Sup. Ct., G.B.; December 4, 1963; 17 *Keishu* 2415.

43. Sup. Ct., G.B.; April 28, 1965; 19 *Keishu* 203.

44. A bribe which a third party to a crime knowingly receives from the accused shall be confiscated. If all or part of the bribe is unable to be confiscated, its price shall be charged.

45. Sup. Ct., G.B.; May 18, 1966; *Hanrei Jiho* No. 445, 1966, p. 15.

46. Customs Code, Article 112, Paragraph 1 reads that either an imprisonment with hard labor of not more than three years or a fine of not more than 300,000 yen or both shall be imposed upon a person who knowingly transports, keeps in storage, acquires with or without compensation, or acts as an intermediary (hereinafter referred to as acts of transporting) in the disposition of cargoes involved in the crime as stipulated in Article 109, Paragraph 1 (the crime of importing contraband goods), or in Article 110, Paragraph 1 (the crime of evading import duties).

47. Sup. Ct., G.B.; October 11, 1950; 4 *Keishu* 2037. See also Kurt Steiner, "A Japanese Cause Celebre: The Fukuoka Patricide Case," in *American Journal of Comparative Law*, Vol. 5, 1956, pp. 106–111.

48. Sup. Ct., G.B.; April 4, 1973; 27 *Keishu* 265.

49. Utsunomiya Dist. Ct.; May 29, 1969; 27 *Keishu* 318.

50. Sup. Ct., 3rd. P.B.; April 28, 1953; 7 *Minshu* 439. The Supreme Court 2nd. petty bench on April 13, 1956, also denied the discretionary power of the local agricultural commission not to give a legal effect to a land lease when a plaintiff was denied by the commission to buy a whole tract, and not a part, of farm land he had leased. See *Governor, Hyogo Prefecture v. Morimoto*, 10 *Minshu* 397.

51. Sup. Ct., G.B.; January 29, 1971; 25 *Minshu* 1.

52. Sup. Ct., 1st. P.B.; October 28, 1971; 25 *Minshu* 1037.

53. Sup. Ct., G.B.; December 20, 1961; 15 *Keishu* 1940.

54. Sup. Ct., G.B.; November 25, 1970; 24 *Keishu* 1670.

55. *Kubota v. Japan;* Sup. Ct., G.B.; October 15, 1952; 6 *Minshu* 827. Also, the Tokyo district court in *Hoshino v. Japan* (September 26, 1969; *Hanrei Jiho* No. 568, p. 14) involving denial of a permit to hold a demonstration in the environs of Diet, passed judgment on the relationship between an injunction against an administrative action and a Prime Minister's objection *(kihi)* thereto. According to the opinion of the court: 1) the power to issue an injunction against an administrative action has been delegated by the executive to the judiciary, and the scope and method of the injunction are deter-

mined at the discretion of the legislature. But this does not render a court's injunction and a Prime Minister's objection thereto in contravention of Article 32 of the Constitution; 2) a Prime Minister's objection does not prevent a judge from exercising his conscience and independence in making a determination on a petition seeking an injunction, nor does it subject the judge to the executive branch of government; thus, a Prime Minister's objection does not violate Article 76, Paragraph 3 of the Constitution; and 3) the judicial grant of an injunction on the strength of Article 25 of the Administrative Litigation Code is not a substitute for judicial judgment on a petition to revoke an administrative action after that petition has become moot because of the time it had taken the court to act on it.

56. Sup. Ct., G.B.; March 9, 1960; 14 *Minshu* 355.

57. Hideo Wada, *Saiko Saibansho Ron* (On the Supreme Court), Tokyo: Nihon Hyoronsha, 1971, p. 105.

58. The judge shall be appointed from among those who possess proper qualifications according to law. No judge shall be deprived of his position, unless by way of criminal sentence or disciplinary punishment. Rules for disciplinary punishment shall be determined by law.

59. Saburo Ienaga, *Shihoken Dokuritsu no Rekishiteki Kosatsu* (The Historical Study of Judicial Independence), Tokyo: Nihon Hyoronshinsha, 1962, pp. 9–10.

60. Gr. Ct. Cass.; May 27, 1891; *Horitsu Shimbun* No. 214.

61. See Sakae Wagatsuma *et al* (eds.), *Nihon Seiji Saibanshi Roku: Showa Zengo* (The Record of the Political Trials in Japan: Around the Showa Era), Tokyo: Daiichi Hoki Shuppan, 1970.

62. Eigoro Aoki, "Saibankan no senso sekinin" (War responsibilities of judges), in *Hogaku Semina*, No. 11, 1962, pp. 2–7.

63. Tokyo Dist. Ct., February 2, 1948 as cited in Yoshihiro Niimura, "Hirano tsuiho teishi karishobun jiken no gaiyo" (An outline of the temporary disposition to depurge Hirano) in 1 *Horitsu Jiho* 1, 1949, pp. 33–38.

64. Masao Nomura (ed.), *Op. Cit.*, *Hoso Fuunroku*, Vol. 2, p. 113.

65. Urawa Dist. Ct.; July 2, 1948; the *Hoso Shimbun* No. 27, 1948, p. 6.

66. Jiro Tanaka, Isao Sato, and Jiro Nomura (eds.), *Sengo Seiji Saibanshiroku* (Postwar Political Trials), Tokyo: Daiichi Hoki Shuppan, 1980, Vol. 1, pp. 415–444.

67. *Ibid.*, Vol. 2, pp. 83–110. The Sapporo district court convicted a Japan Communist Party member who had been charged with the homicide of Police Chief Shiratori in revenge against the police arrest of radical leftist members. His conviction was upheld by both the Sapporo high court and the Supreme Court. The defense labeled it a political trial against the leftist movement.

68. *Murakami v. Japan;* Sup. Ct., 1st. P.B.; May 20, 1975; 29 *Keishu* 177.

69. The Tokyo district court expressed its concern that judicial independence might be grossly impaired by the action of some labor unions and bar associations demanding, by the unlawful methods of distributing fliers and pamphlets, the dismissal of Judge Hidenobu Sonobe, who had screened the admission of spectators to his trials of labor dispute cases. There were similar views expressed from conservative quarters.

70. Gr. Ct. Cass.; March 3, 1937; 16 *Keiroku* 193.

71. Frank O. Miller, *Minobe Tatsukichi: Interpreter of Constitutionalism in Japan*, Berkeley, Cal.: University of California Press, 1965, p. 72.

72. Hirobumi Ito, *Teikoku Kempo Koshitsu Tempangikai* (The Exposition of the Imperial Constitution and Rules), Tokyo: Maruzen, 1935, pp. 99–100.

73. Ad. Ct.; February 24, 1914; 25 *Gyoroku* 109.

74. Gr. Ct. Cass.; October 12, 1917; 23 *Minroku* 1395.

75. Tatsukichi Minobe, *Ruishu Hyoron Gyoseiho Hanrei* (Cases and Comments on Administrative Law), 1925, p. 234, as cited in Masayasu Hasegawa, *Kempo Hanrei no Taikei*, p. 56.

76. Gr. Ct. Cass.; July 11, 1913; 19 *Keiroku* 792.

77. The constitutional breakdown of sixteen cases is as follows: eight cases dealing with open trial (Article 59), two cases with special courts (Article 60), one case with national polity (Article 1), one case with emergency rescript (Article 8), one case with inviolability of the

home (Article 25), one case with judicial review (Article 23), one case with free enterprise (Article 22), one case with police order (Article 9), and one with religious freedom (Article 28). With regard to the last two cases referred to above, for instance, the Great Court of Cassation upheld a prefectural police order to regulate enterprises and gave the opinion that Article 22 of the constitution dealt with freedom of domicile and moving and not the freedom of enterprises. (*Inomata v. Japan;* November 15, 1916; 22 *Keiroku* 1774). Likewise, the Great Court of Cassation ruled that a prefectural ordinance restraining religious acts did not violate religious freedom guaranteed in Article 28 of the constitution. (*Akiyoshi v. Japan;* October 12, 1931; 10 *Keiroku* 445).

78. Gr. Ct. Cass.; March 3, 1937; 16 *Keiroku* 193.

79. Sup. Ct., G.B.; April 2, 1969; 171 *Saibanshu Keiji* 13.

CHAPTER 6

The Conservative Supreme Court

The Constitution of Japan functions not only as the supreme and organic law of the country but also as the basic law, for it delineates the relationship between the rights and freedoms of individual citizens, on the one hand, and the state power of the representative government, on the other. The Constitution, as the basic law, purports to guarantee the rights and freedoms of individuals, family, business, labor, religious organizations, and other groups in the highly pluralistic Japanese society.

The provisions of Articles 10 through 40 of the Constitution enumerate rights and duties of the people, and, combined with Articles 82 and 89 therein, constitute the civil rights and liberties in Japan. Here constitutional rights and freedoms of the people are not absolute but qualified. For instance, Article 11 guarantees fundamental human rights, but Article 12 imposes the duty not to abuse such rights. Likewise, Article 27 provides for both the right and duties to work. Individual rights and liberties are qualified by the consideration for public welfare.

The Constitution has assigned the Supreme Court and lower courts the task of upholding constitutional rights and liberties of individuals. In performing this function the courts are obliged to balance an individual's rights and liberties with public interests such as national security and the public welfare. This chapter attempts to analyze the Supreme Court's decision making in disputes involving civil rights and liberties.

It is assumed that judicial attitudes, judicial attributes, and judicial culture all influence judicial behavior in varying degrees. Judicial attitudes on civil liberties manifest themselves on the dimension of judicial liberalism and conservatism while judicial attributes are an aggregate of, *inter alia,* such social backgrounds as prior occupation of judges, political party affiliations of judicial appointors, and a judge's age at the time of appointment. We shall start with operational definitions of judicial liberalism and conservatism, and a discussion of methods employed in this work.

1. Judicial Attitudes: Liberalism and Conservatism

Constitutional rights and liberties of individuals are semantically divided into either a socioeconomic or sociopolitical type.[1] Article 28 (rights of workers), Article 29 (private property rights and just compensation in land reform), and Article 22 (freedom of occupation) exemplify predominantly socioeconomic civil liberties as from time to time are raised in constitutional litigations. Article 21 (freedom of assembly, association, and expression), Article 23 (academic freedom), and Article 31 (due process) are prime examples of sociopolitical civil liberties enumerated in chapter three of the Constitution. Indeed there are many more provisions of sociopolitical liberties than socioeconomic ones found in the chapter. At the same time Article 13 (the right to life, liberty, and the pursuit of happiness), Article 14 (equality under law), Article 15 (the right to choose and dismiss officials), Article 24 (equality of the sexes in the family life), and Article 25 (minimum standards of wholesome and cultured living) have been invoked by the Supreme Court in relation to both socioeconomic and sociopolitical types of litigation.

First, the dimension of sociopolitical liberalism in Japan is operationally defined as a belief in and support of, *inter alia,* sociopolitical equality (*e.g.,* legislative reapportionment, an abolition of heavier penalty in patricide), sociopolitical freedom (*e.g.*, freedom of expression, free exercise of religion), rights of fair procedure (*e.g.*, right to counsel, open trial) and the right to individual privacy (*e.g.*, protection against illegal search and seizure). Conversely, sociopolitical conservatism is defined as a belief in and support of law and order and the defense of the status quo.

Socioeconomic liberalism in Japan is defined as a defense of, *inter alia*, the rights of workers, freedom of occupation, just compensation under eminent domain, and property rights. It includes the belief in the support of: 1) unions as opposed to employers on the assumption that the former acts as the agent of working men to improve their economic status; 2) fiscal claims of injured workers or their families against employers; 3) a union member as opposed to a union itself inasmuch as the former is the underdog and weaker than the latter; 4) governmental regulations of business activities designed to maintain freedom of competition between small and big businesses and to protect consumers; and 5) such tax laws that are designed to regulate enterprises and condition the effective government program of economic control and services.

Conversely, socioeconomic conservatism is defined as the defense of private enterprise, vested interests, and broad differentials in wealth and income between property owners and workers. For instance, a judge is considered liberal if he acquits a criminally accused person on the ground that the prosecution violated his constitutional rights in a criminal trial. A judge is called conservative when he upholds the conviction of a labor union leader in a labor/management dispute on the grounds of violating the property rights of management besides law and order.

There are some "positive civil liberty" cases in which the government acts as a mediator of conflicting interests between individuals or groups of individuals. Exclusive private organizations whose discriminatory policies with respect to sex, social status, creed, or religion can no longer enjoy constitutional immunity. Here a judge is sociopolitically liberal if he condemns such discrimination. Likewise, a land reform designed to redistribute an absentee land owner's farm among former tenants is clearly a liberal economic policy. However, in a civil case involving a constitutional guarantee of due compensation by the government to a former landlord, a judge who upholds a claim of just compensation for a former land owner is liberal, but a judge who dismisses such a claim becomes conservative even though his support of land reform would render him liberal in another case.

Attitudinal differences in constitutional litigation manifest themselves most distinctly in divided decisions in which at least one justice disagrees with the conclusion of a case. In the present work, a constitutional case is operationally defined to be one in which at least one justice raises a constitutional issue. If one case raises more than one constitutional issue and decisions are made on each issue, each decision is counted separately. The present work primarily analyzes voting behavior in the grand bench because that is where all important constitutional decisions are made. The justices from all three petty benches, as described earlier, participate in the grand bench. Contained in the unabridged reports are 227 divided constitutional decisions made between 1947 and 1980. Since nine cases involve more than one constitutional issue with a decision made on each issue, each decision was counted separately. Thus, 227 divided constitutional decisions include 223 divided decisions or 214 divided cases on civil liberties.

Supreme Court practice in Japan makes analysis of judicial voting behavior very difficult. First, except during the initial period, not all the decisions rendered by the Court have been published. The Supreme Court committee on judicial precedents, which consists of six justices (two justices from each petty bench) and two *chosakan* (one from the criminal section and the other from the civil section), is in charge of selecting and publishing Court decisions. *Chosakan* first read all the decisions rendered by both the petty and grand benches each month, classifying them into two groups. The first group includes those decisions which seem to reflect important legal interpretations that are likely to become new precedents, and also those cases which do not seem important enough to be included in the abridged Supreme Court reports *(saiko saibansho hanreishu)* but which may be useful for legal practitioners. The second group includes those cases which do not show important legal interpretations of the Court, but which are socially important, such as public security, and are worth preserving for future reference. All the cases thus selected by *chosakan* under either one of the two categories are included in the unabridged Supreme Court reports *(saiko saibansho saibanshu)*. Only those cases in the first group which contain important judicial interpretations are submitted for further scrutiny to the six-member judicial committee. The committee meets once a month and selects from the previous month's decisions, which are chosen beforehand by *chosakan* only those cases which it deems appropriate for inclusion in the abridged Supreme Court report. The committee also supervises the summarization of the holding in each case included in the abridged reports.

The Unabridged Supreme Court Report: Criminal Cases (Saikosaibansho Saibanshu Keiji), Vol. 1 contains decisions rendered from November 1947 to April 1948. By July 1987 this series reached 242 volumes (though the number jumps from Vol. 19 to Vol. 35). *The Unabridged Supreme Court Report: Civil Cases (Saikosaibansho Saibanshu Minji)*, Vol. 1, contains decisions from September 1947 to March 1948. By July 1987, 147 volumes had been published.

Any quantitative analysis of judicial behavior based upon the cases published in either report must take into account the statistical reliability of the universe. The unabridged reports are more exhaustive and include even those decisions that are virtually identical. It clearly reflects more closely the numerical magnitudes of the Court's output, and is a better source to use for any quantitative analysis of judicial behavior. For the purpose of the present work, the unabridged reports are used to analyze the divided decisions of the grand bench while the abridged reports are used to analyze the unanimous decisions of the grand bench, as well as both unanimous and divided decisions of the petty benches. Hayakawa and Danelski used the abridged reports and also different criteria in determining each point listed above, and accordingly, caution is needed in comparing their findings with the findings in the present study.

Second, there is the problem of determining the time at which a judicial decision is made. A writer circulates his draft among all other justices including the minority for the purpose of reviews and modifications. When each justice approves the final draft, he signs and affixes his seal to it. The signing by a justice of the final draft is taken as the time of decision making. A justice may change his mind between the time of group discussion and the time of writing his opinions, and therefore, a justice should be considered as having made a final decision when he is ready to sign and affix his seal to the written judgment. This work includes those justices who express their agreement or disagreement with the opinion of the Court, even though they do not sign and seal the written judgment due to illness, official trips, retirement, or other reasons.

Third, the composition of the Supreme Court changes so much that it is impossible to identify which fifteen justices have decided a given case. The absence of the term system in Japan, together with the rapid turnover of justices and, most of all, the time lag between the date of actual decision making and the date the decision is announced often make it difficult to determine the actual decision makers in a given case.

For example, *Iida et al v. Japan* or the *Mitaka* case[2] was decided on December 22, 1954, and was announced on June 22, 1955.[3] The grand bench decision in *Miyata v. Japan*[4] was announced on December 24, 1952. A list of the justices who decided this case shows that twelve justices (*i.e.*, Kuriyama, Sawada, Kotani, Tanimura, Inoue, Mano, Fujita, Shima, Hasegawa, Iwamatsu, Tanaka, and Y. Saito) formed the grand bench. Yet Justice Hasegawa had retired on November 30, 1951. It follows that this case was decided on or prior to November 30, 1951, despite the announced date of December 24, 1952. Furthermore, the list of court membership compiled by use of the appointment and retirement dates for each justice indicates that the twelve justices served together, or formed a grand bench, between October 5, 1951, and

November 30, 1951. This further narrows the period during which the case was decided, but this is as far as we can go. Supposing the case was decided on the day that Justice Hasegawa retired, one year and twenty-four days elapsed between the date of decision and the date the decision was announced. In a more extreme case, the time lag was two years and forty days![5] Furthermore, the Japanese practice of giving only the date of announcement makes it difficult to ascertain the names of the justices who do not participate in deciding a given case although they are on the bench at the time a case is deliberated upon. Any quantitative analysis of the Supreme Court voting behavior should take into consideration these methodological problems.

Judicial attitudes, along with the issues of a case, constitute an important component in converting input into output in judicial decision making. Judicial conversion proceeds through a judge's value system which is known to be relatively consistent and stable. On the assumption that a constitutional issue of a case is an independent variable, and judicial attitude an intervening variable, then judicial voting becomes a dependent variable. So a change in voting behavior comes from a change in either an issue of a case or judicial attitudes or both. A judge may construct factual relations or legal questions in old and new cases differently so as to avoid use of precedents in the old case. Extraneous issues like types of litigants and competence of counsel may cause a change in judicial voting. Also, judges have been known to change their attitudes over the years. A change in the composition of the Court is a prime example of a change in the judicial attitudinal variable. A new judge may project value judgments different from those of his predecessor.

One such occasion arose concerning the increase of penalties which pertained to the constitutional provision of Article 39. *Ozaki v. Japan* (1950)[6] was decided by the thirteen-member grand bench of the Supreme Court. A ten-justice majority held that since the middle term of the indefinite period of imprisonment imposed by the first instance court was one year and nine months, the one-and-one-half year definite period of imprisonment which the court below handed down increased neither the middle nor the long-term imprisonment originally imposed by the first instance court. Three justices dissented by stating that the judgment of the court below increased the penalty imposed by the first instance court, thereby violating the principle of not changing a penalty to the disadvantage of an accused, and that to deny the short term imprisonment granted by the law to the accused violates the spirit of the fair trial clause of the Constitution. In short, the Court was conservative and restrained in relation to the court below but four years later reversed the policy it had established in the *Ozaki* case and became a liberal and activist court in *Doto v. Japan* (1954).[7] This change in precedent resulted from the change of the Court's composition and in some justices' voting behavior.

First, four justices (Tsukasaki, Sawada, Iwamatsu, and Hozumi) who decided against the defendant in the *Ozaki* case and Justice Hasegawa who decided for the defendant retired and were replaced by two new justices (K. Tanaka and Tanimura) who also decided for the defendant. Justices Mano, Kotani, and Shimoyama, who decided against the defendant in the *Ozaki* case, switched their votes in favor of the defendant in the *Doto* case. Inoue, who did not participate in the *Ozaki* case, decided for the defendant in the *Doto* case, while the remaining four justices decided the same way in both cases. Thus, the precedent established by three to ten in the *Ozaki* case was changed by eight to three in the *Doto* case four years later. The eight-member majority established a new policy that accepting a *kokoku* appeal made by the prosecutors and not by the accused in the present case, the court below increased the indefinite period of imprisonment, the middle term of which would have been three years and three months, to four years of imprisonment, thereby violating the principle against increasing a penalty that is disadvantageous to the accused. Three dissenters reasoned that since the sentence below equaled the long term (four years) of imprisonment for an indefinite period imposed by the first instance court, it did not increase the penalty unfavorable to the accused.

Another instance of such a change dealt with the constitutionality of a trial in lieu of conciliation. *Suzuki v. Ishigaki* (1956)[8] dealt with a judicial trial forced on both parties after the failure to solve a dispute through conciliation over the cancelled lease of a rental house. The Tokyo district court conducted a trial in lieu of conciliation under the authority of Article 19, Paragraph 2 of the Monetary Liability Provisional Adjustment Code.[9] Sustaining such a trial in accordance with Articles 32 and 82 of the Constitution, the Supreme Court majority was of the opinion that a trial in lieu of conciliation, though noncontentious in nature, has the same features as judicial adjudication, that appeals are available for review of such a trial and that open trial, confrontation of witnesses, and other requirements of Article 82 of the Constitution are not required. This judgment was made by a narrow margin of eight to seven. Four of the seven dissenting justices held that the provision of the Monetary Liability Provisional Adjustment Code on Forced Conciliation violated Articles 32 and 82 of the Constitution, and that such a trial in lieu of conciliation was unconstitutional. Two other justices dissented by stating that the provisional law was constitutional but was misapplied in the present instance, whereby the lower court contravened Article 82 of the Constitution.

However, four years later the Court changed by nine to six the *Suzuki* ruling when it decided *Nomura v. Yamaki et al* (1960),[10] and became an activist in relation to the lower court. According to the nine-member majority in the case, the lower court, which conducted a trial in lieu of conciliation on purely contentious matters by applying Article 19, Paragraph 2 of the Wartime Civil Matters Special Code and Article 7 of the Monetary Adjustment Code, violated Articles 32 and 82 of the Constitution. The majority elaborated its opinion as follows: Article 10 of the Monetary Adjustment Code provides that a judicial judgment rendered in lieu of conciliation as stipulated in Article 7 is as effective as judicial conciliation. However, such a trial becomes finalized just as a regular trial, although an appeal is instantly available for it. Regardless of the parties involved, it is not different from a trial, and as such, it must be conducted in an open court with a confrontation of witnesses. Whereas the instant trial in lieu of conciliation should have been confined to non-contentious matters like interest rates and time limit and should not be used to decide the rights and duties of contending parties, the lower court ordered an evacuation of the rented house and a splitting of expenses despite disagreement between the two parties over the lease. It had also exceeded the authority of Article 7 of the Monetary Adjustment Code. According to four of the majority justices, Article 7 is not unconstitutional, but a court forcing a trial in lieu of conciliation is. The remaining four of the majority justices held the law unconstitutional as well.

According to Y. Saito, K. Tanaka, and Takahashi, three of the six dissenters, it is purely a legislative matter to place a dispute under civil conciliation and have a judge try it under certain conditions while allowing appeals against such judicial judgment. Such a trial is not only in harmony with Article 32 of the Constitution but should also be encouraged to alleviate delay in trials, and promote the spirit of Article 76, Paragraph 2 of the Constitution. The change of this precedent resulted from the retirement of two liberals (Mano and Iwata) and four conservatives (Kuriyama, Tanimura, Kobayashi, and Motomura), and the addition of four liberals (D. Kawamura, Shimoiizaka, Okuno, and Takagi) and two conservatives (Takahashi and Ishizaka), resulting in a net gain of two liberals. Furthermore, Shima and M. Kawamura switched their earlier votes, respectively, trading off one liberal vote with one conservative vote.

We should also list inconsistency on the side of a judge as another reason for changes in voting. For instance, during the Mano Court (1947–1958) a total of twenty-two decisions were decided by the Supreme Court grand bench mainly on the basis of whether or not Government Ordinance 325, penalizing conduct harmful to the occupation's objectives was still effective even after the San Francisco Peace Treaty went into force. The justices in twenty-one of these decisions voted consistently, either for or against the validity of the government ordinance. In *Japan v. Hamazoe* (1956),[11] however, the Fukuoka district court acquitted the defendant of having violated this ordinance. Upon appeal, the Fukuoka high court rendered a verdict of innocent instead of acquittal by stating that the alleged action of the defendant did not amount to the criminal act of false or destructive criticism against the occupation forces. The Supreme Court later restored the judgment of the Fukuoka district court. Justice Yusuke Saito voted against the defendants who were charged with having violated Government Ordinance 325 in twenty-one cases, but in the *Hamazoe* case he voted for the defendant by dismissing the appeal lodged by the prosecution.

Similarly, twenty-nine decisions made during the Mano Court involved the question of admissibility of a defendant's confession made in open court. In twenty-four decisions Justice Shima consistently upheld the admissibility of such confessions, but in five other decisions he held it unconstitutional to convict a defendant solely on the basis of his own confession in open court without any supporting evidence. Except for these and a few other decisions, most justices showed a high degree of consistency in their votes relating to what they perceived to be identical issues, providing a basis of *stare decisis*.

Since each decision reflects a wide range of values in its policy significance and since judicial decision making does not necessarily use court decisions as an instrument for articulation, it is up to a later judge to decide whether or not a given precedent should govern a principal case. Although no explicitly stated principle of *stare decisis* governs Japanese judges, a real fear that the Supreme Court may reverse its rulings that fail to apply what it regards as precedental value, tends to bind strongly many Japanese judges to precedents.

At the same time, the Supreme Court is very cautious not to violate its own precedents. Specifically, *stare decisis* seems to work at the following three levels among judges.[12] First, the individual *stare decisis* deals with the tendency of an individual judge to follow his own voting pattern in similar cases. In the majority of cases individual judges are usually consistent with themselves and often cite their own prior decisions to support their present position. Second, the local *stare decisis* measures the propensity of some subgroup (usually of similar-minded judges) to follow precedents established by earlier subgroups. Here individual judges of subgroups often feel themselves bound by the prior decisions of subgroups of judges who are currently serving on the same court. Third, the traditional *stare decisis* is concerned with the propensity of the entire court as a small decision-making group to follow its own precedents. A court often feels itself bound by the prior decisions of courts of an equal or higher level. The traditional *stare decisis* has been intensely analyzed in the past.

A total of seventy-eight justices served on the Supreme Court at one time or another between 1947 and 1980. When measured in terms of the definitions suggested previously, the Supreme Court of Japan is found to be conservative on civil rights and liberties in this period of time. The Court decided many more cases unanimously than by divided votes. When the grand bench of the Supreme Court was unanimous on civil rights litigation, it passed 164 conservative decisions against only ten liberal decisions on sociopolitical issues (*i.e.*, a ratio of 16.4 to 1), and seventy-two conservative decisions against seventeen liberal decisions on socioeconomic issues (*i.e.*, a ratio of 4.2 to 1). When the grand bench was divided on constitutional litigation, it made ninety-three conservative decisions against eighty-six liberal decisions on sociopolitical issues, and twenty-two conservative decisions against nineteen liberal decisions on socioeconomic issues. Thus, the grand bench has been extremely conservative when unanimous, and just a trifle conservative when divided. Overall, it ranged from being slightly to very conservative. The rest of this chapter will be devoted to the inquiry into judicial culture as another variable in determining degrees of variation in judicial behavior in Japan.

2. Conservative Judicial Antecedents

The liberal and conservative dimension of legal culture emerged in the Western political tradition. According to De Ruggiero,[13] liberty is an abstract concept signifying the essence of individuality, and absolute liberty would lead to license, denying all authority, law and customs, while negating the legislative and governmental functions. Therefore, liberty becomes possible only in the same conditions which give rise to possible restraints on it. As distinguished from abstract liberty, liberties designate a complex of particular empirical rights and privileges acquired, one by one, in historical contexts. In the most general terms, they range from a right to life, personal liberty and security, the freedom of conscience and religious practice, freedom of speech and expression, including press and assembly, and freedom of association, to the possession and use of private property. The exercise of these liberties gives rise to occasional conflicts which can be resolved in compatibility with freedom only if one keeps a balance between two sides of the same coin. The role of the Constitution in the modern state is to defend liberties and enforce responsibility.

The abstract concept of liberty is necessary to prevent empirical liberties from degenerating into privileges and monopolies, while the empirical liberties are indispensable to prevent abstract liberty from becoming an empty and meaningless formula, De Ruggiero concludes. In the end both must be qualified from country to country in arriving at the reality, as civil liberties vary in time and place. The central concept of classical Western liberalism was faith in rational human nature and a society of egalitarian individuals. Seeing government and law as the main source of restraint on individual freedom, traditional Western liberalism signified the freedom of individuals from the restraint of the state. Eighteenth-century Europe stressed absolute liberty and rejected all external restraints. Adam Smith's laissez faire philosophy typified economic liberalism designed to keep government intervention minimal. At the same time, classical Western liberalism propagated changes, innovations, and social mobility at a fast rate.

In contrast, traditional Western conservatism was based on the inherent shortcomings of human nature, and a hierarchical society composed of individuals with different qualities and characteristics. According to the traditional conservatives, absolute liberty negates law, for law is restraint.

However, the absence of restraint would create anarchy, which, in turn, would leave liberty to the exclusive possession of the strong and the unscrupulous. Therefore, they argued that government by superior individuals is the best means to lead the masses and to coax good out of man on a collective basis. By attaching importance to authority, tradition, and the status quo, they contributed to moderation and prudence, and inhibited progress.

It becomes necessary, then, to examine how law and liberty have evolved in the Japanese legal environment as they affect judicial behavior in balancing the relationship between the individual and the state. We shall start with the analysis of liberalism and conservatism of the Japanese legal culture in three distinctive periods in history: the Tokugawa era (1603–1889), Meiji constitutionalism (1889–1945), and the post-1945 era.

Tokugawa authority was paternalistic and highly structured with defined duties and obligations according to each person's station in the Japanese feudal society. The subordinate had nothing more than authoritarian duties and enjoyed no correlative rights. If there had been any rights, it would have been in a reflection of a mutuality of duties, that is, some implicitly perceived right derived from an awareness of the duties of another person (or status) to oneself (or one's status). Both neo-Confucianism and legalism served the Tokugawa autocratic interests as the official philosophy, and fostered a basically conservative legal tradition. Neo-Confucianism furnished underlying concepts of natural justice *(dori)* and provided social justification for the status quo. Based on the view that the ordinary people were not capable of running the country, neo-Confucianism assigned a ruler the task of providing his people with security and welfare and expected him to exercise his prerogatives benevolently.

The Confucian family formed a microcosm of the Tokugawa feudal society with its multistatus social and political order. There was no sharp distinction between public and private morality, and government and politics were not separate from the moral order, but an extension of the humanistic morality. Treating the family and the state as two different aspects of the same morality, neo-Confucianism provided a model relationship, serving as a means of measuring all men. *Ri* (propriety or ideal standards of conduct) as formulated in Confucianism dictated that men be unequal and that status law treat them accordingly. Classifying all men into the four vocational statutes (warriors, farmers, artisans, and merchants), neo-Confucianism required each person to learn and comply with the preexisting natural principles governing three types of bonds which existed between sovereign and subject, father and son, and husband and wife. It also required each person to learn five relationships: Love in the father and filial piety in son; gentility in the eldest brother and humility and respect in younger; righteous behavior in husband and obedience in wife; humane consideration for elders and deference in junior; and benevolence in rulers and loyalty in subjects.

Like neo-Confucianists, the legalists believed that the ordinary man was not capable of ruling the country and that the ruler must be entrusted with that task. They further believed that the interests of the ruler were paramount and the people were only the means to the ruler's personal end. However, in order for a ruler to remain secure in his position, he would have to take care of the people's welfare and thus used the Confucian axiom of "government for the people" to justify their self-serving rule by law. At the same time, the legalists practiced the principle of surveillance and castigation, and made certain that the people would follow the absolute standards of proper conduct. The wise ruler who practiced such a principle would deal with his people in an authoritarian manner and restrain them by punishment and reward.

While neo-Confucianism and legalism, blended together, have had a strong influence on the Japanese legal tradition, Taoism did not have much impact. The way of *Tao*, which teaches the people to be free from ambition and aggression in pursuit of good fellowship and brotherly love, is essentially a policy of laissez faire which preaches that the government restrain itself from interfering in the lives and freedom of its people.

While there was a body of customary civil law among merchants, the Tokugawa legal system was characterized by the predominance of not only status law but also criminal law. The Tokugawa law, often accompanied by harsh penalties, prohibited a subordinate from making a criminal charge against a feudal or family superior without the latter's permission; it also required an itinerant claimant in a civil suit to obtain prior approval from his landlord. As commercial activities increased, however, so did the unsecured monetary claims by the emerging merchant class. The Shogunate or central government was forced to settle disputes, typically involving money, land, water, and mutual affairs. Courts were viewed as being in charge of discovering natural justice through custom and reason. Although there emerged gradually positive laws in the central government, such laws were instruments of legitimizing the Tokugawa autocracy, instead of effectively controlling Tokugawa policies or official actions.

The making of the Meiji constitution also reveals a continuation of the strong conservative legal antecedent of the Tokugawa era. In an early stage of compiling the Civil Code of 1890, some scholars and lawyers were opposed to the coining of the term civil rights *(minken)* as an equivalent to the French *droit civil,* and argued that commoners were not entitled to any rights in relation to the Emperor.[14] Likewise, at the final stage of the privy council's deliberations on the Meiji constitution, Count Arinori Mori was said to have insisted that the title of chapter two of the Meiji constitution be changed to read "the status of subjects," because the Japanese subject had nothing but obligations and a fixed station in life. The final draft of the Meiji constitution was thickly hedged with many provisions protective of the governmental prerogatives and contained little substance of the people's rights and freedoms. It was an authoritarian law made to govern in the essentially dual status society. Its framers regarded sovereignty as residing in the Emperor and not in the people. The constitution was given to the people by Emperor Meiji as an act of his benevolence, and individuals may be free to petition but may not resort to a legal suit against an administrative action. Although it established a constitutional monarchy, the Meiji constitution was primarily an instrument with which to facilitate imperial rule. The restrictions on the state and the individual freedom were mere displays of the limitations which the state, and not the constitution, imposed on itself. The constitution was void of popular parliamentary control, not to mention judicial review. Under it, the Cabinet was responsible to the Emperor and not to the Diet, which was considered largely perfunctory. At the same time, it is fair to say that the Meiji constitution was a big leap forward from the Tokugawa status- and criminal law-oriented social relationships, and gave a much greater promise of freedom of speech, political association, and religion than the people had ever enjoyed before.

The dichotomy between conservative and liberal ideologies under the Meiji constitution (1889–1945) was represented by two academic groups.[15] One group, initiated by Yatsuka Hozumi and continued by Soichi Sasaki and Shinkichi Uesugi, and the other group, started by Kitokuro Ichiki and carried out by Tatsukichi Minobe, were drawn into the political struggle for academic hegemony. Uesugi and Hozumi devoted themselves to the authoritarian, conservative cause led by the elder statesmen of the Satsuma-Choshu clans. Soichi Sasaki, on his part, believed that constitutionalism did not restrict the power of the Emperor, and that parliamentarism, the rule of law, and judicial review were all subordinate to the unitary imperial sovereign power.

Minobe promoted the libertarian cause led by political parties and the leaders of the new capitalism. Minobe gained predominance after 1912 as Uesugi receded from the mainstream of the constitutional scholarship. Although Minobe could not see the separation of powers and judicial review under the Meiji constitution, he intuitively sensed the march of constitutionalism in Europe at the turn of the century. His liberalism lay in the ethical necessity for the moral and intellectual freedom of the individual. He also strongly advocated the democratization of the electoral process as an important aspect of liberal constitutionalism. More than anything else, however, his juristic concept of the state personality was the most revolutionary aspect of his doctrine, in which he viewed the Emperor as only one organ of the state and rejected the obscure and god-immanent spirit of orthodox, parochial, and tradition-bound Japanese constitutionalism. As the Japanese society was becoming more liberalized and stabler than in the years immediately after the Meiji Restoration (1868), Hirobumi Ito and his colleagues accepted a moderate constitutional monarchy advocated by such German jurists as Ludwig Stein and thereby advanced the liberal movement. Their defense of the people's rights under law was rather progressive, along with their efforts to free civil service from the *han* (fief) patronage.[16]

Minobe represented probably the most rational argument and support for a liberal political order within the basically conservative framework of the imperial constitution. He also provided a great impetus to the libertarian movement through his teaching of future bureaucrats at Tokyo Imperial University. Yet, his thoughts revealed conservative elements as well. For one thing, his adherence to Georg Jellinek's position kept him from adopting a more thorough liberalism. For another, he accepted the pre-Meiji Restoration customary law and orthodox political philosophy in his interpretation of the imperial prerogative. Furthermore, he valued the social responsibility of the state over individual rights and freedoms. Consequently, as a captive of the elitist psychology, he never resolved the conflict between his libertarian constitutional interpretation and his predisposition to look upon government as the business of experts. In the final analysis, his liberal aspiration was "circumvented not so much by the Meiji legal order as by the political inadequacy of the government elite to absorb and prevail over the concurrent and protracted shock of political and social revolution."[17]

When compared with these doctrines of Western, particularly American, liberalism and conservatism, faith in individual initiative and equality, which is central to the classical Western liberalism, is largely absent in the Japanese legal tradition. Laissez faire liberalism did not exist in Japan where the government took all the initiatives in economic industrialization and political modernization of the country.

The preceding analysis of the Japanese legal development has predominantly indicated many traits of the traditional

Western conservatism, and whatever liberal ideology might have been implanted on the Japanese soil was greatly qualified by such a conservative tradition. Indigenous to the Japanese experience is the fusion of individuals and groups. Whereas the Western civil rights movement stresses the autonomy of the individual and the right to fulfillment through individual freedom, the right not to belong and not to assume duties, Japan's civil right is the right of individuals to belong to a group and to become involved in a demanding but protective world of duties. Consequently, the constitutional emphasis in 1947 on individual rights seems to have led as much to a heightened consciousness of the individual rights of separate groups vis-a-vis the government and other groups as to an enhanced appreciation of the rights of the individual.[18]

The inclusion of civil rights and liberties in the 1947 Constitution was not the result of the victory of the civil rights movement among the people against the repressive government of wartime Japan. Although academic debates have long flourished concerning whether or not the Constitution of 1947 was essentially imposed by GHQ, SCAP on the Japanese, it was undoubtedly the result of the defeat in World War II, instead of the victory of the Japanese people over their imperial power elite, that led to an unprecedented amount of individual rights and liberties in the postwar Japan.

Postwar liberalism in Japan is identified with the support of the new constitutional order and its underlying "modern" or Western values, particularly, freedom and equality. The rights and freedoms which the American drafters injected into the new Constitution clearly reflected modern liberalism, which has changed the premises and assertions of the traditional liberalism. The concept of freedom from the state was replaced by the concept of freedom through the state. As the modern liberals see it, absence of external compulsion is merely the beginning of more substantive freedoms realizing man's ability to determine himself; a travesty of freedom by another individual created economic or political underdogs, and impaired the collective interests of the community. Consequently, liberals now accept and even advocate the premise that individuals are subject to government regulations and management designed to enhance public welfare and concomitantly a higher level of individual human life.

The notion of the welfare state epitomizes modern economic liberalism in Japan. Government increased its role in the economic field in order to create a more equitable distribution of wealth, to protect free and fair competition and to strengthen labor unions and workers' social security benefits. The argument that no government can remain committed to the absolute primacy of private rights and freedoms gained increased ground. Private rights have been increasingly qualified and made subordinate to public welfare more than ever before.

The LDP-dominated Diet established in 1956 the Commission on the Constitution to conduct extensive investigations into the process of constitution-making.[19] The commission met 131 times in its plenary sessions, 319 times in committees (with each committee composed of five Diet members and five non-political members) and held fifty-six public hearings during its seven years of existence. The commission completed its final report and submitted it to both the Cabinet and Diet in July 1964. It did not recommend either for or against any constitutional revision, but simply listed both pros and cons with respective opinions. The LDP and the government accepted the report, but failed to mount an effective campaign designed to successfully carry out their cause. Anti-revisionists, primarily composed of the opposition parties, were critical of the commission report favoring a revision, and succeeded in securing one-third of the seats in Diet to block the LDP's attempted revision. Furthermore, anti-revisionists were helped by various opinion polls which verified the lack of public support for revision, especially a total revision. Finally, the LDP found itself in a confusing position, because the pressing need to maintain a united front as the governing party kept the LDP from presenting issues which would cause a split within the party. Therefore, the entire issue of constitutional revision has been laid aside and allowed to rest. At present, the public opinion favoring pacifism and the realistic need for self-defense have made Article 9 symbolic of Japan's pacifist attitude while allowing rearmament without constitutional revision.[20] Likewise, the conservatives have found the way to advance their cause on many domestic issues, ranging from law and order to the concentration of private capital, without resort to constitutional revision.

Like liberalism, Western conservatism has gone through a radical transformation. If modern liberalism has come to accept a positive role of government in the realization of a higher individual value and freedom, modern conservatism has come to reject even a passive role for government. According to the modern conservatives, the moral liberty of individuals and the welfare of the majority will be best served if the domination of the state over the individual and the egalitarian reduction of the individual to a statistic in socioeconomic planning and regulations are minimized, and if free enterprises and free competition and individual self-reliance are strengthened.

Advocates of conservative, traditional values and ethics were clearly a side current in the latter part of the 1940s inasmuch as the purges and the continuation of the occupation suppressed political criticism of the new Constitution. However, the outbreak of the Korean War in 1950 touched off a conservative reaction, starting with a wide debate on the political feasibility of Article 9 renouncing rearmament, and the need to develop the Self-Defense Forces because of pressing international tensions. Criticism encompassed the dislike of Article 9, the impracticality and ineffectiveness of controlling the abuse of power by political parties, and the form and language of the constitutional text due to the repetition in the preamble and chapter three dealing with the rights and duties of the people. The secretive manner in the workings of the draft constitution was also criticized.

Debates, started by the politically rehabilitated bureaucrats and politicians, developed from the practical question of partial revision of the Constitution into the emotional question of revising the entire document.[21] Some favored the revision of one or more particular articles concerning private ownership, Diet's status, and the electorate's rights, while others felt it necessary to amend Article 9. Still others called for a total revision of the Constitution to remove any suspicion of American influence in the document. Prewar bureaucrats whose hostility stemmed from their purge by the occupation, developed a bipartisan activity embracing parliamentary members from both the conservative and progressive parties. The cause of a drastic revision became a particularly important rallying point of the ruling party. They insisted on incorporating in a new Constitution the history, traditions, and national characteristics of the Japanese while retaining the universal principles of democracy and freedom.

Against the background of these ideological developments, liberal and conservative political ideologies have been reflected in liberal and conservative judicial ideologies because Japanese judges share these political ideologies with policy makers to a large degree. Particularly, the influence of political conservatism upon judicial conservatism is significant.

The wartime government relied most often on the Peace Preservation Code of 1925 to hold criminally liable a person who tried to change national polity or aid the Comintern and the Japan Communist Party. Some judges construed, without examining the presence of a clear and present danger deriving from such an act, objectives of the law so broadly as to penalize a person for having intended to support an association organized to effect peaceful changes of national policy or even for having inadvertently aided either the Comintern or the Japan Communist Party.[22] Yoichi Wada of *World Culture (sekaibunka)*, a popular magazine, was convicted on his testimony that he might have unconsciously entertained the idea of realizing a communist society in Japan. Osamu Kuno, a victim of the same law, recalls that judges often were more protective of moral standards and the national religion than guardians of legal order. A journal editor of Kyoto University Poem and leaders of the Holiness Christian Church were convicted respectively on the basis of their confessions exacted by torture.

Many older judges are said to retain the bureaucratic and artisan type of mindset, all inherited from conservative legal antecedents.[23] Authoritarian attitudes and the lack of human rights awareness are believed to be widespread among judges who were trained under the Meiji judicial system. Those judges readily agree with and even follow the political branches, and are unsympathetic toward the people. They often rationalize the supremacy of the government over the people on a supra-rational basis. Referring to a judge who was reluctant to dismiss an involuntary confession of an accused, former Judge Sasaki cites a judge saying that he cannot reject the defendant's confession under the circumstances in which the police deny the defendant's complaint about forced confession which the accused properly signed and sealed. Emphasizing that judges, as part of the Japanese bureaucracy who tend to interpret law from the standpoint of the governing body, Sasaki explains the underlying bureaucratic attitude of such a judge as follows:[24] public servants can be more trusted than a defendant or any other ordinary citizen, including defense counsel. As an agent of the state, a policeman or public prosecutor would not force a confession. Such a judge may even try to protect a policeman and prosecutor because he is just as much afraid of admitting any mistakes committed by his bureaucratic colleagues as his own. Judges of the Great Court of Cassation and the administrative court acted like bureaucrats and were probably biased in favor of government at the expense of civil rights.[25]

The prosecutor in the pre-1945 period dressed like a judge, housed and trained with a judge, and sat at the same level as a judge in a court. A prosecutor, who had been regarded until 1874 as something like the Tokugawa inspector, enjoyed a great deal of discretion in handling criminal complaints and conducting pretrial investigations. The judicial bias, especially during the prewar period, in favor of prosecutors can be partly explained by the prosecutors' function of more frequent, more intensive, and more extensive interactions with judges.

After 1945 the attorney general assigned all government arguments in the Supreme Court among members of his staff, and argued important cases himself. Since the Cabinet is held responsible to the Diet for domestic peace, law, and order, it can influence the prosecutor's work through the justice minister who has jurisdiction over the prosecutor's office, as was exemplified by the cabinet interference in the prosecutors' investigations in the 1954 shipbuilders payoff scandal. Some critics charge that in criminal proceedings a judge maintains friendly attitudes toward prosecutors while being hostile toward the defense counsel.[26] Yet the "situational bias" in favor of prosecutors may be much weaker today because judges are no longer under the control of the ministry of justice.[27] The artisan type of judicial skill has been cherished among many judges of the old generation. There still exists a feeling among judges that what gives a trial prestige and public confidence is the legal experience vital to the correct way of writing the decision, and that legal techniques can be mastered only through experience.

Even today intensive training of the JRTI turns out highly skilled legal technicians. Consequently, some judges would show little interest in improving their techniques of fact-finding. Heavy reliance on their common sense, if not hunch, and routine, cursory fact-finding result in misjudgment when handling unfamiliar types of cases, thus impairing the rights of the criminally accused person. According to the 1969 work of James Dator, who measured attitudes of Japanese high court judges by questionnaire methods, traditional Japanese values are the main cause of judicial conservatism.[28] Included in the traditional values are the superiority of adults over children, the superiority of the Japanese over the Koreans, male superiority, intellectual superiority, and traditional ethics and religion. For instance, reflecting the history of Japanese traditional views on sex, 87 percent of the high court judges responded that men should be allowed greater sexual freedom than women. Furthermore, 96 percent of judges held that ethical education, which was banned by the American occupation government and remained proscribed until the mid-1960s, should be reintroduced in the public schools. Dator found the Japanese judges to be essentially conservative, and several judges to be very conservative, while finding no one who scored at the very liberal end of the scale. This may be a function of the conservative legal culture in Japan. Yet, he is reluctant to conclude that the Japanese judges are more or less conservative than American judges and much less willing to declare how much more or less. Be that as it may, cultural antecedents seem to wield pervasive influence in determining the conservative tendencies of judicial behavior in Japan.

Footnotes to Chapter Six

1. Glendon A. Schubert, *The Judicial Minds: The Attitudes and Ideologies of Supreme Court Justices; 1946-1963*, Evanston, Ill.: Northwestern University Press, 1965, pp. 16–28.

2. *Hanrei Jiho*, No. 52, 1955, p. 1.

3. *Takeuchi et al v. Japan;* Sup. Ct., G.B.; June 22, 1955; 9 *Keishu* 1189.

4. 71 *Saibanshu Keiji* 313.

5. *Yoshino et al v. Japan;* Sup. Ct., G.B.; 8 *Keishu* 1461.

6. Sup. Ct., G.B.; March 15, 1950; 4 *Keishu* 335.

7. Sup. Ct., G.B.; January 20, 1954; 8 *Keishu* 41.

8. Sup. Ct., G.B.; October 31, 1956; 10 *Minshu* 1355.

9. Monetary Debt Provisional Mediation Code of 1932, Article 19, Paragraph 2, reads that upon unsuccessful mediation by the mediation board as stipulated in Article 7, Paragraph 1, a court, if it deems it proper, may hear the board's opinions under its own authority, weigh both parties' interests fairly, take into its consideration the nature of work and resources, processing fees, down payment a debtor has paid, and all other circumstances, and may change deadlines for interest and other terms of liability in lieu of mediation. A court may not order the payment of liabilities or relinquishment of other financial assets.

10. Sup. Ct., G.B.; July 6, 1960; 14 *Minshu* 1657.

11. Sup. Ct., G.B.; January 25, 1956; 112 *Saibanshu Keiji* 131; or 10 *Keishu* 105.

12. Reed C. Lawlor, "What computers can do: Analysis and prediction of judicial behavior," in *American Bar Association Journal*, Vol. XLIX, 1963, pp. 337–344.

13. Guido de Ruggiero, *The History of European Liberalism*, Boston, Mass: Beacon Press, 1964, pp. 348–369.

14. Dan F. Henderson, *Op. Cit.*, "Law and political modernization in Japan," pp. 421–422.

15. Soichi Sasaki, "Kokka koi no junsui gokensei ni taisuru saikosaibansho no ketteiken" (The Supreme Court's power to issue abstract judgment on the constitutionality of state governance), in 61 *Hogaku Ronso* 4, 1955, pp. 1–30. See in contrast, Tatsukichi Minobe, *Kempo Gairon* (An Outline of the Constitution), Tokyo: Yuhikaku, 1966, pp. 192–194.

16. Masayasu Hasegawa, "Kempogakushi" (A history of constitutional studies), in Nobushige Ukai *et al* (eds.), *Nihon Kindaiho Hattatsushi* (Development of Modern Japanese Law), Vol. 9, Tokyo: Keiso Shobo, 1960, p. 211.

17. Frank O. Miller, *Op. Cit.*, *Minobe Tatsukichi*, p. 194.

18. Lawrence W. Beer, "The public welfare standard and freedom of expression in Japan," in Dan F. Henderson (ed.), *The Constitution of Japan: Its First Twenty Years, 1947-67*, Seattle, Wash.: University of Washington Press, 1968, p. 201.

19. John M. Maki, "Documents of Japan's commission on the Constitution," in Dan F. Henderson (ed.), *Ibid.*, *The Constitution of Japan*, p. 279.

20. Haruhiro Fukui, "Twenty years of revisionism," in Dan F. Henderson (ed.), *Op. Cit.*, *The Constitution of Japan*, p. 41.

21. Haruhiro Fukui, *Ibid.*, p. 44.

22. See Shigeo Hatanaka, *Showa Shuppan Dan'atsu Shoshi* (Brief History of the Suppression of the Press in the Showa Era), Tokyo: Tosho Shimbun, 1977.

23. Naoki Kobayashi, *Op. Cit.*, *Nihonkoku Kempo no Mondai Jyokyo*, p. 212.

24. Tetsuzo Sasaki, *Saibankanron* (On Judges), Kyoto: Horitsu Bunkasha, 1960, p. 69.

25. Ushijiro Sato, *Kempo* (The Constitution), Tokyo: Nihon Hyoronsha, 1936, p. 188.

26. Morio Miyahara, "Saiban katei niokeru bengoshi no yakuwari" (The role of lawyers in the judicial process), in Takeyoshi Kawashima (ed.), *Hoshakaigaku koza* Vol. 8, *Shakai to Ho*, Tokyo: Iwanami Shoten, 1973, p. 292. See also Yoshio Ideya, "Kensatsukan kara mita saibankan" (Judges as seen by prosecutors), in *Jurisuto* No. 265, January 1963.

27. Eigoro Aoki, "Saibankan no hoishiki" (The law consciousness of judges), in *Hogaku Semina* No. 76, July 1962, pp. 2–9.

28. James Dator, "Measuring attitudes across cultures: A factor analysis of the replies of Japanese judges to Eysenck's inventory of conservative-progressive ideology," in Schubert and Danelski (eds.), *Op. Cit., Comparative Judicial Behavior*, p. 98.

CHAPTER 7

Judicial Administration

1. Administrative Functions of the Supreme Court

The significance of judicial administration lies in its potential impact on judicial adjudication. Administrative rule making could very well affect the judicial decision making in a courtroom. A fear has often been expressed that the Supreme Court, singly or jointly with judge-bureaucrats in the general secretariat and lower courts, adversely influences the free exercise of the judicial power by lower court judges. According to Naoki Kobayashi, the increasing bureaucratic control of courts has allowed senior judges trained under the Meiji constitution to influence judges of a new generation who are oriented to the new democratic constitutional ideals. In his words, "If prejudice and dogmatic judgments at the top of the judicial hierarchy put psychological pressure on lower court judges, the judiciary will start drifting away from the new constitutional spirit."[1] Whereas senior judges are believed to reveal the legal value judgments acquired through their prewar education and training, a new generation of judges tends to reflect the constitutional ideals of democracy, pacifism, and human rights. As will be revealed shortly in the Hiraga Memorandum incident, pervasive influence can also be wielded by a lower court director or president in favor of judicial restraint and conservatism. Although steadily increasing in number, the new generation of judges is said to be still dominated by the older generation of top judge-administrators. While these contrasts of prewar and postwar judges may be somewhat overdrawn, we examine here administrative decision making and its potential impact on judicial adjudication within the Japanese judiciary.

Judicial administration under the Meiji constitution was structured in such a way that the courts were under the control of the minister of justice within the executive branch, on matters of the judicial budget, and the appointment and promotion of judges. As part of their efforts to establish judicial independence, allied occupation authorities transferred the jurisdiction over judicial administration from the justice minister to the Supreme Court.[2] The judicial reform deliberation council, created by the justice minister, recommended at the August 8, 1946, subcommittee meeting that the budgets for both the courts and the justice ministry be prepared and submitted by the justice minister and be appropriated from separate accounts of the national budget. However, GHQ,SCAP rejected the recommendation and assigned to the Supreme Court the task of preparing the budget for the entire courts and submitting it directly to the Diet.

Likewise, GHQ,SCAP placed under the jurisdiction and supervision of the Supreme Court the newly established Judicial Research and Training Institute (JRTI), contrary to the subcommittee's recommendation that the justice minister keep control over it. Finally, administrative functions of the Supreme Court, as stipulated in Article 77 of the Constitution, have been expanded to include: 1) the rules of procedure and practice, 2) the rules governing attorneys and public prosecutors, 3) internal discipline of the courts and the administration of judicial affairs, and 4) the appointment and transfer of lower court judges.

The Supreme Court performs its administrative functions in its judicial conference, which is composed of all fifteen justices. The Chief Justice convenes and presides over its meeting, the quorum of which is nine. A decision is made by a simple majority vote of those justices who are present, and the Chief Justice breaks tie votes if necessary. The judicial conference was initially held once every month in a closed session. In 1953 a standing committee, made up of a Chief

Justice and one justice from each of the three petty benches, was created to expedite a growing number of routine administrative matters, but except during the Court's summer vacation, it has been less utilized than before. The plenary session began meeting every Wednesday, instead of monthly.

The Court Code, in Article 13, established the general secretariat within the Supreme Court to assist administrative functions of the Court (Supreme Court Rules 5 and 10 of 1947). Headed by a secretary general and a vice-secretary general, the supporting organ has 7 bureaus and 28 divisions, staffed by over 750 personnel. The general secretariat assists the Supreme Court justices in almost every aspect of judicial administration: 1) it prepares, prints, and distributes trial materials for both petty and grand benches; 2) it drafts proposals of procedures, processes and court structures to be decided by the judicial conferences; 3) it prepares the appointment and transfer of lower court judges as well as the budgetary and fiscal matters of all the courts; 4) it prepares conferences for judges and other court personnel at all levels; and 5) it implements the decisions of the judicial conferences.

A Supreme Court Chief Justice spends most of his time on judicial administration. Top officials of the general secretariat have also been instrumental in making a wide range of administrative decisions, thereby affecting adjudicative functions of both the Supreme Court and the lower courts. The secretary general attends the judicial conferences, and the vice-secretary general and heads of bureaus and divisions also brief the judicial conferences from time to time. The bureau and division heads of personnel are always present whenever the judicial conference deals with personnel matters. Referring to the pervasive influence of judicial bureaucrats, former Justice Shunzo Kobayashi complained in 1959 that the general secretariat thwarted structural reform plans which had been supported by the majority of justices.

The general secretariat regularly organizes seminars for lower court judges to study judicial precedents established by other courts on civil, criminal, and administrative cases. It chooses topics for seminars, collects judicial precedents, directs discussions, and summarizes conclusions of seminars. Directly or indirectly the civil, criminal, family, or administrative bureau of the general secretariat has been in a position to affect the judicial decision making of lower court judges.

Procedural rules made by the Supreme Court should be considered as an important influence on judicial decision making. As Jerome Frank argued, both substantive and procedural laws may be looked at as "procedural" in the sense that they are all merely weapons in the courtroom fight, and procedural laws are known to affect substantive laws and the outcome of judicial decision making. The old Court Organization Code in Article 125, Paragraph 1 conferred upon the minister of justice the authority to make rules of conduct for the courts and prosecutors' offices, and to oversee the Great Court of Cassation. The Supreme Court, however, has been given directly by the new Constitution (Article 77) the authority and responsibility to make two types of rules. One deals with internal operations including the assignment of lower court judges, discipline of judicial personnel, and the jurisdiction of both the Supreme Court and lower courts. The other deals with the procedure and practice of the courts such as Civil Litigation Rules and Domestic Non-litigation Rules, as well as matters relating to practicing attorneys and public prosecutors.

To what extent a rule can be made by the Court to supplement legislative codes like rules of evidence remains unclear. Initially the Supreme Court's rule-making power was not believed to be subordinate to the Diet's legislative power, but now it is generally believed that it is up to the Diet to make new rules for the courts. The Supreme Court has been extremely reluctant to initiate new rules either for itself or for the lower courts. But, in reality important rules of both kinds have been made by the Court. Fully aware of the significance of procedural rules in judicial decision making, the Court has taken special care not to let procedural rules adversely affect substantive rule making which is reserved for the legislature. Whenever the judicial conference of the Supreme Court has made important procedural rules, it has invited reactions from judges, prosecutors, attorneys, scholars, and government agencies.

The Criminal Litigation Rules (Supreme Court Rule 32) of 1948 have significantly supplemented the Criminal Litigation Code. The constitutional rights of the criminally accused persons, however, have been left to law instead of a Supreme Court Rule. Upholding the provision of Article 218 of the Supreme Court Criminal Procedural Rule which allowed a trial court to cite from a prosecutor's indictment a defendant's alleged criminal act, the Court in *Otaki et al v. Japan* (1953)[3] ruled that the Criminal Procedural Rule did not change the meaning of the provision of Article 335, Paragraph 1 of the Criminal Procedural Code which required a court to cite an alleged criminal act whenever it convicted an accused. In the opinion of the Court, the code did not restrict the manner in which a court cited such factual relations.[4]

The Supreme Court may delegate to lower courts the power to make their own rules. But the Supreme Court has delegated little of the rule-making power stipulated in Article 77 to the judicial conferences of the lower courts. Initially all lower court judges participated in administrative rule making of their courts as members of their own judicial conferences. They advised the Supreme Court in the selection of their department heads who, in turn, would assign cases and administrative tasks to each judge. However, participatory decision making by all lower court judges in administrative matters came under criticism as being dysfunctional. First, some judges were found to be inept at administrative matters. Second, collective decision making by a large group of judges sometimes slowed down administrative functions and added to an already overburdened judge's trial work load. Finally, the Supreme Court decided to establish a line of administrative command and responsibility within a lower court as well as between the Supreme Court and the lower courts. Thus, the Supreme Court judicial conference in 1955 revised Rule 10 of the Inferior Courts Business Disposition, and transferred the authority of the judicial conference to the president and director of each high court, district court, and family court.[5] Ever since then presidents and directors of lower courts have come to assume the task of recommending judicial appointments and also acting as channels through which the Supreme Court disseminates its own instructions and information to all lower court judges. This revision of Rule 10 widened the separation between adjudicative and administrative functions among lower court judges.

Concentration of administrative power in the hands of the Supreme Court Chief Justice, high-ranking judge-bureaucrats of the Supreme Court general secretariat and the directors and presidents of lower courts have created a judicial environment in which administrative functions have come to be regarded as more prestigious and important than adjudicative functions, and in which an appointment to an administrative position has come to be highly valued by many judges as a promotion. This is not something new because many judges used to identify their career goals with appointment to and promotion in an administrative position within the justice ministry in prewar days. Although judges are no longer under the administrative control of the minister of justice, the recruitment policy of administrative personnel within the judiciary has revived much of the influence of prewar judicial bureaucrats who have retained their administrative grip over judicial adjudication. Consequently, the initial composition of the general secretariat consisted largely of bureaucrats of the prewar justice ministry. Except for the first secretary general Kiichi Honma, lawyer and professor at Hitotsubashi University in Tokyo, the secretaries general have predominantly been recruited from among bureaucrats in the general secretariat or the former justice ministry.

Bureaucratization of judicial administration is reinforced by another personnel policy of shifting "elite" judges between administrative and adjudicative assignments. On the one hand, one of a small number of competent judges is appointed chief judge of a district court and then promoted to presiding judge in a high court of their own. A still smaller number of career judges are lucky enough to become presidents of high courts of their own. Often judges and assistant judges of high

Judicial Administration

courts, district courts, or summary courts in major metropolitan areas, particularly Tokyo, have been appointed to such important administrative positions as vice-secretary general or bureau chiefs of the general secretariat. On the other hand, many high ranking judge-bureaucrats in the general secretariat have returned to full-time judgeships in important, centrally located courts. Ex-secretary generals, for instance, rank equally with a high court president in the metropolis, and most of the vice-secretary generals, department heads, and personnel section chiefs become secretary generals or even chief judges of high courts. Some of them have become Supreme Court justices or even Chief Justice. Specifically Masatoshi Yokota (third Chief Justice) and Kazuto Ishida (fourth Chief Justice) came to the Supreme Court with backgrounds as high judicial bureaucrats. Finally, a small number of newly recruited judges is believed to be earmarked for the future judicial elite such as high court president and Supreme Court justice. They are posted near the Supreme Court, and are appointed judges in Tokyo. When they are transferred to remote places like Hokkaido, they are soon called back to Tokyo. Sometimes they are appointed judicial administrators in the Supreme Court general secretariat, instructors at JRTI, or *chosakan* for Supreme Court justices.

These personnel policies have caused the emergence of tightly knit working relationships between the Supreme Court judicial conference and the top echelon of both judge-administrators in the general secretariat and the lower courts. Their common interest in judicial administration sets them apart from a large majority of judges whose primary function lies in courtroom adjudication. This practice often affects the attitude of rank and file judges engaged in adjudication. Some are resigned to their lot and accept it. Others have become increasingly dissatisfied and begun to behave defiantly and recalcitrantly even against Supreme Court precedents, the informal doctrine of *stare decisis* notwithstanding. Ideological differences between the top judicial administrators and some new radical judges became magnified and came to assume political tones as the international politics surrounding Japan became intensified in the late 1940s and early 1950s. The

255

ideological confrontation between the two groups manifested itself in the disciplinary problems of lower court judges as well as the appointment and reappointment of the latter.

2. Judicial Decision Making and Activist Judges

The Supreme Court judicial conference is empowered by the Court Code (Article 80, Item 1) to supervise judicial proceedings and the personnel of the lower courts so long as it does not interfere with nor restrict an adjudicative function of lower court judges (Article 81). In a few instances the Supreme Court has taken supervisory actions and in so doing has invited wide criticism that it has impaired the judicial independence of lower court judges.

Such was the case in the Osaka district court trial in the *Suita* case[6] and the Supreme Court reaction to it. This incident took place against the general background of a series of widespread disturbances by leftist groups designed to turn the courtroom into a political arena for their cause, and heated debates over the tightening of order in the courtroom. On June 25, 1952, in the midst of the Korean War, a group of radicals affiliated with the Japan Communist Party and sympathetic with North Korea clashed with police near Suita City of Osaka. One hundred and eleven leftist rioters were arrested and later charged with causing a public disturbance. While their mass public trial was underway, presiding Judge Tetsuzo Sasaki of the Osaka district court, upon the strong demand by the defendants and sympathizers among the audience, allowed them to applaud and pray for the victory of North Korea during the trial. He was aware that he could declare them in contempt of court for obstruction of a court proceeding, which would have made the demonstrators subject to one year or less of confinement and/or a fine of up to 4,000 yen. He could have also requested the mobilization of police to maintain order in the courtroom, as happened in the case of the Tokyo University riot trial of 1969.[7]

The Osaka district prosecutors immediately reported, with

taped and stenographic proceedings of the trial, Judge Sasaki's action to the Supreme Court and the supreme prosecutor in Tokyo.[8] While the proceedings in the Suita trial were still going on, the Supreme Court judicial conference headed by Chief Justice Kotaro Tanaka on September 26, 1953, issued to all the judges of lower courts a memorandum entitled "On the Prestige of the Courtroom." In the memorandum the Supreme Court stated as follows:[9]

> Last June during a public hearing of the *Suita* case at the Osaka district court, many defendants and spectators prayed and applauded. The presiding Judge Tetsuzo Sasaki had no intention of stopping such conduct but let them continue with it. We have taken every opportunity to stress the importance of maintaining order inside a courtroom, one of the serious problems within the judiciary, and also told all the judges of techniques to cope with this kind of problem. In the light of it, Judge Sasaki's conduct in the *Suita* trial is regrettable. This should present an opportunity to consider the danger that a judge who presides over a proceeding in a courtroom can impair the prestige of a court, the authority of law, and the public respect for law. This memorandum, however, should not be construed to affect by any means the ongoing *Suita* trial.

Many judges, lawyers, and legal scholars took this Supreme Court memorandum as an act of administrative interference with Judge Sasaki, and expressed their concern over the ramifications of this administrative guidance. At the same time, this incident in the *Suita* trial reflects significant developments of judicial ideologies among Japanese judges.

Kotaro Tanaka was appointed by Prime Minister Shigeru Yoshida of the Liberal Party (predecessor of the LDP) as a new Supreme Court Chief Justice in March 1950, a few months before the outbreak of the Korean War. Coupled with the 1949 communist takeover of China, the Korean War sharpened the confrontation between the American occupation authorities and the Japanese government, on the one hand, and leftist groups, on the other. The GHQ's Red purge was followed by communist demonstrations against the Yoshida Cabinet, as exemplified in the Sunagawa and Matsukawa incidents.[10] Later on, the Tokyo ordinance to regulate leftist radical activities was met by massive riots and disturbances against the proposed revision of the United States-Japan security treaty, eventually forcing the resignation of Prime Minister Nobusuke Kishi in 1960. Soon after his appointment in 1950, Chief Justice Tanaka began to make distinctively political pronouncements. Often quoted is his 1952 annual New Year's address to the judicial conference of directors and presidents of the lower courts, which read, in part, as follows:[11]

> The red imperialism of communism has expanded beyond the place of its origin and started to reveal its ambition to conquer the world. Although disguised as a pseudo-science, it is no less authoritarian and despotic than Nazi fascism. No time has been more dangerous than the present to human beings. Fortunately, many peace-and freedom-loving nations began uniting themselves to prevent invasions by the vicious international gangsters. . . . Anyone who believes in neutrality must be criticized for his lack of moral belief because goodness, justice, and freedom can never be compromised with evil, injustice, and slavery. Suppose a burglar breaks into our neighborhood and rapes women; can we be allowed to stand by idly in fear of getting involved?

The end of the occupation in 1952 touched off heated debates on constitutional revisions ranging from the no-war clause (Article 9) to the entire document. Particularly, prewar politicians and bureaucrats within the LDP advocated a reintroduction in the 1947 Constitution of traditional values and nationalistic ideology. The above-quoted statement of Chief Justice Tanaka has been taken by many people to strongly reflect the anti-communist, conservative ideology of Prime Minister Yoshida and his Liberal Party. It should be also noted that the inauguration of the Tanaka Court coincided with the retirement of liberal judges like Tsuyoshi Mano, Katsushige Kotani, Shunzo Kobayashi, and Tadaichiro Tanimura who had been appointed by the Socialist Katayama Cabinet in 1947.

As if to counter the anti-communist ideology and judicial restraint of the Tanaka Court, some 270 young lawyers, scholars, and judges organized the junior legal association (JLA) (*seinen horitsu kyokai*) in 1954. Their objective was to defend the 1947 Constitution against what they perceived to be reactionary revisionist attempts. By 1971 JLA membership had grown to over 2,150 (1,500 lawyers, 230 judges, 170 or more JRTI trainees, 250 scholars and intellectuals). This steady growth was reflected in the judicial behavior of some lower courts in that 43 percent of lawyers, judges, and prosecutors were graduated from JRTI by 1965, and that during 1969 and 1970 some trial court judges of this new breed made a series of libertarian, anti-governmental decisions in cases involving such politically hot issues as public safety ordinances, labor management disputes, and the United States-Japan security treaty.

The active administrative role of the Tanaka Court and the general secretariat was strengthened and even institutionalized by Chief Justice Kazuto Ishida in the late 1960s and early 1970s. The Ishida Court took a series of disciplinary actions against eight JLA-affiliated judges in 1970. Between 1970 and 1976, twenty-four trainees were denied appointment to judgeships, of which seventeen were JLA members. On May 2, 1970, Ishida told the press that a person who was an ultranationalist, nihilist, militarist, or communist was not qualified to be a desirable type of judge, at least as a matter of ethics,[12] and urged an extremely careful use of judicial review. Ishida apparently had in mind some judges who were affiliated with the leftist-oriented JLA. Article 52, Paragraph 1 of the Court Code prohibits a judge to hold an office in the Diet or any other public offices. The LDP's judicial committee contemplated amending the Court Code to forbid judges from party membership and any political activities. It is not clear, however, whether the contemplated amendment would keep him from becoming an active member of a political party. On June 29, 1970, this remark of Ishida was made the grounds for an impeachment lodged against him by twenty-nine legal scholars and lawyers who complained that his remarks against "ists" threatened judicial freedom of thought and conscience. Also, a petition containing the signature of 2,208 lawyers demanding Ishida's resignation was submitted to the Supreme

Court by a group called the liaison conference to protect judicial independence. Like all previous attempts to impeach justices, this charge against Chief Justice Ishida was dismissed by the Diet impeachment committee.

Some JRTI trainees staged a protest demonstration against the Supreme Court action denying appointment of some judge trainees by reasons of their membership in JLA. On the occasion of the JRTI's commencement ceremony in 1970, Tokuo Sakaguchi, one of the graduating trainees, snatched a microphone away from Director Tadashi Morita, who was about to make a commencement address, and proceeded to discuss discriminatory actions of the Supreme Court. He was dismissed on the same day by the Supreme Court for this disruptive action. The Supreme Court action was quickly endorsed by both the general secretariat and the judicial conference of directors and presidents of the lower courts. Secretary General Kishi echoed Chief Justice Ishida by stating that a judge who joined a political organization might create suspicions in the public mind that his judgment might be biased by his political ideology. He urged the judges to hold themselves to a position of strict neutrality lest their courtrooms and judicial process should become arenas in which political opposition to government policies were carried out. This was followed by the unanimous resolution by the national judicial conference of high, district, and family courts that judges should withdraw from JLA. The resolution forced ten assistant judges attached to the Supreme Court general secretariat to leave the association.

Various critical reactions followed immediately from many quarters. On the one hand, the Japan Federation of Employers backed up the Supreme Court by denouncing its action as exposing the subversive character of JLA. On the other hand, the Japan Science Council deplored the Court's action as a violation of judicial freedom, and the General Council of Japan Labor Unions launched a nationwide campaign against the reactionary judiciary. The Federation of Japan Bar Associations, although split between young activists and older or moderate members, issued an official statement that the Court should not discriminate on the basis of thought, creed, or association and should disclose its reasons for the suspected discriminatory action taken against JLA members. These critics feared a trend toward domination of judicial administration over judicial adjudication, which would determine, from the top down, undesirable judicial thought. Undaunted by these criticisms, Chief Justice Ishida on May 1, 1971, defended his action and criticized "abusive and defamatory remarks intended to arouse suspicion of the judiciary." The secretary general also protested what he called interference with the independent exercise of judicial administration.

3. Judicial Administration In Turmoil

The Ishida Court came under severe attack in the spring of 1971, when Yasuaki Miyamoto, an assistant judge of the Kumamoto district court, was denied reappointment as a district court judge although no fewer than four other judges affiliated with JLA were reappointed. According to Article 80, Paragraph 1 of the Constitution, "the judges of the inferior courts shall be appointed by the Cabinet from a list of persons nominated by the Supreme Court and such judges shall have ten-year terms of office and shall be eligible for reappointment. . . ." An established practice of the Supreme Court has been that the Court nominates no more persons than the number of judgeships necessary to fill vacant posts with the result that the Cabinet will not be given latitude to pick and choose among the nominees. Moreover, in preparing a list of nominees for lower court judgeships, the Court retains complete discretion in nominating or rejecting whomever it pleases, and its discretion is virtually nonreviewable by the political branches of the government.

It was widely speculated that Miyamoto was not reappointed because of his membership in JLA, but the secretary general refused to respond to Miyamoto's request for reasons why his name was not submitted to the Cabinet for reappointment. Granted the complete discretion of the Court in handling the Miyamoto case, many court observers have come to express doubts on whether the Court has given the rejected nominee due process. A series of mass meetings were held in Tokyo and elsewhere, including scholars, lawyers, students, and concerned citizens to safeguard the Constitution and judicial prestige, demanding a disclosure of reasons behind the denied reappointment. The judicial committee of the House of Representatives summoned Secretary General Yoshida and the personnel director, but both men declined to give the Court's reason for non-reappointment. When the opposition parties like the Japan Socialist Party and the Clean Government Party of the House of Councillors moved to summon Chief Justice Kazuto Ishida for questioning, the LDP members blocked them. Indeed, it was the lack of an impression of fairness which attracted the attention of many Japanese to the Miyamoto case. In 1972 all judicial applicants for reappointment were approved except for one member who withdrew his application apparently in fear that he could not be reappointed because of his membership with JLA. Charles Stevens states a ramification of the Miyamoto case as follows:[13]

> The career nature of Japanese judges would probably mean that Miyamoto, once rejected for reappointment, has lost his chosen life's career as a judge although he may still be able to become a practicing attorney. Denying him any statement of the reason for non-reappointment seems to have impaired whatever respect the Court has enjoyed among the public as an impartial and fair tribunal.

If the non-reappointment of Assistant Judge Miyamoto reflected the Supreme Court's displeasure with leftist-oriented judges, the Hiraga Memorandum incident, and the impeachment and dismissal of Assistant Judge Shiro Kito of Kyoto district court seemed to depict the Court's embarrassment with rightist judges. The Kito incident resulted from the Lockheed Aircraft Company's payoff scandal. Former Prime Minister Kakuei Tanaka was suspected as a recipient of a payoff and was arrested on July 27, 1976, on the charge of a violation of the Foreign Currency Code. Shortly afterward the United States justice department handed over to the Miki government a confidential listing of those high-ranking Japanese officials who allegedly were involved in the payoff scandal. The Japanese press quickly reported that Yasuhiro Nakasone, LDP secretary general and a political ally of Prime Minister Takeo Miki, was included in the list, thereby raising a doubt about the credibility of Prime Minister Miki who had vowed to get to the bottom of the scandal.

Against this background, a man who identified himself as Supreme Prosecutor Fuse made a phone call to Miki's residence and sought the Prime Minister's instructions concerning the ongoing Lockheed payoff criminal investigations. Specifically, he wanted to extract from Miki a word that the Prime Minister would intervene in the ongoing investigations and prosecute former Prime Minister Tanaka but not Secretary General Nakasone. The caller recorded the entire conversation, which lasted almost an hour. Shortly afterward Shiro Kito, a forty-three-year old assistant judge of Kyoto district court, contacted the *Yomiuri* Press in Tokyo, indicating that he had a tape containing the phone conversation between Supreme Prosecutor Fuse and Prime Minister Miki, and would like to meet some *Yomiuri* reporters to play back the tape for them. Following such a meeting with two *Yomiuri* reporters in the Palace Hotel room in Tokyo on August 10, 1976, Kito was arrested as a man who made the fake call to Miki and was criminally charged. Kito was also charged with a gross violation of professional duties, excessive negligence of his professional responsibilities, and a reprehensible act resulting in a loss of his dignity as a judge. At the hearings conducted by the Supreme Court, Kito denied the charge that he was the man who made the fake call.

Whereas a judge can be dismissed for reasons of mental or physical incompetency, public impeachment (Article 78 of the Constitution), or popular review (Article 79, Paragraph 2), Kito was formally arraigned for an indictment and impeachment by Diet.[14] In conformity to the Diet Code each House appointed seven members to act as judges of the impeachment court, and appointed an equal number of members to act as members of the judicial indictment committee. Each House also appointed ten members and five alternate members to the judicial indictment committee and seven regular and four alternate members to the judicial impeachment court.

The indictment committee began non-public investigations, called witnesses, and subsequently indicted Kito for impeachment by a two-thirds majority vote of the committee members present, as required by law. Then a fourteen-man impeachment committee conducted a public hearing attended by the accused judge, who elected to represent himself for defense. Any dismissal or disciplinary judgment can only be entered after a statement of the affected judge has been heard, and any such judgment must be based upon proof and accompanied with reasons. Accordingly, the committee summoned and cross-examined Kito, who often declined to answer the committee's questions, but who implied that he did intend to make a newspaper article out of the taped phony telephone call, a point he did not dispute during the Supreme Court inquiry. The committee also obtained evidence and summoned witnesses with compulsory subpoenas. One of the two *Yomiuri* reporters who had listened to the tape at the Palace Hotel testified before the committee that Kito approached him by saying that he wanted to have it reported in the newspaper. Suspecting the caller was not a real supreme prosecutor, the reporter questioned Kito, who in turn admitted that he had made the call, but asked the reporter not to identify the caller when writing a newspaper article.

According to the committee's findings, Kito had been known for his close associations with an anti-communist, ultra-conservative magazine, *The Comprehensive View (Zembo)* to which he had contributed articles from time to time. He was critical of Prime Minister Miki who was selling out the LDP's conservative causes by exposing former Prime Minister Tanaka and the mainstream of the LDP. Kito saw an opportunity to discredit Miki and force his resignation by fabricating the Prime Minister's intervention and whitewash in the pending criminal investigation of the Lockheed payoff scandal. Fully aware that once made public, the recorded telephone conversation with the supreme prosecutor would raise a doubt about Miki's political credibility and give a deadly blow to

Judicial Administration

Nakasone's political life, Kito deliberately framed Prime Minister Miki by faking the supreme prosecutor's voice and attempted to disrupt national politics.

The impeachment committee concluded that he neglected his judicial duty and gravely impaired the prestige of judges by meddling into politics, as proscribed in Article 49 and Article 52, No. 1 of the Court Code. Whereas any dismissal or disciplinary judgment must be made by a two-thirds majority, the present impeachment committee on March 23, 1977, voted unanimously to impeach and dismiss Kito whose term of office as assistant judge would have expired on April 6, 1977. No further recourse was available as the Tokyo district court earlier[15] dismissed a charge lodged against an accused judge, and ruled that, since the decision of the judge impeachment committee was administrative in nature, a court could not make the committee a defendant nor issue an injunction against it inasmuch as the Judge Impeachment Code did not provide for any complaint against the committee's decision. So, the impeachment and dismissal of Kito had the effect of stripping him of his legal qualifications foreclosing any career as prosecutor or practicing attorney in the future. Be that as it may, following his dismissal, Kito ran unsuccessfully for a seat in the House of Councillors in July 1977, counting on ultraconservative votes!

Granting that the Kito affair was a bizarre and unprecedented event as judicial involvement in politics, critics of the Supreme Court trace the cause of this kind of political activity by an incumbent judge to the biased judicial administration in that the Court has created an environment in which fanatic reactionaries like Assistant Judge Kito could play their political game. One critic[16] accuses the Court of double standards: permissive attitudes toward right-wing judges and an intolerant and severe punishment of leftist judges. The Hiraga Memorandum incident is the case in point. This incident seems to reveal that the Supreme Court placed blame on a wrong party when a lower court director tried to influence his subordinate judge in an ongoing trial involving a national security issue.

Takashi Ito and some 200 farmers at Naganuma in Hokkaido

filed suit with the Sapporo district court seeking a court injunction against the minister of agriculture and forestry to rescind the minister's designation of a tract of land as a national forest reserve where the defense agency had planned to build an air defense force Nike Hercules missile base. In granting a temporary injunction pending the court's ruling on the constitutionality of the proposed missile base in *Ito et al v. Agricultural Minister* (1973),[17] a three-judge bench headed by Chief Judge Shigeo Fukushima upheld the petitioners' contention that the proposed missile base would put the petitioners' livelihoods in jeopardy and that no urgent self-defense needs would justify such a missile installation. The Sapporo high court chaired by Judge Yasoji Koga on August 5, 1976, reversed this decision of the district court and remanded the case for proceedings on the original suit to reverse.[18] In so doing, the high court resorted to the doctrine of state governance barring the standing to sue, without reference to the constitutionality of the Self-Defense Force itself.

Meanwhile, to the great surprise of the public, major newspapers disclosed what was later to be known as the Hiraga Memorandum incident. According to the press, while the Ito case was being tried at the Sapporo district court, Kenta Hiraga, director of the court, sent a memorandum to Presiding Judge Shigeo Fukushima and Assistant Judge Hiroshi Hirata giving them "friendly advice from a senior colleague" on the case. After he publicly announced his decision in the case, Presiding Judge Fukushima brought the memorandum to the attention of his colleagues and the judicial conference of his court. It appears that he held the memorandum in strict confidence until after the sealing of the decision. Both the Sapporo district court and the Supreme Court issued statements regretting that Hiraga exceeded the limit of judicial propriety and brought public doubts upon judicial independence and fairness of a trial. Hiraga was transferred to the Tokyo high court as a disciplinary measure, a measure which looked more like a promotion than a demotion! The Supreme Court also mildly admonished Judge Fukushima when it stated that "judges should not fall into the error of self-importance, but should always be humble enough to try to build up character and competence by exchanging experience and knowledge among themselves."[19] Thereupon the Federation of Bar Associations held a special meeting in protest against the Supreme Court's support for disciplinary action against Judge Fukushima.

At the same time of the reprimand of Director Hiraga by the Supreme Court, a strong defense for him was brought by Shigeto Iimori, a presiding judge at the Kagoshima district court. Judge Iimori has long been known as an outspoken defender of conservative causes, so much so that he invited official discipline from the judicial conference of the Supreme Court in 1961 when he publicly commented on a case in which a boy belonging to a radical right-wing group murdered two family members of the *Chuokoron* Publishing Company president in Tokyo. Also, in 1966 the judicial committee of the House of Representatives took up anti-constitutional remarks which Judge Iimori, then chief judge of the Kagoshima district court, had made in a court bulletin.

In an article published in the LDP organ paper, this time he criticized the Supreme Court for having censored Hiraga and said that over half of the Sapporo district court judges were members of the JLA which he identified as a conspiratorial anti-establishment organization. Judge Iimori was joined by prominent spokesmen for the LDP right-wing Diet members like Tadao Kuraishi and Isoji Tanaka and the Japan Federation of Employers, who all regarded JLA as a source of judicial obstruction and willful exercise of judicial review for radical political causes. Both the Fukuoka high court and the Supreme Court were especially annoyed by Iimori when he stated that Hiraga's action in advising Judge Fukushima was by no means without precedent in judicial decision making.

When the Sapporo high court remanded the present case to Judge Fukushima for a proceeding on an original suit to reverse, the minister of justice sought to have Fukushima removed from the case on the grounds that his membership in JLA would impair judicial fairness, because the group of left-wing attorneys was supporting the cause of the petitioners. The minister was turned down by the Sapporo district court and the high court on the grounds that Fukushima's affiliation with JLA would not impair his uprightness as a judge. Also, the ministry's attempt to have him dismissed was in vain, for he had secured reappointment to a second ten years which was to last until 1977.

Meanwhile, a Diet impeachment court was formed upon the petition entered by the Tokyo and Sapporo Bar Associations, and on October 9, 1976, voted no impeachment against Hiraga but deferred judgment upon Fukushima until it would have in its hands all the returns on an inquiry it had sent to over 200 judges whose membership in JLA was being made a basis for an impeachment inquiry. The majority of the judges who had received such an inquiry refused to respond by not affirming or denying their membership in JLA. Subsequently, the committee chairman stated that although his committee would not draw the conclusion that a failure to respond to the inquiry would automatically imply membership in the association if the judges did not respond, he would have to undertake other means of investigation. The committee dominated by LDP members proceeded to impeach Fukushima on the charge of having violated judicial propriety in publishing the Hiraga memorandum, but suspended the proceedings against him during good behavior. When the Sapporo high court responded to the Diet decision with a similar oral reprimand to him, Judge Fukushima submitted his resignation by stating that the court abandoned judicial independence and bowed to political pressure. After persuasion by his friends and colleagues, he withdrew his resignation and retracted the above statement, although he still refused to comply with a summons from the Diet impeachment committee to testify on the matter of his resignation.

More than the Miyamoto incident or the Kito scandal, the Hiraga Memorandum incident revealed administrative influence upon the substance of an ongoing judicial decision-making matter in a gross manner. Hiraga acknowledged his attempt to influence, and Fukushima perceived such influence. Judging from the final court decision of the influenced, the influencer seemed to have failed to bring about the desired court decision in the *Naganuma Nike Missile Base* case.[20] Whether such an influence had any impact on the final outcome was one issue. Another issue was the propriety of the mere display of administrative interference into an ongoing judicial decision-making matter itself. At the same time, the Supreme Court compounded the problem by imposing a much stiffer disciplinary action against the influenced than the influencer.

4. The Supreme Court and Lower Courts Compared

The provisions of Article 81 confer upon not only the Supreme Court but also lower courts the power of judicial review. Upholding judicial review exercised by the Tokyo high court in *Yanagi v. Japan* (1950)[21] involving violation of the Foodstuff Control Code, the Court was of the opinion that in applying a law or an ordinance to a concrete legal dispute, a judge, whether at the Supreme Court or a lower court level, has both the authority and the responsibility to determine the constitutionality of such a law or an ordinance. But, at the same time, the constitutional judgment by a lower court is subject to Supreme Court review. Interpreting the provision of Article 17, Paragraph 1 of the Code of Criminal Procedural Temporary Measure, which stated in part that a high court judgment made on a first instance court ruling could be *jokoku*-appealed to the Supreme Court only when the constitutionality of a law, order, regulation, or official act was challenged, the Court in *Komatsu v. Japan* (1948)[22] ruled that judicial judgment is included in Articles 81 and 98 of the Constitution.

It is often alleged that the higher a court is, the more conservative and self-restrained it becomes in regard to popular sovereignty, pacifism, and fundamental human rights, all underlying the 1947 Constitution. Judicial conservatism and judicial restraint of the Supreme Court are attributed to not only judicial ideologies but also different judicial processes involved between the lower courts and the Supreme Court. Whereas a lower court, especially a district court, conducts a constitutional litigation centering on fact-findings in oral hearings, the Supreme Court's review of lower court proceedings tends to become abstract and formalistic, often resulting in conservative and self-restrained decisions. Testing of the widely-held allegations would require a comparison of liberal/conservative ideological differences between the Supreme Court and the lower courts.

From time to time the Supreme Court has been criticized for having replaced a prewar justice minister who dominated judicial administration. The cleavage between the Supreme Court and the lower courts is said to be much greater than what the Supreme Court purports to occupy in the judicial hierarchy. As the court of last resort the Supreme Court affects lower courts' decisions through appeals. This type of influence is perfectly justifiable from the very nature of judicial decision making, but a key question is the influence of judicial administration upon a lower court's proceedings in a courtroom. As we saw, the Supreme Court determines the structure, personnel, and operation of the lower courts. In this context the Supreme Court and judge-administrators of lower courts are in the position to adversely affect lower court trials. In view of a strict confidentiality required of judicial decision making in a courtroom, it is not possible to verify any actual influence in a specific case. However, a potential influence can be inferred from the revelation in the Hiraga memorandum of the *Missile Base* case and Judge Iimori's remarks alluding to similar practices among some judges. At the same time, the widely held view that the direction of influence is only from the top down should be examined. After all, judicial policy making is a continuous process of conflict resolution and reallocation of values, goods, and services for the entire political system. Much as the Supreme Court influences lower court policy making, both positive and negative reactions from lower courts could very well serve as a very important input to the Supreme Court's policy making. It would appear that persistent lower court decisions could influence the Supreme Court's decision making on some constitutional issues.

The most notable example of such an influence can be found in the patricide cases. In 1971 the Court reversed its earlier decision established in the *Yamato* case (1950) and this reversal is widely attributed to the decision of the Utsunomiya district court. The Supreme Court grand bench in the *Yamato* case upheld the constitutionality of Article 200 of the Criminal Code, thereby approving discriminatory treatments in patricide. This decision was bitterly criticized by a large majority of scholars. When the Utsunomiya district court defied the *Yamato* ruling and held Article 200 unconstitutional in violation of the equality clause, and applied Article 199 instead, it was applauded by many scholars and the mass media. Although the Tokyo high court reversed the Utsunomiya district court decision on the strength of the *Yamato* ruling, the Supreme Court by this time had changed its membership composition and became more receptive to the strong public reaction supportive of the Utsunomiya district court decision, and gradually and subtly changed its policy on patricide. The Supreme Court basically accepted the judgment of the Utsunomiya district court which held that the provision in the Criminal Code which imposed imprisonment at forced labor for life or for not less than three years, upon a manslaughter committed against a lineal ascendant of the offender or of his or her spouse while imposing an imprisonment at forced labor for not less than two years upon other types of manslaughter, violated the equality clause of the Constitution.

A series of decisions involving public employees' union disputes reveal a mutual influence between the Supreme Court and the lower courts. Several lower courts handed down in 1960 and 1961 decisions all favorable to labor activities of public employees.[23] However, the Supreme Court second petty bench on March 15, 1963, restricted public employees' rights, and invited wide criticism from scholars and organized labor. Then, in defiance of the above-mentioned Supreme Court petty bench ruling, the Niigata high court, Nagaoka branch on February 28, 1964, approved the application of Article 1, Paragraph 2 of the Labor Union Code to public utility employees, thereby allowing collective bargaining and other labor activities of public employees. This lower court ruling was strongly supported by many people, and apparently laid a foundation for the Supreme Court grand bench decision in *Toyama et al v. Japan* (1966),[24] better known as the *Tokyo Central Post Office* case.

Involved in this case were officials of the National Postal Service Labor Union who were charged with inciting a labor disruption of postal workers during the 1958 spring labor offensive for higher wages and better working conditions. The Tokyo district court on March 30, 1962,[25] dismissed the prosecution charge, holding that although Article 17 of the Public Enterprise Labor Relations Code (PELRC) prohibits disputes by public employees, certain kinds of acts are justifiable under Article 1, Paragraph 2 of the Labor Union Code and that the act of failing to carry out postal work, an offense under Article 79 of the Postal Code, is justifiable because the action of the defendants fell in the category of a labor dispute. However, the Tokyo high court[26] reversed the ruling below, on the strength of the 1963 Supreme Court petty bench precedent, and held that Article 17 of the PELRC, and not Article 1, Paragraph 2 of the Labor Union Code, should govern the present case. Reversing this Tokyo high court ruling for a further review, the Supreme Court grand bench called for minimal restrictions of public employees' rights, and minimal penalties for such violators.

This liberal decision was followed in *Hasegawa et al v. Japan* (1969),[27] known as the *Tokyo Teachers Union* case involving the executive chairman and other leaders of the Tokyo Teachers Union, who directed distribution of pamphlets urging a concerted walkout and other forms of sabotage in protest against a teaching evaluation by the board of education. Weighing a balance between the freedom of thought and conscience, freedom of expression, and teachers' rights as workers on the one hand, and teachers' obligations as public employees on the other hand, the Supreme Court grand bench acquitted the defendants on the grounds that their actions were of the kind which normally accompanied labor disputes.

However, four years later the Supreme Court shifted to the conservative direction once again in a labor dispute by union officials of the National Agricultural and Forestry Labor Union, which was a public employees organization. In

Tsurusono et al v. Japan (1973),[28] the Court prohibited labor disputes or any incitement thereof by public employees and subjected them to criminal punishment when the accused incited union members to participate in an on-the-job rally as part of the protest against the proposed revision of the Police Duty Performance Code. Only Justice Irokawa dissented, defending political activities of public employees. This changing of Supreme Court policies is largely due to the change of the Supreme Court's membership, and the change of some justices' opinions, but it is also the result of persistent lower court decisions contrary to Supreme Court policies. Such an influence from below is especially conceivable in constitutional policy making involving highly politicized ideologies. In civil and criminal laws in which many case laws have been established since the Great Court of Cassation, the influence of lower court decisions or scholars' support thereof has not been so visible, but in such new fields as the constitutional law, the administrative law and the labor law and procedural codes thereof, all of which grew under the 1947 Constitution, some lower court judges, particularly younger ones, with the support of legal scholars in these fields, have succeeded in influencing judicial policies of the Supreme Court. Thus, the widely held view that the direction of influence is only from the top down should be qualified by evidence, however little it may be, of influences by lower court judges.

At the same time, liberal decisions of the Supreme Court should also be noted. In *Sudo v. Japan* (1953), *Matsunaga v. Japan* (1958), and the *Konoura* case (1957),[29] all involving manslaughter and theft in Shizuoka prefecture, trial judges in the first and second instance courts adopted police testimony and defense confessions and sentenced the accused in each case to capital punishment or life imprisonment. Upon appeal, the Supreme Court reversed their convictions and remanded each case, thereby acquitting the accused. These cases reveal one thing in common, namely, the inadequacy of judicial fact-findings by trial courts.[30] First, in all of the three cases, judges of the first and second instances failed to question the involuntary confessions the police forced from the accused. Police investigators induced confessions by leading questions, flattery, and even false testimony. Furthermore, the judges of the second instance court failed to examine the accused's complaints about torture and decoy investigation. In all three cases, the accused were arrested months after the alleged crimes. The accused complained that the police forced their confessions on the burglary and homicide charge while they were ostensibly investigating other petty crimes. Second, the court of the second instance failed to suspect the credibility of the forced confession as against the material evidence despite the fact that the accused began to change their story and became increasingly irrational and contradictory. Instead, the changing of confessions was taken as further evidence of the criminals' psychology in trying to evade punishment. Third, the second instance court in each case shifted the burden of proving the involuntary nature of confession to the defense by requiring definite evidence of alleged torture and decoy investigation. Finally, hearings and the court opinions at the second instance courts were extremely poor and biased, partly reflecting the resentment among the local people against the accused in each case.

Ushiomi attributes the libertarian behavior of the Supreme Court in some criminal and labor cases like the *Matsukawa* case (1959) and the *Tokyo Central Post Office* case (1966)[31] to a relatively wide variety of backgrounds of the justices and also to the political sensitivity of the Supreme Court. In his view, a wide variety of social backgrounds of justices, ranging from career judges, ex-practicing attorneys, and ex-prosecutors, to law professors and ex-bureaucrats, can be more susceptible to public sentiment than the career judges of lower courts.

Lower court judges are evaluated partly on the basis of work efficiency of case loads and decisions that can withstand review by a higher court. An upshot of these criteria is to sacrifice quality in favor of quantity of trial and also make lower court judges follow precedents without question. Should they try to do otherwise, it is often said that lower courts render public acts or actions unconstitutional, only to be reversed by the Supreme Court. Against this widely held view, it is revealing to examine the propensity of agreement and disagreement between the Supreme Court and the lower courts, as measured by the incidence with which the former sustains or reverses the latter's decisions.

On the basis of constitutional civil rights and liberties cases found in the abridged Supreme Court reports between 1947 and 1980, the Supreme Court grand bench, when it was unanimous, was found to have sustained decisions below in an overwhelmingly large majority of instances (92 percent); on sociopolitical issues, 161 decisions below were sustained while 15 decisions below were reversed; on socioeconomic issues, 74 decisions below were upheld while only seven decisions below were overruled. Likewise, on the basis of constitutional civil rights and liberties cases found in the unabridged Supreme Court reports, the Supreme Court grand bench, when it was divided, was found to have reversed decisions below in almost half of the cases, i.e., 103 decisions, or 50.4 percent, reversed against 111 decisions, or 49.6 percent, sustained; on sociopolitical issues, the Court reversed 83 decisions below while sustaining 92 decisions; on socioeconomic issues, the Court reversed 20 decisions below while sustaining 19.

Thus, the divided Court reversed decisions below 4.67 times more often than the unanimous Court. This finding, however, should be qualified by much larger numbers of unanimous decisions than those of divided decisions that are not reported in the unabridged Supreme Court reports. It would be fair to say that the Supreme Court agreed with the court below in constitutional litigations more often than the relatively high percentage of reversed decisions might lead us to believe.[32]

An analysis of constitutional cases in the abridged Supreme Court reports indicates that the Supreme Court grand bench, when it was unanimous, was no more conservative or liberal than courts below; it became liberal by overruling them in eleven conservative decisions below (i.e., nine sociopolitical and two socioeconomic ones), and became conservative by reversing eleven liberal decisions below (i.e., six sociopolitical and five socioeconomic ones). According to the same data, the unanimous grand bench was more liberal than courts below on sociopolitical issues at a rate of nine to six, and was more conservative than courts below on socioeconomic issues at a rate of five to two. A similar analysis of divided constitutional decisions reported in the unabridged Supreme Court reports between 1947 and 1980 shows the Supreme Court grand bench to be more liberal than courts below 2.6 times, eighty-two liberal Supreme Court decisions against thirty-one conservative decisions. On sociopolitical issues, the Court was liberal in sixty-four decisions and conservative in nineteen compared to courts below, while on socioeconomic issues the Court was liberal in eighteen decisions and conservative in two of them, rendering the grand bench more liberal than courts below at a rate of 3.3 to 1 on sociopolitical issues and 9 to 1 on socioeconomic issues. Overall, the present analysis would render the Supreme Court grand bench more liberal in relation to lower courts than many Japanese scholars would make us believe.

5. Concluding Remarks

In conclusion, the present work attempted to describe as typically as possible the structure and process of constitutional decision making by the Japanese Supreme Court, and also to explain causal relationships among some basic variables and parameters. We viewed the Supreme Court as a system made up of a set of variables with different degrees of interrelationships among them. We categorized and described both legal and extra-legal variables that influence judicial decision making. In so doing, we have discovered hitherto unnoticed variables and classified existing data into an integrated and meaningful whole.

Yet, while attempting to explain possible causal relationships of variables through empirical research, the present work is still incomplete in correlating the objective reality of judicial process with its empirical referents. For instance, a counsel, through his briefs and oral presentations, can limit or expand judicial selection of alternative judgments and rationalization thereof. Likewise, a lower court can influence the Supreme Court which is sometimes reluctant to change its own precedents unless initiated by a lower court. Probably more than anybody else, *chosakan* are in a position to significantly affect the amount and content of information available to justices, and a justice in charge is also capable of influencing his colleagues. More and more constitutional cases are being disposed of by the petty benches. All these variables are among the more important determinants in Supreme Court decision making, but how they are interrelated and how much they affect the final resolution of constitutional disputes remain unanswered. As we noticed among Japanese court observers, many hypotheses have been formulated generally rather than specifically, so operational definitions are yet to be devised for precise identification and measurement of variables.

If judicial attitudes manifest themselves in divided decisions, rapidly decreasing numbers of divided constitutional decisions make quantitative analyses of judicial attitudes among the Supreme Court justices virtually impossible. Initially, the Supreme Court was busily engaged in constitutional policy making through interpreting and applying the newly enacted constitutional provisions. The Supreme Court grand bench especially was sharply divided on civil rights and liberties. The Mibuchi Court was divided in thirty-one decisions, the K. Tanaka Court was split in 144 decisions and K. Yokota in thirty-two, but after the K. Yokota Court the grand bench drastically decreased its divided decisions. The M. Yokota Court was divided in only three decisions, the Ishida Court in six decisions, and the Murakami and Fujibayashi Courts in two. The Okahara and Hattori Courts produced no divided decisions at all. It seems that by the mid-1970s the Court had very few new civil liberty issues to deal with. Also, with the departure of chief justices with strong personalities and judicially conservative ideologies, like K. Tanaka and K. Ishida, such staunch and vocal liberals like Mano and Irokawa also disappeared.

Conversely, one gets an impression that the traditional mode of consensus-building seems to have become the dominant type of Supreme Court decision making since the mid-1960s. In the absence of the divided Court, the judicial response to a hypothetical case may have to be analyzed to explain the linkage between judicial role expectation and judicial behavior. Thus, research frontiers of theory-building can be further advanced by refining the existing structural/functional model, devising new research techniques, and increasing the empirical data compiled of judicial decision making.

Judicial policy making is a continuous process of conflict resolution and allocation of values for a wider political system. As we saw, the Supreme Court has settled constitutional disputes in a self-restrained manner in relation to political branches, and conservatively in respect to civil rights and liberties. The way the Court has decided constitutional policies has often evoked much reaction, critical and sympathetic, from various quarters. Many progressive constitutional scholars have been highly critical of the Court's sparing use of judicial review and its frequent use of legal concepts that render constitutional issues non-justiciable. They argue that an activist liberal Supreme Court would be by far conducive to advancement of the rule of law and democracy in Japan.

Yet, the judiciary is often dubbed as the weakest branch of all. The Supreme Court might have acted the way it did as self-defense and self-preservation against the much stronger political branches. By upholding the constitutionality of governmental acts and actions, and by favoring law and order at the expense of civil rights and liberties, the Court might have minimized conflicts with Diet and the executives. In so doing, the Court seems to have consolidated itself in the Japanese political system.

At the same time, from the standpoint of system maintenance, the self-restrained, conservative Court has played important roles. Under the long reign of the conservative LDP, the government has single-mindedly devoted itself to political stability and growth of the national economy. Justices have also accepted it as their important role to contribute to the stability of the national polity and socioeconomic goal attainments. Situated at the apex of the judiciary, the Court has resolved societal conflicts to achieve those goals through constitutional litigation.

The Court has also performed other functions like providing legitimacy and generating support for the political system. In many instances the Supreme Court has placed a seal of legitimacy and credibility upon the acts and actions of the political branches. Traditionally the courts, judges, and the law have carried a great deal of prestige and respect among the people. Hence judicial recognition and endorsement of governmental policies enhance the legitimacy and credibility of the government, thereby contributing to the stability of the political system. Often the public trust of the judiciary has been translated into public support of the government and its policies. The court has been one of the most trusted institutions in the country, and judges are among the most respected of professionals. The highly favorable impressions seem to have permeated deeply and widely among the public.

Finally the self-restrained conservative Court has established a considerable degree of predictability toward conflict resolution in the future. In this respect, the Court has increased the stability of law itself. Just like public policies of the political branches, judicial precedents which the Supreme Court has created for the past forty-some years have firmly been embedded in the Japanese civil law tradition, and the self-restrained, conservative tendency of the Court is clearly to stay in Japan for many years to come.

Footnotes to Chapter Seven

1. Naoki Kobayashi, *Op. Cit., Nihonkoku Kempo no Mondai Jyokyo,* p. 155.

2. See Kotaro Tanaka, "Democracy and judicial administration in Japan," in 2 *Japanese International Commission of Jurists* 2, 1959–1960, pp. 7–19.

3. Sup. Ct., 3rd. P.B.; February 10, 1953; 7 *Keishu 199. Likewise, Mori v. Komaki et al* (Sup. Ct., G.B.; July 10, 1958; 12 *Minshu* 1747) ruled that Article 77 of the Constitution is not violated by Article 50 of the Civil Procedural Rule of the Supreme Court, which stipulates that a *jokoku* appellant shall submit an appeal brief within fifty days after having an appeal granted.

4. *Shimazaki v. Japan* (Sup. Ct., G.B.; October 25, 1950; 19 *Saibanshu Keiji* 987, or 4 *Keishu* 2151) upheld the constitutionality of the provision of Article 3, Item 3 of the Criminal Procedures Enforcement Rule (Supreme Court Rule No. 34 of 1948) as being within the scope of the rule-making power of the Supreme Court, granted by Article 77 of the Constitution. For a similar ruling, see *Nobuchi v. Japan* (Sup. Ct., G.B.; November 15, 1950; 37 *Saibanshu Keiji* 645).

5. Hideo Wada, *Op. Cit., Saiko Saibansho Ron*, p. 167.

6. *Hanrei Jiho* No. 357, 1964, p. 13.

7. Tokyo Dist. Ct.; May 14, 1970; *Hanrei Jiho* No. 598, 1970, p. 45.

8. The *Asahi Shimbun*, August 4, 1953.

9. Kanji Kondo, "Nijyunen o keikashite" (20 years since its establishment), *Jurisuto* No. 385, December 1967, p. 14.

10. The *Sunagawa* case, Sup. Ct., G.B.; December 16, 1959; 13 *Keishu* 3225. The *Matsukawa* case, Sup. Ct., G.B.; August 10, 1959; 13 *Keishu* 1419.

11. Wada, *Op. Cit., Saiko Saibansho Ron*, p. 217.

12. Takeo Hayakawa, "The Japanese judiciary in the whirlwind of politics," in *Kobe University Law Review* Vol. 7, 1971, p. 17.

13. Charles R. Stevens, "The Miyamoto incident: A legal analysis," paper delivered at the 1974 annual meeting of the Association for Asian Studies in New York City.

14. Chuichi Suzuki, "Problems of disqualification of judges in Japan," in *American Journal of Comparative Law* Vol. 18, 1970, pp. 727–743.

15. *Mori v. Diet Impeachment Committee;* Tokyo Dist. Ct.; June 13, 1968; *Hanrei Jiho* No. 529, p. 45.

16. Toshitaka Ushiomi, "Saikosai no sekinin" (The responsibility of the Supreme Court), in the *Mainichi Shimbun*, March 24, 1977.

17. Sapporo Dist. Ct.; September 7, 1973; *Hanrei Jiho No.* 712, p. 26.

18. Hanrei Jiho, No. 821, 1976, p. 23.

19. Frank O. Miller, "The Naganuma case: Judge Fukushima and the seihokyo," paper presented at the 1974 Association for Asian Studies meeting in New York City, p. 24.

20. Sapporo Dist. Ct.; September 7, 1973; Hanrei Jiho No. 712, 1973, p. 26.

21. Sup. Ct., G.B.; February 1, 1950; 4 Keishu 73.

22. Sup. Ct., G.B.; July 8, 1948; 2 Keishu 801.

23. See Hakodate district court on March 5, 1960 (first instance) and Sapporo high court, Hakodate branch on February 21, 1961 (second instance); and Yamaguchi district court, Shimonoseki branch on March 30, 1960 (first instance) and Hiroshima high court, Matsue branch on December 1, 1961 (second instance).

24. Sup. Ct., G.B.; October 26, 1966; 161 Saibanshu Keiji 185.

25. Hanrei Jiho No. 308, 1962, pp. 2–5.

26. Tokyo H. Ct.; November 27, 1963; Hanrei Jiho No. 363, 1964, pp. 48–49.

27. Sup. Ct., G.B.; April 2, 1969; 23 Keishu 305.

28. Sup. Ct., G.B.; April 25, 1973; 27 Keishu 547.

29. The so-called Konoura case involved a criminal trial of three defendants suspected of manslaughter and theft. Shizuoka Dist. Ct., Hamamatsu branch, April 27, 1950; Tokyo H. Ct., May 8, 1951; Sup. Ct., 1st. P.B.; January 14, 1957. Sudo v. Japan, Shizuoka Dist. Ct., Hamamatsu branch, December 27, 1950; Tokyo H. Ct., September 29, 1951; Sup. Ct., 2nd. P.B.; November 27, 1953; 7 Keishu 2303. Matsunaga v. Japan, Shizuoka Dist. Ct., February 18, 1952; Tokyo H. Ct., September 13, 1956, Sup. Ct., 2nd. P.B.; June 1958; 12 Keishu 2009.

30. Takeshichiro Otake et al., "Jijitsu nintei niokeru saibankan no handan: Konoura, Futamata, Kojima jiken hanketsu no jisshoteki kenkyu" (A judicial fact-finding: An empirical study of the Konoura, Futamata, and Kojima cases), in 36 Horitsu Jiho 2, 1964, pp. 30–49.

31. Sup. Ct., G.B.; October 26, 1966; 20 Keishu 901.

32. During the ten years (1957–1966), an average of 3 to 4 percent of the decisions below in civil cases reviewed by the Supreme Court were reversed, while the Great Court of Cassation reversed more than 10 percent of the decisions it reviewed. In criminal cases, the rates of decisions below which were reversed by the Court were 0.8 percent, in 1960, 0.6 percent in 1961 and 1.2 percent in 1962. Tsugio Nakano, "Saikosaibansho no saibanjimu no genkyo to jakkan no mondai ten" (Judicial administration of the Supreme Court: Present conditions and some problems), in *Jurisuto* No. 385, December 1967, pp. 88, 90–91.

Appendix

The Constitution of Japan*
(Nihonkoku Kempo)

We, the Japanese people, acting through our duly elected representatives in the National Diet, determined that we shall secure for ourselves and our posterity the fruits of peaceful cooperation with all nations and the blessings of liberty throughout this land, and resovled that never again shall we be visited with the horrors of war through the action of government, do proclaim that sovereign power resides with the people and do firmly establish this Constitution. Government is a sacred trust of the people, the authority for which is derived from the people, the powers of which are exercised by the representatives of the people, and the benefits of which are enjoyed by the people. This is a universal principle of mankind upon which this Constitution is founded. We reject and revoke all constitutions, laws, ordinances, and rescripts in conflict herewith.

We, the Japanese people, desire peace for all time and are deeply conscious of the high ideals controlling human relationship, and we have determined to preserve our security and existence, trusting in the justice and faith of the peace-loving peoples of the world. We desire to occupy an honored place in an international society striving for the preservation of peace, and the banishment of tyranny and slavery, oppression and intolerance for all time from the earth. We recognize that all peoples of the world have the right to live in peace, free from fear and want.

We believe that no nation is responsible to itself alone, but that laws of political morality are universal; and that obedience to such laws is incumbent upon all nations who would sustain their own sovereignty and justify their sovereign relationship with other nations.

We, the Japanese people, pledge our national honor to accomplish these high ideals and purposes with all our resources.

CHAPTER I. THE EMPEROR

Article 1. The Emperor shall be the symbol of the State and of the unity of the people, deriving his position from the will of the people with whom resides sovereign power.

Article 2. The Imperial Throne shall be dynastic and succeeded to in accordance with the Imperial House Law passed by the Diet.

Article 3. The advise and approval of the Cabinet shall be required for all acts of the Emperor in matters of state, and the Cabinet shall be responsible therefor.

Article 4. The Emperor shall perform only such acts in matters of state as are provided for in this Constitution and he shall not have powers related to government.

2. The Emperor may delegate the performance of his acts in matters of state as may be provided by law.

Article 5. When, in accordance with the Imperial House Law, a Regency is established, the Regent shall perform his acts in matters of state in the Emperor's name. In this case, paragraph one of the preceding article will be applicable.

Article 6. The Emperor shall appoint the Prime Minister as designated by the Diet.

2. The Emperor shall appoint the Chief Judge of the Supreme Court as designated by the Cabinet.

Article 7. The Emperor, with the advice and approval of the Cabinet, shall perform the following acts in matters of state on behalf of the people:

(1) Promulgation of amendments of the constitution, laws, cabinet orders and treaties.
(2) Convocation of the Diet;
(3) Dissolution of the House of Representatives;
(4) Proclamation of general election of members of the Diet:
(5) Attestation of the appointment and dismissal of Ministers of State and other officials as provided for by law, and of full powers and credentials of Ambassadors and Ministers;
(6) Attestation of general and special amnesty, commutation of punishment, reprieve, and restoration of rights;
(7) Awarding of honors;
(8) Attestation of instruments of ratification and other diplomatic documents as provided for by law;
(9) Receiving foreign ambassadors and ministers;
(10) Performance of ceremonial functions.

Article 8. No property can be given to, or received by, the Imperial House, nor can any gifts be made therefrom, without the authorization of the Diet.

Appendix

CHAPTER II. RENUNCIATION OF WAR

Article 9. Aspiring sincerely to an international peace based on justice and order, the Japanese people forever renounce war as a sovereign right of the nation and the threat or use of force as a means of settling international disputes.

    2. In order to accomplish the aim of the preceding paragraph, land, sea, and air forces, as well as other war potential, will never be maintained. The right of belligerency of the state will not be recognized.

CHAPTER III. RIGHTS AND DUTIES OF THE PEOPLE

Article 10. The conditions necessary for being a Japanese national shall be determined by law.

Article 11. The people shall not be prevented from enjoying any of the fundamental human rights. These fundamental human rights guaranteed to the people by this Constitution shall be conferred upon the people of this and future generations as eternal and inviolate rights.

Article 12. The freedoms and rights guaranteed to the people by this Constitution shall be maintained by the constant endeavor of the people, who shall refrain from any abuse of these freedoms and rights and shall always be responsible for utilizing them for the public welfare.

Article 13. All of the people shall be respected as individuals. Their rights to life, liberty, and the pursuit of happiness shall, to the extent that it does not intefere with the public welfare, be the supreme consideration in legislation and in other governmental affairs.

Article 14. All of the people are equal under the law and there shall be no discrimination in political, economic or social relations because of race, creed, sex, social status or family origin.

    2. Peers and peerage shall not be recognized.

    3. No privilege shall accompany any award of honor, decoration or any distinction, nor shall any such award be valid beyond the lifetime of the individual who now holds or hereafter may receive it.

Article 15. The people have the inalienable right to choose their public officials and to dismiss them.

    2. All public officials are servants of the whole community and not of any group thereof.

    3. Universal adult suffrage is guaranteed with regard to the election of public officials.

    4. In all elections, secrecy of the ballot shall not be violated. A voter shall not be answerable, publicly or privately, for the choice he has made.

Article 16. Every person shall have the right of peaceful petition for the redress of damage, for the removal of public officials, for the enactment, repeal or amendment of laws, ordinances or regulations, and for other matters, nor shall any person be in any way discriminated against for sponsoring such a petition.

Article 17. Every person may sue for redress as provided by law from the State or a public entity, in case he has suffered damage through illegal act of any public official.

Article 18. No person shall be held in bondage of any kind. Involuntary servitude, except as punishment for crime, is prohibited.

Article 19. Freedom of thought and conscience shall not be violated.

Article 20. Freedom of religion is guaranteed to all. No religious organization shall receive any privileges from the State nor exercise any political authority.

2. No person shall be compelled to take part in any religious acts, celebration, rite or practice.

3. The State and its organs shall refrain from religious education or any other religious activity.

Article 21. Freedom of assembly and association as well as speech, press and all other forms of expression are guaranteed.

2. No censorship shall be maintained, nor shall the secrecy of any means of communication be violated.

Article 22. Every person shall have freedom to choose and change his residence and to choose his occupation to the extent that it does not interfere with the public welfare.

2. Freedom of all persons to move to a foreign country and to divest themselves of their nationality shall be inviolate.

Article 23. Academic freedom is guaranteed.

Article 24. Marriage shall be based only on the mutual consent of both sexes and it shall be maintained through mutual cooperation with the equal rights of husband and wife as a basis.

2. With regard to choice of spouse, property rights, inheritance, choice of domicile, divorce and other matters pertaining to marriage and the family, laws shall be enacted from the standpoint of individual dignity and the essential equality of the sexes.

Article 25. All people shall have the right to maintain the minimum standards of wholesome and cultured living.

2. In all spheres of life, the State shall use its endeavors for the promotion and extension of social welfare and security, and of public health.

Article 26. All people shall have the right to receive an equal education correspondent to their ability, as provided by law.

2. All people shall be obligated to have all boys and girls under their protection receive ordinary educations as provided for by law. Such compulsory education shall be free.

Article 27. All people shall have the right and the obligation to work.

Appendix

2. Standards for wages, hours, rest and other working conditions shall be fixed by law.
3. Children shall not be exploited.

Article 28. The right of workers to organize and to bargain and act collectively is guaranteed.

Article 29. The right to own or to hold property is inviolable.
2. Property rights shall be defined by law, in conformity with the public welfare.
3. Private property may be taken for public use upon just compensation therefor.

Article 30. The people shall be liable to taxations as provided by law.

Article 31. No person shall be deprived of life or liberty, nor shall any other criminal penalty be imposed, except according to procedure established by law.

Article 32. No person shall be denied the right of access to the courts.

Article 33. No person shall be apprehended except upon warrant issued by a competent judicial officer which specified the offense with which the person is charged, unless he is apprehended, the offense being committed.

Article 34. No person shall be arrested or detained without being at once informed of the charges against him or without the immedate privilege of counsel,; nor shall he be detained without adequate cause; and upon demand of any person such cause must be immediately shown in open court in his presence and the presence of his counsel.

Article 35. The right of all persons to be secure in their homes, papers and effects against entries, searches and seizures shall not be impaired except upon warrant issued for adequate cause and particularly describing the place to be searched and things to be seized, or except as provided by Article 33.
2. Each search or seizure shall be made upon separate warrant issued by a competent judicial officer.

Article 36. The infliction of torture by any pubic officer and cruel punishments are absolutely forbidden.

Article 37. In all criminal cases the accused shall enjoy the right to a speedy and public trial by an impartial tribunal.
2. He shall be permitted full opportunity to examine all witnesses, and he shall have the right of compulsory process for obtaining witnesses on his behalf at public expense.
3. At all times the accused shall have the assistance of competent counsel who shall, if the accused is unable to secure the same by his own efforts, be assigned to his use by the State.

Article 38. No person shall be compelled to testify against himself.

2. Confession made under compulsion, torture or threat, or after prolonged arrsest or detention shall not be admitted in evidence.

3. No person shall be convicted or punished in cases where the only proof against him is his own confession.

Article 39. No person shall be held criminally liable for an act which was lawful at the time it was committed, or of which he has been acquitted, nor shall he be placed in double jeopardy.

Article 40. Any person, in case he is acquitted after he has been arrested or detained, may sue the State for redress as provided by law.

CHAPTER IV. THE DIET

Article 41. The Diet shall be the highest organ of state power, and shall be the sole law-making organ of the State.

Article 42. The Diet shall consists of two Houses, namely the House of Representatives and the House of Councillors.

Article 43. Both Houses shall consist of elected members, representative of all the people.

2. The number of the members of each House shall be fixed by law.

Article 44. The qualifications of members of both Houses and their electors shall be fixed by law. However, there shall be no discrimination because of race, creed, sex, social status, family origin, education, property or income.

Article 45. The term of office of members of the House of Representatives shall be four years. However, the term shall be terminated before the full term is up in case the House of Representatives is dissolved.

Article 46. The term of office of members of the House of Councillors shall be six years, and election for half the members shall take place every three years.

Article 47. Electoral districts, method of voting and other matters pertaining to the method of election of members of both Houses shall be fixed by law.

Article 48. No person shall be permitted to be a member of both Houses simultaneously.

Article 49. Members of both Houses shall receive appropriate annual payment from the national treasury in accordance with law.

Article 50. Except in cases provided by law, members of both Houses shall be exempt from apprehension while the Diet is in session, and any members apprehended before the opening of the session shall be freed during the term of the session upon demand of the House.

Article 51. Members of both Houses shall not be held liable outside the House for speeches, debates or votes cast inside the House.

Appendix

Article 52. An ordinary session of the Diet shall be convoked once per year.

Article 53. The Cabinet may determine to convoke extraordinary sessions of the Diet. When a quarter of more of the total members of either House makes the demand, the Cabinet must determine on such convocation.

Article 54. When the House of Representatives is dissolved, there must be a general election of members of the House of Representatives within forty (40) days from the date of dissolution, and the Diet must be convoked within thirty (30) days from the date of the election.

2. When the House of Representatives is dissolved, the House of Councillors is closed at the same time. However, the Cabinet may in time of national emergency convoke the House of Councillors in emergency session.

3. Measures taken at such session as mentioned in the proviso of the preceding paragraph shall be provisional and shall become null and void unless agreed to by the House of Representatives within a period of ten (10) days after the opening of the next session of the Diet.

Article 55. Each House shall judge disputes related to qualifications of its members. However, in order to deny a seat to any member, it is necessary to pass a resolution by a majority to two-thirds or more of the members present.

Article 56. Business cannot be transacted in either House unless one-third or more of total membership is present.

2. All matters shall be decided, in each House, by a majority of those present, except as elsewhere provided in the Constitution, and in case of a tie, the presiding officer shall decide the issue.

Article 57. Deliberation in each House shall be public. However, a secret meeting may be held where a majority of two-thirds or more of those members present passes a resolution therefor.

2. Each House shall keep a record of proceedings. This record shall be published and given general circulation, excepting such parts of proceedings of secret session as may be deemed to require secrecy.

3. Upon demand of one-fifth or more of the members present, votes of the members on any matter shall be recorded in the minutes.

Article 58. Each House shall select its own president and other officials.

2. Each House shall establish its rules pertaining to meetings, proceedings and internal discipline, and may punish members for disorderly conduct. However, in order to expel a member, a majority of two-thirds or more of those members present must pass a resolution thereon.

Article 59. A bill becomes a law on passage of both Houses, except as otherwise provided by the Constitution.

2. A bill which is passed by the House of Representatives, and upon which the House of Councillors makes a decision different from that of the House of Representatives, becomes a law when passed a second time by the House of Representatives by a majority of two-thirds or more of the members present.

3. The provision of the preceding paragraph does not preclude the House of Representatives from calling for the meeting of a joint committee of both Houses, provided for by law.

4. Failure by the House of Councillors to take final action within sixty (60) days after receipt of a bill passed by the House of Representatives, time in recess excepted, may be determined by the House of Representatives to constitute a rejection of the said bill by the House of Councillors.

Article 60. The Budget must first be submitted to the House of Representatives.

2. Upon consideration of the budget, when the House of Councillors makes a decision different from that of the House of Representatives, and when no agreement can be reached even through a joint committee of both Houses, provided for by law, or in the case of failure by the House of Councillors to take final action within thirty (30) days, the period of recess excluded, after the receipt of the budget passed by the House of Representatives, the decision of the House of Representatives shall be the decision of the Diet.

Article 61. The second paragraph of the preceding article applies also to the Diet approval required for the conclusion of treaties.

Article 62. Each House may conduct investigations in relation to government, and may demand the presence and testimony of witnesses, and the production of records.

Article 63. The Prime Minister and other Ministers of State may, at any time, appear in either House for the purpose of speaking on bills, regardless of whether they are members of the House or not. They must appear when their presence is required in order to give answers or explanation.

Article 64. The Diet shall set up an impeachment court from among the members of both Houses for the purpose of trying those judges against whom removal proceedings have been instituted.

2. Matters relating to impeachment shall be provided by law.

CHAPTER V. THE CABINET

Article 65. Executive power shall be vested in the Cabinet.

Article 66. The Cabinet shall consist of the Prime Minister, who shall be its head, and other Ministers of State, as provided for by law.

2. The Prime Minister and other Ministers of State must be civilians.

3. The Cabinet, in the exercise of executive power, shall be collectively responsible to the Diet.

Article 67. The Prime Minister shall be designated from among the members of the Diet by a resolution of the Diet. This designation shall precede all other business.

2. If the House of Representatives and the House of Councillors disagree and if no agreement can be reached even through a joint committee of both Houses, provided for by law, or the House of Councillors fails to make designation within ten (10) days, exclusive of the period of recess, after the House of Representatives has made designation, the decision of the House of Representatives shall be the decision of the Diet.

Article 68. The Prime Minister shall appoint the Ministers of State. However, a majority of their number must be chosen from among the members of the Diet.

2. The Prime Minister may remove the Ministers of State as he chooses.

Article 69. If the House of Representatives passes a nonconfidence resolution, or rejects a confidence resolution, the Cabinet shall resign en masse, unless the House of Representatives is dissolved with ten (10) days.

Article 70. When there is a vacancy in the post of Prime Minister, or upon the first convocation of the Diet after a general eletion of members of the House of Representatives, the Cabinet shall resign en masse.

Article 71. In the cases mentioned in the two preceding Articles, the Cabinet shall continue its functions until the time when a new Prime Minister is appointed.

Article 72. The Prime Minister, representing the Cabinet, submits bills, reports on general national affairs and foreign relations to the Diet and exercises control and supervision over various administrative branches.

Article 73. The Cabinet, in addition to other general administrative functions, shall perform the following functions:

(1) Administer the law faithfully; conduct affairs of state;
(2) Manage foreign affairs;
(3) Conclude treaties. However, it shall obtain prioror, depending on circumstances, subsequent approval of the Diet;
(4) Administer the civil service, in accordance withstandards established by law;
(5) Prepare the budget, and present it to the Diet;
(6) Enact cabinet orders in order to execute theprovisions of this Constitution and of the law. However, it cannot include penal provisions insuch cabinet orders unless authorized by such law.

(7) Decide on general amnesty, special amnesty, commutation of punishment, reprieve, and restoration of rights.

Article 74. All laws and cabinet orders shall be signed by the competent Minister of State and countersigned by the Prime Minister.

Article 75. The Ministers of State, during their tenure of office, shall not be subject to legal action without the consent of the Prime Minister. However, the right to take that action is not impaired hereby.

CHAPTER VI. JUDICIARY

Article 76. The whole judicial power is vested in a Supreme Court and in such inferior courts as are established by law.

2. No extraordinary tribunal shall be established, nor shall any organ or agency of the Executive be given final judicial power.

3. All judges shall be independent in the exercise of their conscience and shall be bound only by this Constitution and the laws.

Article 77. The Supreme Court is vested with the rule-making power under which it determines the rules of procedure and of practice, and of matters relating to attorneys, the internal discipline of the courts and the administration

2. Public procurators shall be subject to the rule-making power of the Supreme Court.

3. The Supreme Court may delegate the power to make rules for inferior courts to such courts.

Article 78. Judges shall not be removed except by public impeachment unless judicially declared mentally or physically incompetent to perform official duties. No disciplinary action against judges shall be administered by any executive organ or agency.

Article 79. The Supreme Court shall consist of a Chief Judge and such number of judges as may be determined by law; all such judges excepting the Chief Judge shall be appointed by the Cabinet.

2. The appointment of the judges of the Supreme Court shall be reviewed by the people at the first general election of members of the House of Representatives following their appointment, and shall be reviewed again at the first general election of members of the House of Representatives after a lapse of ten (10) years, and in the same manner thereafter.

3. In cases mentioned in the foregoing paragraph, when the majority of the voters favors the dismissal of a judge, he shall be dismissed.

4. Matters pertaining to review shall be prescribed by law.

5. The judges of the Supreme Court shall be retired upon the attainment of the age as fixed by law.

6. All such judges shall receive, at regular stated intervals, adequate compensation which shall not be decreased during their terms of office.

Article 80. The judges of the inferior courts shall be appointed by the

Appendix

Cabinet from a list of persons nominated by the Supreme Court. All such judges shall hold office for a term of ten (10) years with privilege of reappointment, provided that they shall be retired upon the attainment of the age as fixed by law.

2. The judges of the inferior courts shall receive, at regular stated intervals, adequate compensation which shall not be decreased during their terms of office.

Article 81. The Supreme Court is the court of last resort with power to determine the constitutionality of any law, order, regulation or official act.

Article 82. Trials shall be conducted and judgement declared publicly. Where a court unanimously determines publicity to be dangerous to public order or morals, a trial may be conducted privately, but trials of political offenses, offenses involving the press or cases wherein the rights of people as guaranteed in Chapter III of this Constitution are in question shall always be conducted publicly.

CHAPTER VII. FINANCE

Article 83. The power to administer national finances shall be exercised as the Diet shall determine.

Article 84. No new taxes shall be imposed or existing ones modified except by law or under such conditions as law may prescribe.

Article 85. No money shall be expended, nor shall the State obligate itself, except as authorized by the Diet.

Article 86. The Cabinet shall prepare and submit to the Diet for its consideration and decision a budget for each fiscal year.

Article 87. In order to provide for unforeseen deficiencies in the budget, a reserve fund may be authorized by the Diet to be expended upon the responsibility of the Cabinet.

2. The Cabinet must get subsequent approval of the Diet for all payments from the reserve fund.

Article 88. All property of the Imperial Household shall belong to the State. All expenses of the Imperial Household shall be appropriated by the Diet in the budget.

Article 89. No public money or other property shall be expended or appropriated for the use, benefit or maintenance of any religious institution or association, or for any charitable, educational or benevolent enterprises not under the control of public authority.

Article 90. Final accounts of the expenditures and revenues of the State shall be audited annually by a Board of Audit and submitted by the Cabinet to the Diet, together with the statement of audit, during the fiscal year immediately following the period covered.

2. The organization and competency of the Board of Audit shall be determined by law.

Article 91. At regular intervals and at least annually the Cabinet shall report to the Diet and the people on the state of national finances.

CHAPTER VIII. LOCAL SELF-GOVERNMENT

Article 92. Regulations concerning organization and operations of local public entities shall be fixed by law in accordance with the principal of local autonomy.

Article 93. The local public entities shall establish assemblies as their deliberative organs, in accordance with law.

2. The chief executive officers of all local public entities, the members of their assemblies, and such other local officials as may be determined by law shall be elected by direct popular vote within their several communities.

Article 94. Local public entities shall have the right to manage their property, affairs and administration and to enact their own regulations within law.

Article 95. A special law, applicable only to one local public entity, cannot be enacted by the Diet without the consent of the majority of the voters of thealocal public entity concerned, obtained in accordance with law.

CHAPTER IX. AMENDMENTS

Article 96. Amendments to this Constitution shall be initiated by the Diet, through a concurring vote of two-thirds or more of all the members of each House and shall thereupon be submitted to the people for ratification, which shall require the affirmative vote of a majority of all votes cast thereon, at a special referendum or at such election as the Diet shall specify.

2. Amendments when so ratified shall immediately be promulgated by the Emperor in the name of the people. as an integral part of this Constitution.

CHAPTER X. SUPREME LAW

Article 97. The fundamental human rights by this Constitution guaranteed to the people of Japan are fruits of the age-old struggle of man to be free; they have survived the many exacting tests for durability and are conferrd upon this and future generations in trust, to be held for all time inviolate.

Article 98. This Constitution shall be the supreme law of the nation and no law, ordinance, imperial rescript or other act of govenrment, or part

Appendix

thereof, contrary to the provisons hereof, shall have legal force or validity.

2. The treaties concluded by Japan and established laws of nations shall be faithfully observed.

Article 99. The Emperor or the Regent as well as Ministers of State, members of the Diet, jduges, and all other public officials have the obligation to respect and uphold this Constitution.

CHAPTER XI. SUPPLEMENTARY PROVISIONS

Article 100. This Constitution shall be enforced as from the day when the period of six months will have elapsed counting from the day of its promulgation.

2. The enactment of laws necessary for the enforcement of this Constitution, the election of members of the House of Councillors and the procedure for the convocation of the Diet and other preparatory procedures for the enforcement of this Constitution may be executed before the day prescribed in the preceding paragraph.

Article 101. If the House of Councillors is not constituted before the effective date of this Constitution, the House of Representatives shall function as the Diet until such time as the House of Councillors shall be constituted.

Article 102. The term of office for half the members of the House of Councillors serving in the first term under this Constitution shall be three years. Members falling under this category shall be determined in accordance with law.

Article 103. The Ministers of State, members of the House of Representatives, and judges in office on the effective date of this Constitution, and all other public officials, who occupy positions corresponding to such positions as are recognized by this Constitution shall not forfeit their positions automatically on account of the enforcement of this Constitution unless otherwise specified by law. When, however, successors are elected or appointed under the provisions of this Constitution, they shall forfeit their positions as a matter of course.

Abbreviations

Ad. Ct. Administrative Court
Cri. Div. Criminal Division
Dist. Ct. District Court
Gr. Ct. Cass. Great Court of Cassation
H. Ct. High Court
Sup. Ct., G. B. Supreme Court Grand Bench
Sup. Ct., P. B. Supreme Court Petty Bench

Gyoroku Gyosei Saibansho Hanketsuroku (Records of Judgments of the Administrative Court)

Gyosai Reishu Gyosei Jiken Saiban Reishu (Selected Records of Judgments on Administrative Affairs)

Kakyu Keishu Kakyu Saibansho Keiji Saibanreishu (Reports of Judicial Precedents of Inferior Courts: Criminal Cases)

Keiroku Taishin'in Hanketsu Roku Keiji (Records of Judgments of the Great Court of Cassation: Criminal Cases)

Keishu Saikosaibansho Hanreishu Keiji (The Collection of Selected Supreme Court Decisions: Criminal Cases)

Minroku Taishin'in Hanketsuroku Minji (Rec-

	ords of Judgments of the Great Court of Cassation: Civil Cases)
Minshu	Saikosaibansho Hanreishu Minji (The Collection of Selected Supreme Court Decisions: Civil Cases)
Saibanshu Keiji	Saikosaibansho Saibanshu Keiji (The Collection of the Supreme Court Decisions: Criminal Cases)
Saibanshu Minji	Saikosaibansho Saibanshu Minji (The Collection of the Supreme Court Decisions: Civil Cases)
GHQ, SCAP	The General Headquarters, Supreme Commander for the Allied Forces
JCP	The Japan Communist Party
JLA	The Junior Legal Association
JPCBWU	The Japanese Press, Communication, and Broadcasting Workers Union
JRTI	The Judicial Research and Training Institute
JSP	The Japan Socialist Party
LDP	The Liberal Democratic Party
LPEC	The Local Public Employees Code
NPAR	The National Personnel Authority Rule

Abbreviations

NPEC The National Public Employees Code

PELRC The Public Enterprises Labor Relations Code

Legends

Asahi Janaru	The Asahi Journal
Asahi Shimbun	The Asahi Press
Hanrei Jiho	The Case Journal
Hanrei Taimuzu	The Case Times
Hogaku Kyokai Zasshi	The Journal of the Jurisprudence Association, Tokyo University
Hogaku Kenkyu	The Journal of Law, Politics, and Sociology, Keio University
Hogaku Ronso	The Kyoto Law Review
Hogaku Semina	The Law Seminar
Ho no Shihai	The Rule of Law
Horitsu Jiho	The Law Journal
Ho no Hiroba	The Law Square
Horitsu Shimbun	The Law Press
Hoso Shimbun	The Lawyers Association Press
Jiyu to Seigi	Liberty and Justice

Jurisuto	The Jurists
Keiho Zasshi	The Journal of Criminal Law
Keiji Saiban Geppo	The Monthly Criminal Trials
Koho Kenkyu	The Public Law Review
Koto Saibansho Keiji Saiban Tokuho	The Special Reports of the High Court Criminal Decisions
Mainichi Shimbun	The Mainichi Press
Shimbun	The Mainichi Press
Toki no Horei	The Contemporary Law and Regulations

Selected Bibliography

The Japanese Language Sources

Masayasu Hasegawa, Hiroshi Miyauchi, Yozo Watanabe (eds.), *Nihon no Horitsuka* (Legal Professionals in Japan), Tokyo: San'ichi Shobo, 1962.

Masayasu Hasegawa, *Seiji to Saiban* (Politics and Trial), Tokyo: Nihon Hyoronsha, 1978.

Yoichi Higuchi, *Shiho no Sekkyokusei to Shokyokusei* (Judicial Activism and Restraint), Tokyo: Keiso Shobo, 1978.

Hogaku Semina (ed.), *Saiko Saibansho* (The Supreme Court: Comprehensive Special Series 4), Tokyo: Nihon Hyoronsha, December 1977.

Hogaku Semina (ed.), *Kon'nichi no Saiko Saibansho: Genten to Genten* (The Supreme Court Today: The Past and Present), Tokyo: Nihon Hyoronsha, February 1988.

Jurisuto (ed.), *Nihon no Horitsuka* (Legal Professionals in Japan), Tokyo: Yuhikaku, September 1977.

Michitaka Kaino, *Saiban* (Trial), Tokyo: Nihon Hyoronsha, 1977.

Takashi Kakuma, *Nihon no Shiho: Saibankan, Kensatsukan, Bengoshi* (The Judiciary in Japan: Judges, Prosecutors, and Lawyers), Tokyo: Sankei Shuppan, 1977.

Naoki Kobayashi, *Shimpan: Kempo Kogi* (The Lecture on the Constitution: New Edition), Tokyo: Tokyo Daigaku Shuppankai, 1980 (Vol. 1), 1981 (Vol. 2).

Nihon Bengoshi Rengokai (ed.), *Saiko Saibansho* (The Supreme Court), Tokyo: Nihon Hyoronsha, 1980.

Nihon Bunka Kaigi (ed.), *Nihonjin no Hoishiki: Chosa Bunseki* (Legal Consciousness of the Japanese: Survey Analysis), Tokyo: Shiseido, 1973.

Heiji Nomura *et al* (eds.), *Nihon no Saiiban* (The Trial in Japan), Tokyo: Nihon Hyoronsha, 1968.

Jiro Nomura, *Hoso Anokoro* (Legal Professionals Now and Then), Tokyo: Nihon Hyoronsha, 1978 (Vol. 1), 1981 (Vol. 2).

Osaka Bengoshi Kai (ed.), *Ho, Saiban, Bengoshi: Kokumin no Hoishiki* (Law, Trial, and Lawyers: The Public Consciousness of Law), Kyoto: Mineruba Shobo, 1977.

Mitsuo Riko, Seiichi Mori, and Yasunori Sone, *Manjo Icchi to Tasuketsu: Mono no Kimekata no Rekishi* (The Unanimity and Majority Votes: A History of Decision Making), Tokyo: Nihon Keizai Shimbunsha, 1980.

Hideo Saito, *Saibankan Ron* (On Judges), Tokyo: Ichiryusha, 1979.

Tetsuzo Sasaki, *Saibankan Ron* (On Judges), Kyoto: Horitsu Bunkasha, 1960.

Hideo Wada, *Kempo to Saiko Saibansho* (The Constitution and the Supreme Court), Tokyo: Gakuyo Shobo, 1975.

Hideo Wada, *Saiko Saibansho Ron* (On the Supreme Court), Tokyo: Nihon Hyoronsha, 1971.

Zenmei Yoshida *et al* (eds.), *Sengo Kempogaku no Tenkai*

(The Postwar Development of the Study of the Constitution), Tokyo: Nihon Hyoronsha, 1988.

The English Language Sources

Theodore L. Becker, *Comparative Judicial Politics: The Political Functionings of Courts*, Chicago, Ill.: Rand McNally & Company, 1970.

Lawrence W. Beer, *Freedom of Expression in Japan: A Study in Comparative Law, Politics, and Society*, Tokyo: Kodansha International, 1984.

Shigemitsu Dando, *Japanese Criminal Procedure* (tr. by B.J. George, Jr.), South Hackensack, N.J.: Fred B. Rothman, 1965.

Mary T. Espey, Masashi Nishihara, Frank J. Shulman, and Robert E. Ward (eds.), *The Allied Occupation of Japan, 1945–1952*, Chicago, Ill.: The American Library Association, 1974.

Takaaki Hattori and Dan F. Henderson, *Civil Procedure in Japan*, New York: Matthew Bender, 1983.

Dan F. Henderson, *Law and Legal Process in Japan*, Seattle, Wash.: University of Washington, School of Law, 1978.

Dan F. Henderson and John O. Haley (comp. and eds.), *Law and the Legal Process in Japan: Materials for an Introductory Course on Japanese Law*, Seattle, Wash.: University of Washington, School of Law, 1978.

Hiroshi Itoh (ed.), *Japanese Politics: An Inside View*, Ithaca, NY: Cornell University Press, 1973.

Hiroshi Itoh and Lawrence W. Beer (eds.), *The Constitutional Case Law of Japan: Selected Supreme Court Decisions, 1961–70*, Seattle, Wash.: University of Washington Press, 1978.

Chalmers Johnson, *Conspiracy at Matsukawa*, Berkeley, Cal.: University of California Press, 1972.

John M. Maki (ed.), *Court and Constitution in Japan: Selected Supreme Court Decisions: 1948–60*, Seattle, Wash.: University of Washington Press, 1964.

John M. Maki (ed.), *Japan's Commission on the Constitution: The Final Report*, Seattle, Wash.: University of Washington Press, 1980.

Frank O. Miller, *Minobe Tatsukichi: Interpreter of Constitutionalism in Japan*, Berkeley, Cal.: University of California Press, 1965.

Yoshiyuki Noda, *Introduction to Japanese Law* (tr. and ed. by Anthony H. Angelo), Tokyo: Tokyo University Press, 1976.

Alfred C. Oppler, *Legal Reform in Occupied Japan: A Participant Looks Back*, Princeton, N.J.: Princeton University Press, 1976.

Glendon A. Schubert, *Judicial Policy Making: The Political Role of the Courts*, Glenview, Ill.: Scott, Foresman, 1965 and 1974.

Glendon A. Schubert, *The Judicial Mind Revisited: Psychometric Analysis of Supreme Court Ideology*, New York: Oxford University Press, 1974.

Glendon A. Schubert and David J. Danelski (eds.), *Comparative Judicial Behavior: Cross-Cultural Studies of Political Decision Making in the East and West*, New York: Oxford University Press, 1969.

Hideo Tanaka (ed.), *The Japanese Legal System: Introductory Cases and Materials* (tr. by Malcolm H. Smith), Tokyo: Tokyo University Press, 1976.

Selected Bibliography

Frank K. Upham, *Law and Social Change in Postwar Japan*, Cambridge, Mass.: Harvard University Press, 1988.

Arthur T. von Mehren (ed.), *Law in Japan*, Cambridge, Mass.: Harvard University Press, 1963.

Robert E. Ward and Yoshikazu Sakamoto (eds.), *Democratizing Japan: The Allied Occupation*, Honolulu: University of Hawaii Press, 1987.